THE FOUNDATIONS
OF SOCIAL RESEARCH

THE FOUNDATIONS OF SOCIAL RESEARCH

Meaning and perspective in the research process

Michael Crotty

Los Angeles | London | New Delhi
Singapore | Washington DC

First published 1998

by Allen & Unwin
9 Atchison Street
St Leonards NSW 2065
Australia

SAGE Publications Ltd
1 Oliver's Yard
55 City Road
London EC1Y 1SP

SAGE Publications Inc
2455 Teller Road
Thousand Oaks
California 91320

SAGE Publications India Pvt. Ltd
B 1/I Mohan Cooperative Industrial Area
Mathura Road
New Delhi 110 044

SAGE Publications Asia-Pacific Pte Ltd
3 Church Street
#10-04 Samsung Hub
Singapore 049483

British Library Cataloguing in Publication data

A catalogue record for this book is
available from the British Library

ISBN 978 0 76196 106 2

Library of Congress catalog record available

Printed in Great Britain by Ashford Colour Press Ltd, Gosport, Hants

12 11 10 9 8 7

CONTENTS

PREFACE

This book emerges from several years of teaching a subject entitled *Qualitative Research Methods*. I have been guided by what students in that subject, and students whose research I have supervised, have found useful. I thank them for their feedback.

Some of the authors quoted in this book wrote at a time when there was little awareness of the oppression borne along in language. They quite happily write of 'man' when they mean women and men. They make use of the generic masculine whenever they need pronouns. Since my readers need no help to recognise and deplore these usages, I have refrained from interrupting the text with [sic] many times over to point them out.

My wife, Christina, is a musician. She has rifled through the text for the odd allusion to music and art.

My sons, Martin and Luke, are technologists, one an audio engineer and the other on the way to becoming an electronic engineer. Some time or other, they tell me, they might be tempted to look at Chapter 2.

'Life's unfair!' my daughter, Mikaila, declared at the age of six. In this same vein, ten years on, she feels Chapter 6 and Chapter 7 may have something of interest if she ever gets around to reading them.

The book is dedicated to them, all the same.

MICHAEL CROTTY
APRIL 1998

Introduction:
THE RESEARCH PROCESS

. . . many arrows, loosèd several ways,
Fly to one mark . . .

William Shakespeare, *Henry V*

They call it 'scaffolded learning'. It is an approach to teaching and learning that, while careful to provide an initial framework, leaves it to the learner to establish longer term structures.

What is presented here is offered in this spirit. It is to be seen as in no way a definitive construction of the social research process but merely a framework for the guidance of those wishing to explore the world of research.

Research students and fledgling researchers—and, yes, even more seasoned campaigners—often express bewilderment at the array of methodologies and methods laid out before their gaze. These methodologies and methods are not usually laid out in a highly organised fashion and may appear more as a maze than as pathways to orderly research. There is much talk of their philosophical underpinnings, but how the methodologies and methods relate to more theoretical elements is often left unclear. To add to the confusion, the terminology is far from consistent in research literature and social science texts. One frequently finds the same term used in a number of different, sometimes even contradictory, ways.

In response to this predicament, here is one reasonably clear-cut way of using terms and grasping what is involved in the process of social research. It is obviously not the only way in which these terms are used, nor is it being suggested that it is the only defensible way to use them. Equally, it is not the only way of analysing and understanding the research process. This is scaffolding, not an edifice. Its aim is to provide researchers with a sense of stability and direction as they go on to do their own building; that is, as they move towards understanding and expounding the research process after their own fashion in forms that suit their particular research purposes.

FOUR ELEMENTS

As a starting point, it can be suggested that, in developing a research proposal, we need to put considerable effort into answering two questions in particular. First, what methodologies and methods will we be employing in the research we propose to do? Second, how do we justify this choice and use of methodologies and methods?

The answer to the second question lies with the purposes of our research—in other words, with the research question that our piece of inquiry is seeking to answer. It is obvious enough that we need a process capable of fulfilling those purposes and answering that question.

There is more to it than that, however. Justification of our choice and particular use of methodology and methods is something that reaches into the assumptions about reality that we bring to our work. To ask about these assumptions is to ask about our theoretical perspective.

It also reaches into the understanding you and I have of what human knowledge is, what it entails, and what status can be ascribed to it. What kind of knowledge do we believe will be attained by our research? What characteristics do we believe that knowledge to have? Here we are touching upon a pivotal issue. How should observers of our research—for example, readers of our thesis or research report—regard the outcomes we lay out before them? And why should our readers take these outcomes seriously? These are epistemological questions.

Already our two initial questions have expanded. We find ourselves with four questions now:

- What *methods* do we propose to use?
- What *methodology* governs our choice and use of methods?
- What *theoretical perspective* lies behind the methodology in question?
- What *epistemology* informs this theoretical perspective?

At issue in these four questions are basic elements of any research process, and we need to spell out carefully what we mean by each of them.

- *Methods*: the techniques or procedures used to gather and analyse data related to some research question or hypothesis.
- *Methodology*: the strategy, plan of action, process or design lying behind the choice and use of particular methods and linking the choice and use of methods to the desired outcomes.
- *Theoretical perspective*: the philosophical stance informing the methodology and thus providing a context for the process and grounding its logic and criteria.
- *Epistemology*: the theory of knowledge embedded in the theoretical perspective and thereby in the methodology.

In social research texts, the bulk of discussion and much of the terminology relate in one way or another to these four elements. What one often finds, however, is that forms of these different process elements are thrown together in grab-bag style as if they were all comparable terms. It is not uncommon to find, say, symbolic interactionism, ethnography and constructionism simply set side by side as 'methodologies', 'approaches', 'perspectives', or something similar. Yet they are not truly comparable. Lumping them together without distinction is a bit like talking about putting tomato sauce, condiments and groceries in one basket. One feels compelled to say, 'Hang on a moment! Tomato sauce is one of many forms of condiment. And all condiments are groceries. Let's do some sorting out here'. Similarly, one may feel urged to do some sorting out when confronted by items like symbolic interactionism, ethnography and constructionism all slung together.

Ethnography, after all, is a *methodology*. It is one of many particular research designs that guide a researcher in choosing methods and shape the use of the methods chosen. Symbolic interactionism, for its part, is a *theoretical perspective* that informs a range of methodologies, including some forms of ethnography. As a theoretical perspective, it is an approach to understanding and explaining society and the human world, and grounds a set of assumptions that symbolic interactionist researchers typically bring to their methodology of choice. Constructionism[1] is an *epistemology* embodied in many theoretical perspectives, including symbolic interactionism as this is generally understood. An epistemology, we have already seen, is a way of understanding and explaining how we know what we know. What all this suggests is that symbolic interactionism, ethnography and constructionism need to be *related* to one another rather than merely set side by side as comparable, perhaps even competing, approaches or perspectives.

So there are epistemologies, theoretical perspectives and methodologies.

If we add in *methods*, we have four elements that inform one another, as depicted in Figure 1.

Figure 1

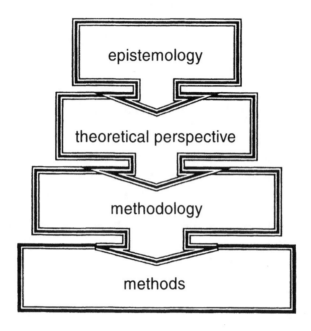

One or other form of constructionism is the epistemology found, or at least claimed, in most perspectives other than those representing positivist and post-positivist paradigms. As we have just noted, the epistemology generally found embedded in symbolic interactionism is thoroughly constructionist in character. So, if we were to write down the four items we are talking about, we would be justified in drawing an arrow from constructionism to symbolic interactionism to indicate this relationship. Ethnography, a methodology that sprang in the first instance from anthropology and anthropological theory, has been adopted by symbolic interactionism and adapted to its own purposes. For that reason, our next arrow may go from symbolic interactionism to ethnography. Ethnography, in turn, has its methods of preference. Participant observation has traditionally been accorded pride of place. So, out with the pen for yet another arrow. Here, then, we have a specific example of an epistemology, a theoretical perspective, a methodology and a method, each informing the next as suggested in Figure 2.

The textbooks describe several epistemological positions, quite a number of theoretical stances, many methodologies, and almost countless

Figure 2

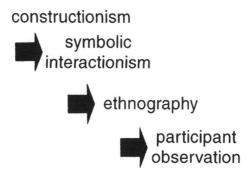

methods. An attempt to list a representative sampling of each category might result in something like Table 1. (But note the several 'etceteras' occurring in this table. It is not an exhaustive listing.)

To denote another typical string, an arrow could start with 'objectivism'. Objectivism is the epistemological view that things exist as *meaningful* entities independently of consciousness and experience, that they have truth and meaning residing in them as objects ('objective'

Table 1

Epistemology	Theoretical perspective	Methodology	Methods
Objectivism	Positivism (and	Experimental	Sampling
Constructionism	post-positivism)	research	Measurement and
Subjectivism	Interpretivism	Survey research	scaling
(*and their variants*)	• Symbolic	Ethnography	Questionnaire
	interactionism	Phenomenological	Observation
	• Phenomenology	research	• participant
	• Hermeneutics	Grounded theory	• non-participant
	Critical inquiry	Heuristic inquiry	Interview
	Feminism	Action research	Focus group
	Postmodernism	Discourse analysis	Case study
	etc.	Feminist standpoint	Life history
		research	Narrative
		etc.	Visual ethnographic
			methods
			Statistical analysis
			Data reduction
			Theme identification
			Comparative analysis
			Cognitive mapping
			Interpretative
			methods
			Document analysis
			Content analysis
			Conversation analysis
			etc.

herefore), and that careful (scientific?) research can
truth and meaning. This is the epistemology under-
t stance. Research done in positivist spirit might
rvey research and employ the quantitative method
(see Figure 3). Once again the arrows go across the
last.

Figure 3

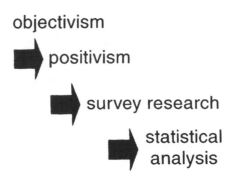

What purpose can these four elements serve?

For one thing, they can help to ensure the soundness of our research
and make its outcomes convincing. Earlier we recognised the need to
justify the methodologies and methods employed in our research. Setting
forth our research process in terms of these four elements enables us to
do this, for it constitutes a penetrating analysis of the process and points
up the theoretical assumptions that underpin it and determine the status
of its findings.

How might we outline our research proposal in these terms?

RESEARCH METHODS

First, we describe the concrete techniques or procedures we plan to use.
There will be certain activities we engage in so as to gather and analyse
our data. These activities are our research methods.

Given our goal of identifying and justifying the research process, it is
important that we describe these methods as specifically as possible. To this
end, we will not just talk about 'carrying out interviews' but will indicate
in very detailed fashion what kind of interviews they are, what interviewing
techniques are employed, and in what sort of setting the interviews are
conducted. We will not just talk about 'participant observation' but will
describe what kind of observation takes place and what degree of partici-

pation is involved. We will not just talk about 'identifying themes in the data' but will show what we mean by themes, how the themes emerge, how they are identified, and what is done with them when they do.

RESEARCH METHODOLOGY

We now describe our strategy or plan of action. This is the research design that shapes our choice and use of particular methods and links them to the desired outcomes.

What is called for here is not only a description of the methodology but also an account of the rationale it provides for the choice of methods and the particular forms in which the methods are employed. Take ethnographic inquiry, for instance. Ethnographic inquiry in the spirit of symbolic interactionism seeks to uncover meanings and perceptions on the part of the people participating in the research, viewing these understandings against the backdrop of the people's overall worldview or 'culture'. In line with this approach, the researcher strives to see things from the perspective of the participants. It is this that makes sense of the researcher's stated intention to carry out *unstructured* interviews and to use a *non-directive* form of questioning within them.

THEORETICAL PERSPECTIVE

Next we describe the philosophical stance that lies behind our chosen methodology. We attempt to explain how it provides a context for the process and grounds its logic and criteria.

Inevitably, we bring a number of assumptions to our chosen methodology. We need, as best we can, to state what these assumptions are. This is precisely what we do when we elaborate our theoretical perspective. Such an elaboration is a statement of the assumptions brought to the research task and reflected in the methodology as we understand and employ it. If, for example, we engage in an ethnographic form of inquiry and gather data via participant observation, what assumptions are embedded in this way of proceeding? By the very nature of participant observation, some of the assumptions relate to matters of language and issues of intersubjectivity and communication. How, then, do we take account of these assumptions and justify them? By expounding our theoretical perspective, that is, our view of the human world and social life within that world, wherein such assumptions are grounded.

Symbolic interactionism is a theoretical perspective that grounds these assumptions in most explicit fashion. It deals directly with issues such as language, communication, interrelationships and community. As we shall see in more detail in Chapter 4, symbolic interactionism is all about those basic social interactions whereby we enter into the perceptions, attitudes and values of a community, becoming persons in the process. At its heart is the notion of being able to put ourselves in the place of others—the very notion we have already expressed in detailing our methodology and have catered for in the choice and shaping of our methods.

EPISTEMOLOGY

Finally, we need to describe the epistemology inherent in the theoretical perspective and therefore in the methodology we have chosen.

The theoretical perspective we have described is a way of looking at the world and making sense of it. It involves knowledge, therefore, and embodies a certain understanding of what is entailed in knowing, that is, *how we know what we know*. Epistemology deals with 'the nature of knowledge, its possibility, scope and general basis' (Hamlyn 1995, p. 242). Maynard (1994, p. 10) explains the relevance of epistemology to what we are about here: 'Epistemology is concerned with providing a philosophical grounding for deciding what kinds of knowledge are possible and how we can ensure that they are both adequate and legitimate'. Hence our need to identify, explain and justify the epistemological stance we have adopted.

There are, of course, quite a range of epistemologies. For a start, there is objectivism. Objectivist epistemology holds that meaning, and therefore meaningful reality, exists as such apart from the operation of any consciousness. That tree in the forest is a tree, regardless of whether anyone is aware of its existence or not. As an object of that kind ('objectively', therefore), it carries the intrinsic meaning of 'tree-ness'. When human beings recognise it as a tree, they are simply discovering a meaning that has been lying there in wait for them all along. We might approach our piece of ethnographic research in that spirit. Much of the early ethnography was certainly carried out in that spirit. In this objectivist view of 'what it means to know', understandings and values are considered to be objectified in the people we are studying and, if we go about it in the right way, we can discover the objective truth.

Another epistemology—constructionism—rejects this view of human knowledge. There is no objective truth waiting for us to discover it. Truth, or meaning, comes into existence in and out of our engagement with the realities in our world. There is no meaning without a mind. Meaning is not discovered, but constructed. In this understanding of knowledge, it is clear that different people may construct meaning in different ways, even in relation to the same phenomenon. Isn't this precisely what we find when we move from one era to another or from one culture to another? In this view of things, subject and object[2] emerge as partners in the generation of meaning.

We will be discussing objectivism in the context of positivism and post-positivism. We will deal with constructionism at some length (Chapter 3) since it is the epistemology that qualitative researchers tend to invoke. A third epistemological stance, subjectivism, comes to the fore in structuralist, post-structuralist and postmodernist forms of thought (and, in addition, often appears to be what people are actually describing when they claim to be talking about constructionism). In subjectivism, meaning does not come out of an interplay between subject and object but is imposed on the object by the subject. Here the object as such makes no contribution to the generation of meaning. It is tempting to say that in constructionism meaning is constructed out of something (the object), whereas in subjectivism meaning is created out of nothing. We humans are not that creative, however. Even in subjectivism we make meaning out of something. We import meaning from somewhere else. The meaning we ascribe to the object may come from our dreams, or from primordial archetypes we locate within our collective unconscious, or from the conjunction and aspects of the planets, or from religious beliefs, or from . . . That is to say, meaning comes from anything *but* an interaction between the subject and the object to which it is ascribed.

Much more can be said about possible epistemological stances, and the three we have referred to are not to be seen as watertight compartments. Hopefully, enough has been said here for us to recognise that epistemology bears mightily on the way we go about our research. Is there objective truth that we need to identify, and can identify, with precision and certitude? Or are there just humanly fashioned ways of seeing things whose processes we need to explore and which we can only come to understand through a similar process of meaning making? And is this making of meaning a subjective act essentially independent of the object, or do both subject and object contribute to the construction of meaning? Embedded in these questions is a range of epistemological stances, each of which implies a profound difference in how we do our researching and how we present our research outcomes.

What about ontology?

In the research literature there is frequent mention of ontology and you might be wondering why ontology does not figure in the schema developed to this point.

Ontology is the study of being. It is concerned with 'what is', with the nature of existence, with the structure of reality as such. Were we to introduce it into our framework, it would sit alongside epistemology informing the theoretical perspective, for each theoretical perspective embodies a certain way of understanding *what is* (ontology) as well as a certain way of understanding *what it means to know* (epistemology).

Ontological issues and epistemological issues tend to emerge together. As our terminology has already indicated, to talk of the construction of meaning is to talk of the construction of meaningful reality. Because of this confluence, writers in the research literature have trouble keeping ontology and epistemology apart conceptually. Realism (an ontological notion asserting that realities exist outside the mind) is often taken to imply objectivism (an epistemological notion asserting that meaning exists in objects independently of any consciousness). In some cases we even find realism identified with objectivism. Guba and Lincoln (1994, p. 108) certainly posit a necessary link between the two when they claim that 'if, for example, a "real" reality is assumed, the posture of the knower must be one of objective detachment or value freedom in order to be able to discover "how things really are" and "how things really work"'. In the chapters that follow, you and I will be listening to a large number of scholars who disagree with this position. Heidegger and Merleau-Ponty, for instance, frequently invoke a 'world always already there', but they are far from being objectivists.

True enough, the world is there regardless of whether human beings are conscious of it. As Macquarrie tells us (1973, p. 57): 'If there were no human beings, there might still be galaxies, trees, rocks, and so on—and doubtless there were, in those long stretches of time before the evolution of *Homo sapiens* or any other human species that may have existed on earth'. But what kind of a world is there before conscious beings engage with it? Not an intelligible world, many would want to say. Not a world of meaning. It becomes a world of meaning only when meaning-making beings make sense of it.

From this point of view, accepting a world, and things in the world, existing independently of our consciousness of them does not imply that meanings exist independently of consciousness, as Guba and Lincoln seem to be saying. The existence of a world without a mind is conceiv-

able. Meaning without a mind is not. Realism in ontology and constructionism in epistemology turn out to be quite compatible. This is itself
an example of how ontological issues and epistemological issues arise
together. Given that state of affairs, it would seem that we can deal with
the ontological issues as they emerge without expanding our schema to
include ontology.

This is borne out when we look at literature that plays up the
importance of the ontological dimension in research. In many instances
the authors are not talking about ontology at all. Blaikie (1993, p. 6),
for example, acknowledges that the 'root definition of *ontology* is the
"science or study of being"'. However, 'for the purposes of the present
discussion', he takes ontology to mean 'the claims or assumptions that
a particular approach to social enquiry makes about the nature of social
reality' (p. 6). This, in itself, is unexceptionable. We need to recognise,
however, that this is no longer ontology in its philosophical sense.
Blaikie's use of the term roughly corresponds to what you and I are
calling 'theoretical perspective'. It refers to how one views the world.
Blaikie tells us that positivism 'entails an *ontology* of an ordered universe
made up of atomistic, discrete and observable events' (p. 94). He tells
us that, in the ontology of critical rationalism (the approach launched
by Karl Popper), nature and social life 'are regarded as consisting of
essential uniformities' (p. 95). He tells us that interpretivism 'entails an
ontology in which social reality is regarded as the product of processes
by which social actors together negotiate the meanings for actions and
situations' (p. 96). This is stretching the meaning of ontology well and
truly beyond its boundaries.

It would seem preferable to retain the usage of 'theoretical perspective'
and reserve the term 'ontology' for those occasions when we do need to
talk about 'being'. This is something you and I cannot avoid doing when
we come to grapple with, say, the philosophy of Martin Heidegger, for
that is a radical ontology and needs to be dealt with in strictly ontological terms. Happy days ahead!

In the Middle Ages, the great ontological debate was between realists
and nominalists and concerned the extramental reality, or irreality, of
'universals'. Are there, for example, just individual human beings or does
'humankind' have real existence too? Does humankind as such denote
a reality in the world or is it just something that exists only in the mind?
In more recent centuries, the major ontological debate has been between
realists and idealists and concerns the extramental reality, or irreality,
of anything whatsoever. While neither debate is without relevance to
an analysis of the research process, it still seems the case that ontological

issues can be dealt with adequately without complicating our four-column schema further by expressly introducing ontology.

IN ALL DIRECTIONS

Back we go to our arrows. We have been drawing arrows from left to right—from one item in one column to another item in the next column to the right. We should feel very free to do this.

First of all, there are few restrictions on where these left-to-right arrows may go. Any limitations that exist would seem to relate to the first two columns. We need to rule out drawing an arrow from constructionism or subjectivism to positivism (or, therefore, post-positivism), since positivism is objectivist by definition. Without a thoroughly objectivist epistemology, positivism would not be positivism as we understand it today. Nor would we want to draw an arrow from objectivism or subjectivism to phenomenology. Constructionism and phenomenology are so intertwined that one could hardly be phenomenological while espousing either an objectivist or a subjectivist epistemology. And postmodernism well and truly jettisons any vestiges of an objectivist view of knowledge and meaning. Other than that, as we draw our arrows from column to column, it would seem that 'the sky's the limit'. Certainly, if it suits their purposes, any of the theoretical perspectives could make use of any of the methodologies, and any of the methodologies could make use of any of the methods. There are typical strings, to be sure, and we have noted two of them in Figure 2 and Figure 3, but 'typical' does not mean 'mandatory'.

Secondly, we can draw arrows from a particular item to more than one item in the column to the right. Historically, objectivism, constructionism and subjectivism have each informed quite a number of different perspectives. Similarly, one theoretical perspective often comes to be embodied in a number of methodologies. Symbolic interactionism is a case in point. It has informed both ethnography and grounded theory and we might well draw arrows from that theoretical perspective to each of those methodologies. Again, while critical inquiry will certainly be linked to action research, we can also draw an arrow from critical inquiry to ethnography. Yes, the critical form of inquiry has come to be embodied in ethnography too, transforming it in the process. Now it is no longer a characteristically uncritical form of research that merely seeks to understand a culture. It is critical ethnography, a methodology that strives to unmask hegemony and address oppressive forces. In the same way, there can be a feminist ethnography or a postmodernist ethnography.

Still, we should not be so carried away with our sense of freedom in drawing arrows from left to right that we forget to draw arrows in other directions as well. Our arrows can fly from right to left too. In terms of what informs what, going from left to right would seem a logical progression. At the same time, in describing our piece of research, we found our starting point in methods and methodology. This suggests that, to mark the chronological succession of events in our research, the arrows may need to be drawn from right to left as well.

Certainly, they may. Not too many of us embark on a piece of social research with epistemology as our starting point. 'I am a constructionist. Therefore, I will investigate . . .' Hardly. We typically start with a real-life issue that needs to be addressed, a problem that needs to be solved, a question that needs to be answered. We plan our research in terms of that issue or problem or question. What, we go on to ask, are the further issues, problems or questions implicit in the one we start with? What, then, is the aim and what are the objectives of our research? What strategy seems likely to provide what we are looking for? What does that strategy direct us to do to achieve our aims and objectives? In this way our research question, incorporating the purposes of our research, leads us to methodology and methods.

We need, of course, to justify our chosen methodology and methods. In the end, we want outcomes that merit respect. We want the observers of our research to recognise it as sound research. Our conclusions need to stand up. On some understandings of research (and of truth), this will mean that we are after objective, valid and generalisable conclusions as the outcome of our research. On other understandings, this is never realisable. Human knowledge is not like that. At best, our outcomes will be suggestive rather than conclusive. They will be plausible, perhaps even convincing, ways of seeing things—and, to be sure, helpful ways of seeing things—but certainly not any 'one true way' of seeing things. We may be positivists or non-positivists, therefore. Either way, we need to be concerned about the process we have engaged in; we need to lay that process out for the scrutiny of the observer; we need to defend that process as a form of human inquiry that should be taken seriously. It is this that sends us to our theoretical perspective and epistemology and calls upon us to expound them incisively. From methods and methodology to theoretical perspective and epistemology, then. Now our arrows are travelling from right to left.

Speaking in this vein sounds as if we create a methodology for ourselves—as if the focus of our research leads us to devise our own ways of proceeding that allow us to achieve our purposes. That, as it happens, is precisely the case. In a very real sense, every piece of research is unique and calls for a unique methodology. We, as the researcher, have to develop it.

If that is the case, why are we bothering with the plethora of methodologies and methods set forth for us so profusely that they seem like William James's 'blooming, buzzing confusion'? Why don't we just sit down and work out for ourselves how we are to go about it?

In the end, that is precisely what we have to do. Yet a study of how other people have gone about the task of human inquiry serves us well and is surely indispensable. Attending to recognised research designs and their various theoretical underpinnings exercises a formative influence upon us. It awakens us to ways of research we would never otherwise have conceived of. It makes us much more aware of what is *possible* in research. Even so, it is by no means a matter of plucking a methodology off the shelf. We acquaint ourselves with the various methodologies. We evaluate their presuppositions. We weigh their strengths and weaknesses. Having done all that and more besides, we still have to forge a methodology that will meet *our* particular purposes in *this* research. One of the established methodologies may suit the task that confronts us. Or perhaps none of them do and we find ourselves drawing on several methodologies, moulding them into a way of proceeding that achieves the outcomes we look to. Perhaps we need to be more inventive still and create a methodology that in many respects is quite new. Even if we tread this track of innovation and invention, our engagement with the various methodologies in use will have played a crucial educative role.

Arrows right to left as well as left to right. What about arrows up and down? Yes, that too. Renowned critical theorist Jürgen Habermas carried on a debate with hermeneuticist Hans-Georg Gadamer over many years and out of that interplay there developed for Habermas a 'critical hermeneutics'. Here we have critical theory coming to inform hermeneutics. In our four-column model, the arrow would rise up the same column ('theoretical perspective') from critical inquiry to hermeneutics. Similarly, we can talk of critical feminism or feminist critical inquiry, of postmodernist feminism or postmodernist critical inquiry. There is plenty of scope for arrows up and down.

THE GREAT DIVIDE

In the model we are following here, you will notice that the distinction between qualitative research and quantitative research occurs at the level of methods. It does not occur at the level of epistemology or theoretical perspective. What does occur back there at those exalted levels is a distinction between objectivist/positivist research, on the one hand, and constructionist or subjectivist research, on the other. Yet, in most research textbooks, it is qualitative research and quantitative research that are set against each other as polar opposites. Just as the student of Latin is taught very early on via the opening lines of Caesar's Gallic Wars that 'All Gaul is divided into three parts', so every beginning researcher learns at once that all research is divided into two parts—and these are 'qualitative' and 'quantitative', respectively.

Our model suggests that this divide—objectivist research associated with quantitative methods over against constructionist or subjectivist research associated with qualitative methods—is far from justified. Most methodologies known today as forms of 'qualitative research' have in the past been carried out in an utterly empiricist, positivist manner. This is true, as we have already noted, of the early history of ethnography. On the other hand, quantification is by no means ruled out within non-positivist research. We may consider ourselves utterly devoted to qualitative research methods. Yet, when we think about investigations carried out in the normal course of our daily lives, how often measuring and counting turn out to be essential to our purposes. The ability to measure and count is a precious human achievement and it behoves us not to be dismissive of it. We should accept that, whatever research we engage in, it is possible for either qualitative methods or quantitative methods, or both, to serve our purposes. Our research can be qualitative or quantitative, or both qualitative and quantitative, without this being in any way problematic.

What would seem to be problematic is any attempt to be at once objectivist and constructionist (or subjectivist). On the face of it, to say that there is objective meaning and, in the same breath, to say that there is no objective meaning certainly does appear contradictory. To be sure, the postmodernist world that has grown up around us calls all our cherished antinomies into question, and we are invited today to embrace 'fuzzy logic' rather than the logic we have known in the past with its principle of contradiction. Nevertheless, even at the threshold of the 21st century, not too many of us are comfortable with such ostensibly blatant contradiction in what we claim.

To avoid such discomfort, we will need to be consistently objectivist or consistently constructionist (or subjectivist).

If we seek to be consistently objectivist, we will distinguish scientifically established objective meanings from subjective meanings that people hold in everyday fashion and that at best 'reflect' or 'mirror' or 'approximate' objective meanings. We will accept, of course, that these subjective meanings are important in people's lives and we may adopt qualitative methods of ascertaining what those meanings are. This is epistemologically consistent. It has a downside, all the same. It makes people's everyday understandings inferior, epistemologically, to more scientific understandings. In this way of viewing things, one cannot predicate of people's everyday understandings the truth claims one makes for what is scientifically established.

If we seek to be consistently constructionist, we will put all understandings, scientific and non-scientific alike, on the very same footing. They are all constructions. None is objective or absolute or truly generalisable. Scientific knowledge is just a particular form of constructed knowledge designed to serve particular purposes—and, yes, it serves them well. Constructionists may indeed make use of quantitative methods but their constructionism makes a difference. We need to ask ourselves, in fact, what a piece of quantitative research looks like when it is informed by a constructionist epistemology. What difference does that make to it? Well, for a start, it makes a big difference to the truth claims proffered on its behalf, all the more so as one moves towards subjectivism rather than constructionism. No longer is there talk of objectivity, or validity, or generalisability. For all that, there is ample recognition that, after its own fashion, quantitative research has valuable contributions to make, even to a study of the farthest reaches of human being.

Is this scaffolding proving helpful? If so, let us go on to examine the items in some of its columns. We will confine ourselves to the first two columns. We will look at epistemological issues and issues relating to theoretical perspectives.

As already foreshadowed, the epistemological stance of objectivism will be considered in the context of positivism, with which it is so closely allied. Constructionism, as the epistemology claimed in most qualitative approaches today, deserves extended treatment. Our discussion of the constructionist theorising of knowledge will set it against the subjectivism only too often articulated under the rubric of constructionism and found self-professedly in much structuralist, post-structuralist and postmodernist thought.

After our discussion of positivism, the theoretical perspectives we go on to study are interpretivism, critical inquiry, feminism and postmodernism. Thinking about postmodernism will make it necessary for us to delve also into structuralism and post-structuralism.

As we discuss these perspectives and stances, we should remind ourselves many times over that we are not exploring them for merely speculative purposes. You and I will allow ourselves to be led at times into very theoretical material indeed. Nevertheless, we will refuse to wear the charge of being abstract intellectualisers, divorced from experience and action. It is our very inquiry into human experience and action that sends us this far afield. The long journey we are embarking upon arises out of an awareness on our part that, at every point in our research—in our observing, our interpreting, our reporting, and everything else we do as researchers—we inject a host of assumptions. These are assumptions about human knowledge and assumptions about realities encountered in our human world. Such assumptions shape for us the meaning of research questions, the purposiveness of research methodologies, and the interpretability of research findings. Without unpacking these assumptions and clarifying them, no one (including ourselves!) can really divine what our research has been or what it is now saying.

Performing this task of explication and explanation is precisely what we are about here. Far from being a theorising that takes researchers from their research, it is a theorising embedded in the research act itself. Without it, research is not research.

2

POSITIVISM:
THE MARCH OF SCIENCE

Truth is truth
To the end of reckoning.

William Shakespeare, *Measure for Measure*

Inherent in the methodologies guiding research efforts are a number of theoretical perspectives, as the previous chapter has suggested and Table 1 has exemplified. Furthermore, there is a range of epistemological positions informing the theoretical perspectives. Each epistemological stance is an attempt to explain how we know what we know and to determine the status to be ascribed to the understandings we reach.

In Chapter 1 we tried our hand at establishing some relationships among these elements. We connected epistemologies to perspectives to methodologies to methods. In the history of the natural and social sciences, some connections of this kind occur more frequently than others. Certainly, as we look back over the last century-and-a-half, there is one very common string that emerges across our columns. It starts with objectivism (as epistemology), passes through positivism (as theoretical perspective), and is found, historically, informing many of the methodologies articulated within social research.

This positivist perspective encapsulates the spirit of the Enlightenment, the self-proclaimed Age of Reason that began in England in the seventeenth century and flourished in France in the century that followed. Like the Enlightenment that gave it birth, positivism offers assurance of unambiguous and accurate knowledge of the world. For all that, we find it adopting a number of guises. This chapter is concerned with the various meanings that positivism has assumed throughout the history of the concept and with the post-positivism that has emerged to attenuate its claims without rejecting its basic perspective.

POSITIVISM

The coining of the word 'positivism' is often attributed to Auguste Comte. Unjustifiably, it seems. While he did make up the word 'sociology' (and its predecessor, 'social physics'), he cannot be credited with 'positivism'. We are on safer ground in seeing Comte as a populariser of the word, especially through the *Société Positiviste*, which he founded in 1848. Populariser is an apt term to use here, for positivism undoubtedly became a vogue word and soon replaced the earlier usages 'positive science' and 'positive philosophy'.

These latter terms were used by Comte himself, following his mentor Henri de Saint-Simon. One of Comte's major works is the six-volumed *Cours de philosophie positive*, which appeared between 1830 and 1842. However, by the time Comte began talking of positive philosophy and positive science, the terms already had a very long history. They can be found centuries earlier in the writings of Francis Bacon (1561–1626).

'Positive science' sounds strange to our ears. We may have to resist the temptation to ask what negative science would look like. Yet, if *positive* is not being used here in contradistinction to *negative*, in what sense is it being used? To answer that question, we need to look to the traditional use of the word in comparable terms such as 'positive religion' and 'positive law'. There the word serves to distinguish positive religion from natural religion and positive law from natural law.

Natural religion? This is religion that people reason their way to. They work out the existence of God (or of many gods), the duty of divine worship, and so on, by rational argument based on their knowledge of the world. It is styled 'natural' because it is seen to stem from the nature of things. Positive religion, to the contrary, is not the outcome of speculation. It is essentially *something that is posited*. What is posited, thereby forming the starting point and foundation for positive religion, is divinely revealed truth. Positive religion is not arrived at by reasoning. It is a 'given'.

Positive law, too, finds its basis in *something that is posited*. In this case, what has been posited is legislation enacted by a lawgiver. Drawing its authority from an existing code of prescriptions and proscriptions, positive law contrasts sharply with the traditional notion of natural law. While the concept of natural law has a long and ambiguous history, for our purposes here it can be seen as a complex of responsibilities and obligations that, starting from the nature of the world and human nature within the world, people reason their way to. Once again, it is 'natural' because it is seen to stem from the nature of things. Thus, actions seen as wrongful in terms of natural law are considered to be wrong by their very nature. As the old principle has it, such acts are 'prohibited because they are evil' (*prohibita quia mala*). On the other hand, an action considered wrongful in terms of positive law is not regarded as wrong in itself. It is wrong because it has been forbidden by a legislator. In other words, acts of that kind are 'evil because they are prohibited' (*mala quia prohibita*). The concept of positive law is very different. Here there is no cerebral process reasoning about nature or natures. Positive law, like positive religion, is founded on a 'given'.

What does all this have to do with science? Quite a lot, as it happens. Those speaking and writing of 'positive science' were using the word in the same vein. They were talking of a science—*scientia*, 'knowledge'— that is not arrived at speculatively (as in the metaphysics of philosophical schools) but is grounded firmly and exclusively in *something that is posited*. The basis of this kind of science is direct experience, not speculation. Rather than proceeding via some kind of abstract reasoning process, positive science proceeds by a study of the 'given' (in Latin *datum* or, in the plural, *data*).

For many adherents of positive science ('positivists', therefore), what is posited or given in direct experience is what is observed, the observation in question being scientific observation carried out by way of the scientific method. This is certainly the understanding of positivism that prevails today. Although this contemporary understanding assigns a quite definite meaning to positivism, it is not in itself a univocal concept. As many as twelve varieties of positivism have been distinguished by some authors. There is not scope here to deal with the whole bewildering array of positivisms, but we can perhaps touch on some important historical forms that positivism has assumed.

COMTE'S POSITIVISM

Auguste Comte (1798–1857) saw himself at all times as a scientist. A largely self-taught and independent scientist, to be sure, for his formal training was short-lived and he never held an academic post of any standing. In 1814 he began studies at France's leading scientific school, the *École Polytechnique* in Paris. Less than two years after his enrolment, student unrest led to the closure of the school and a far-reaching reorganisation of its program. When it opened its doors once more,

Comte did not seek readmission but devoted himself instead to private tutoring in mathematics.

Much more influential than his year or two at the *École Polytechnique* was his association from 1817 to 1824 with Henri de Saint-Simon. A bizarre, yet fascinating, figure in French intellectual life around the turn of the nineteenth century, Saint-Simon had a long-standing concern for the reconstruction of society. He was convinced that no worthwhile social reorganisation could take place without the reconstruction of intellectual understanding. What Comte imbibed from Saint-Simon was, above all else, this concern for the emergence of a stable and equitable society—and therefore for the development of its *sine qua non*, a valid and comprehensive social science. Despite his bitter parting from Saint-Simon and a total rejection of his mentoring, this goal continued to inspire all of Comte's subsequent endeavours. To the positivism of his science he brought a passionate zeal for social reform. His dedication to society's wellbeing was as fervent as that of any religious zealot and led him in the end to promulgate an utterly secular Religion of Humanity, incorporating a priesthood and liturgical practice all its own. For all the disdain he evinced for the 'theological stage' of societal development and for the religious aspirations of Saint-Simon's latter days, and not-withstanding his eagerness for a thoroughly 'positive' science to replace the ratiocinations of the philosophers, there are metaphysical and quasi-religious assumptions aplenty in what Comte wrote and did. It was certainly on the basis of a well-elaborated worldview that he felt able to call upon all people to become positivists and thereby play their part in establishing the just society.

The kind of social reorganisation Comte envisages requires the human mind to function at its very best. This, he feels, can happen only when all have embraced one scientific method. True enough, there is no one general law obtaining in all the sciences to give them substantive unity. Comte is no reductionist. Nevertheless, there is a universality of method that can unify the practice of science. The scientific method he has in mind is the method emanating from positivism. Not that it is a uniform method to be woodenly applied. Rather, it is a flexible method that succeeds in remaining homogeneous in a multitude of contexts. It is this desire for unity-via-method that moves Comte to set all the sciences in a hierarchy, leading from the most basic science—mathematics—through astronomy, and then physics, to chemistry and biology, culminating in what he sees as the highest science of all, his beloved sociology. Hence Comte's belief that scientific method retains the same essential features whether one is speaking of the natural sciences or the human sciences.

What are these essential features of the scientific method?

Given the contemporary identification of positivism with quantitative methods of research, and in view of Comte's known skills in mathematics, one might be forgiven for expecting the essential features of his scientific method to be couched in mathematical terms. That would be a mistake, nonetheless.

> When Comte talks about positivism, it cannot too often be stressed that he means an attitude of mind towards science and the explanation of man, nature, and society, and not some predilection for mathematical precision, especially not in sociology. In fact, Comte expressly makes a distinction between the search for certainty in science and the mistaken search for numerical precision. (Simpson 1982, p. 69)

Comte, in fact, warns against the dangers of an overly mathematical approach. 'The most perfect methods may, however, be rendered deceptive by misuse and this we must bear in mind. We have seen that mathematical analysis itself may betray us into substituting signs for ideas, and that it conceals inanity of conception under an imposing verbiage' (in Simpson 1982, p. 80).

Nor is Comte to be linked to some crude kind of objectivism. For him, scientific knowledge is not a matter of grasping an objective meaning independent of social thought and social conditions. Comte recognised, like Marx (and like Hegel before Marx), that human consciousness is determined by 'the social'. There is an interdependence here, as Simpson points out in expounding Comte's thought on this matter:

> Only long struggles for positivistic ideology by men of foresight serve to achieve social conditions under which metaphysical propositions give way to positivistic ones. Conversely, the positivistic stage is reached in any science—and especially in sociology—through a continual reorganization of society made possible by the pursuit of sociology and its application to practical problems, particularly problems in the organization of knowledge, its propagation, and its being passed on from generation to generation. (1982, p. 70)

Comte's quarry is the order he believes can be found in the world. Not for him the quest for first causes and last ends so beloved of the metaphysicians. Whether one is focused on nature or society, his positive science bids us look instead to 'laws' that can be scientifically established; that is, to facts that regularly characterise particular types of beings and constant relationships that can be shown to obtain among various phenomena. The direct methods whereby these laws can be established scientifically are observation, experiment and comparison.

At long last! This is finally beginning to sound like what we have always known as positivism. Yet even here we find Comte warning us,

'No social fact can have any scientific meaning till it is connected with some other social fact; without such connection it remains a mere anecdote, involving no rational utility' (in Simpson 1982, p. 78). Nor by 'experiment' does he necessarily mean what we know today as controlled experimentation. He includes under this rubric the study of events that just happen to happen and over which the sociologist has no control. And the 'comparison' he suggests is multifaceted: it includes cross-cultural comparison and especially historical comparison. Comte is, in fact, eminently historical in his approach. As Raymond Aron puts it (1965, p. 70), Comte holds that 'the different phases of human history are characterized by their way of thinking, and the present and final stage will be marked by the universal triumph of positive thought'.

Auguste Comte is seen as the founder of positivism. He did not see himself in that light. As he understood his role, it was that of passing on a torch that had been lit centuries before his time. Certainly, what he had to say about observation and experiment and the establishment of scientific laws can be found centuries earlier in Bacon. Yet, whether we see Comte as the source or merely the channel, it appears clear enough that positivism has changed dramatically since he first appropriated the word. One of the factors in its evolution has been its passing from the hands of working scientists to those of theoretical scientists and philosophers. The former are anxious to determine whether they can use in the human sciences the methods that are being used in the natural sciences. The latter's concern is different. It has to do directly with epistemology and logic. It is a concern to determine what truth claims can be made about scientific findings—or, indeed, about anything.

THE VIENNA CIRCLE AND LOGICAL POSITIVISM

The roots of the Vienna Circle lie in discussions that began in the first decade of the twentieth century, involving social philosopher Otto Neurath, mathematician Hans Hahn and physicist Philip Frank. The Circle came to prominence in the 1920s when Moritz Schlick assumed its leadership. Schlick, who had begun his academic life as a physicist, turned to philosophy and in 1922 was appointed to the chair of philosophy of the inductive sciences at the University of Vienna. It was the discussions that took place within the Vienna Circle, and between the Vienna Circle and its counterparts at Warsaw and Berlin, that gave birth to the philosophy of logical positivism.

The Vienna Circle flourished throughout the 1920s but the coming of Nazism spelled its doom, most of its members being Jewish or Marxist (or both). Many went abroad in the early 1930s, Schlick was assassinated on the steps of the University of Vienna in 1936, and the Circle was officially dissolved in 1938. Its voice was not stifled, however. In fact, the scattering of Circle members—Rudolf Carnap to Chicago, Kurt Gödel to Princeton, Otto Neurath and Friedrich Waisman to Oxford, and so on—served to ensure that logical positivism had world-wide impact. Even before the demise of the Vienna Circle, its philosophy had been popularised in the English-speaking world by A.J. Ayer's *Language, Truth and Logic*, which appeared in 1936.

What was the Vienna Circle's focus of interest, then? As we have seen, Comte and his associates wanted to introduce the methods of the natural sciences to the practice of the social sciences. Now the Vienna Circle was seeking to introduce the methods and exactitude of mathematics to the study of philosophy (as had already happened in the field of symbolic logic).

The Circle certainly appeared to have the expertise it needed for this task. Within its membership, besides an array of empiricist philosophers, there were a number of individuals with outstanding expertise in the field of mathematics (Gödel, for one) and logic (Rudolf Carnap, for instance). There were also eminent scientists whose science was highly mathematical in character.

The work of Gottlob Frege, Bertrand Russell and Alfred North White-head provided the Vienna Circle with an infrastructure for their discussions in the field of logic. An even more important influence on its developing philosophy was the thought of Ludwig Wittgenstein (1889–1951). Wittgenstein, a native of Vienna, came into contact with the Circle in the late 1920s. His *Tractatus Logico-Philosophicus*, published in 1921, had been studied intensely by several members of the Vienna Circle and the Circle shared his interest in the logical analysis of propositions. Wittgenstein's thought was probably not fully under-stood within the Vienna Circle and, in any case, he went on to reverse his position quite radically, as his posthumous work *Philosophical Investi-gations* dramatically reveals. All this notwithstanding, the early Wittgensteinian position was a crucial influence in the development of the Circle's viewpoint. Its membership constructed from it a basis for linking truth to meaning in a way that allows no pathway to genuine knowledge other than that of science. Thereby they excluded meta-physics, theology and ethics from the domain of warrantable human knowledge.

One of the notions drawn from Wittgenstein was what came to be known as the 'verification principle' (or 'principle of verifiability'). Schlick and Ayer embraced this principle enthusiastically and made it a central tenet of logical positivism. According to the verification principle, no statement is meaningful unless it is capable of being verified.

How does one verify a statement, then? As logical positivism would have it, there are only two ways.

In some cases, a statement can be verified because what is predicated of the subject is nothing more than something included in the very definition of the subject. A very obvious instance of this would be the statement, 'A doe is a female deer'. This can be verified simply by examining the definition of a doe. Mathematical statements can also be seen in this light. 'Two-plus-two equals four', or 'three-plus-one equals four', is a statement in this category, since the term 'four' is one that we have created to stand for 'two-plus-two' and 'three-plus-one'. Following terminology that derives from Immanuel Kant, such statements are known as *analytic* statements. An analytic proposition is one whose ascription of a predicate to a subject can be verified, and its meaningfulness thereby established, simply via an analysis of what the subject is.

Analytic statements are far from earth-shattering. They do no more than spell out what is already contained, or not contained, in the definition of the subject. To say that 'A' is 'A', or that 'not-A' is not 'A' is hardly an almighty contribution to human knowledge. Logical positivists would agree. Analytic propositions are either tautologies or contradictions. Nothing more, nothing less. On this accounting, logic and mathematics are merely formal in character. They are quite empty of factual content. In the language of the early Wittgenstein, their content is 'senseless'.

'Senseless' does not mean 'nonsense'. The early Wittgenstein and the logical positivists reserve the latter epithet for non-analytic, or *synthetic*, statements that prove incapable of verification. As one would expect from what has been said already, synthetic statements are propositions in which what is predicated of the subject is *not* included in its definition. Something new is being said about the subject, therefore. Not surprisingly, it is in synthetic statements that logical positivism is primarily interested.

Can synthetic statements be verified and thereby rendered meaningful? If so, how? The logical positivists have a clear-cut answer. Synthetic propositions are verified by experience—and only by experience. Experience? Here too logical positivism is quite definite. Experience means sense-data. What we experience through our senses (immediately, or by way of the instruments of science that extend the operation of our senses) is verified knowledge. This knowledge is 'factual'—and facts are what logical positivism is concerned with before all and above all.

It is, of course, the role of science to establish facts. Philosophy has the task of clarifying and analysing propositions made in the wake of scientific findings.

This line of thought excludes metaphysics, ethics, aesthetics and religion from the purview of genuine philosophy. Metaphysical viewpoints, ethical values, aesthetic judgments and religious beliefs are, as such, unverifiable in the empirical manner demanded by logical positivism. They do not deal in facts and are therefore of no interest to logical positivism. Emotionally, perhaps even spiritually, they may be of great value to people, but cognitively they are meaningless—nonsense, even.

From the viewpoint of logical positivism, the philosopher and the scientist must remain ever alert to the cognitive meaninglessness of views and beliefs of this kind. A clear disjunction must be maintained at all times between fact and value. If we want to deal in human knowledge that has validated meaning, the pathway is that of observation and experiment invoking the evidence of the senses. We need to be thoroughgoing empiricists. (Logical positivism is also known as *logical empiricism*, although some reserve this latter term more strictly for the combination of traditional empiricism and symbolic logic, whether in logical positivism or elsewhere.)

Since physics is the science where such thoroughgoing empiricism is most obvious, we should not be surprised that logical positivism makes particular use of its language. It uses the language of physics both as a tool for analysing and clarifying philosophical issues and as a way to unify scientific terminology. This reflects a certain reductionism within logical positivism: the other disciplines or areas of study are considered to be built upon, and to derive their validity from, the findings of empirical science.

POSITIVISM TODAY

Quite clearly, the meaning of the term 'positivism' has changed and grown over time. So much so that, from the standpoint of the Vienna Circle and in terms of the contemporary understanding of positivism, its acknowledged founder, Auguste Comte, hardly makes the grade.

In the history of ideas, the pathway trodden by positivism turns out to be long, tortuous and complex. Logical positivism has obviously played a major role in developing the concept of positivism that obtains at the present time. For a while, logical positivism looked set not only to dominate the understanding of science but also, in some places at least, to occupy centre stage within the discipline of philosophy itself. Of course, there have been many other factors in the development of the contemporary understanding of positivism. Rather than tracing that development in close detail, we will have to be content to set down positivism's principal features as it is most generally understood today.

One thing is certain: positivism is linked to empirical science as closely as ever. The logical positivists have always been great lovers of science. It has been said of them that they are infatuated with science. Be that as it may, the positivist spirit at the present time continues to adhere to a philosophy of science that attributes a radical unity to all the sciences and sets few bounds to what science is capable of achieving.

Since the time of the Enlightenment, a melioristic spirit has been abroad. There is a widespread notion that we are on a path of inevitable progress. 'Every day, in every way, I'm getting better and better'—Émile Coué's famous dictum parallels a comparable optimism at the societal and even global level. Positivism not only shares this optimistic faith in progress but also presents scientific discovery, along with the technology it begets, as the instrument and driving force of the progress being achieved.

This supreme confidence in science stems from a conviction that scientific knowledge is both accurate and certain. In this respect scientific knowledge contrasts sharply with opinions, beliefs, feelings and assumptions that we gain in non-scientific ways. The principal point of difference is the alleged objectivity of scientific knowledge. It is unlike the subjective understandings we come to hold. Those subjective understandings may be of very great importance in our lives but they constitute an essentially different kind of knowledge from scientifically established facts. Whereas people ascribe subjective meanings to objects in their world, science really 'ascribes' no meanings at all. Instead, it *discovers* meaning, for it is able to grasp objective meaning, that is, meaning already inherent in the objects it considers. To say that objects have such meaning is, of course, to embrace the epistemology of objectivism. Positivism is objectivist through and through. From the positivist viewpoint, objects in the world have meaning prior to, and independently of, any consciousness of them.

From this same viewpoint, scientists are required to keep the distinction between objective, empirically verifiable knowledge and subjective, unverifiable knowledge very much in mind. It emerges as the distinction between fact and value and founds the goal of value-neutral science, which positivistically minded scientists tend to uphold with a significant degree of fervour.

What kind of world, then, is the world of the positivist? Were we to answer, 'A *mathematised* world', we would find ourselves in good company. We would be following the lead given by Edmund Husserl, the founder of phenomenology. Husserl (1970b) attributes this alleged mathematisation of the world to Galileo, in the first instance. He recalls how Galileo dealt with attributes in which there is a clearly subjective element. Such attributes (colour, taste and smell, for instance) he refused to accept as real properties, dismissing them instead as mere secondary properties and not the concern of the scientist. For Galileo, the primary properties of things—'real' properties, therefore—are those that can be measured and counted and thereby quantified. Size, shape, position, number—only properties like these make the grade scientifically. The real world, for the Galilean scientist, is a quantifiable world.

This scientific world is not, of course, the everyday world that people experience. Not even scientists experience it that way in their everyday mode of being. Various authors have considered the example of Tycho Brahe and Johannes Kepler standing together on a hill at sunrise. These two seventeenth-century astronomers held very different views. Brahe thought that the sun circles the earth; Kepler believed that the earth circles the sun. As they watch the sun appear at daybreak, what do they see? Does Brahe see the sun move above the earth's horizon, while Kepler sees the horizon dip below the sun? Norwood Russell Hanson (1972) makes a case for this being so. Others, such as Gerhart and Russell (1984) demur, asserting that, whatever the differences in their scientific stance, Brahe's and Kepler's human experience of a sunrise will be the same in this respect. Most would surely agree. We may believe that the earth is round, and 'Flat Earthers' may be our favourite epithet for people we judge to be behind the times—yet, unless we are doing something like buying a round-the-world air ticket, we do think and act as if the earth were flat. And we are expected to do so. In buying a road map for my trip from Adelaide to Cairns, I would be looked at askance were I to complain to the supplier that the map I am given is flat and not curved.

In other words, the world addressed by positivist science is not the everyday world we experience. As Husserl points out, the scientific world is an abstraction from the 'lived' world; it has been distilled from the world of our everyday experiences, distances us from the world of our everyday experiences, and takes us further still from the world of immediate experience lying behind our everyday experiences. Science imposes a very tight grid on the world it observes. The world perceived through the scientific grid is a highly systematic, well-organised world. It is a world of regularities, constancies, uniformities, iron-clad laws, absolute principles. As such, it stands in stark contrast with the uncertain, ambiguous, idiosyncratic, changeful world we know at first hand.

Making this scientific abstraction from lived reality is not to be criticised. It serves eminently useful purposes, as the history of science and the development of technology witness so forcefully. While there is a downside to the achievements of science and this needs to be kept in mind as well, most of us have abundant reason to be grateful to science.

If we want to quarrel with the positivist view, our quarrel will not be, in the first instance, with what positivist science does. Rather, it will have to do with the status positivism ascribes to scientific findings. Articulating scientific knowledge is one thing; claiming that scientific knowledge is utterly objective and that only scientific knowledge is valid, certain and accurate is another. Since the emergence of positivist science, there has never been a shortage of philosophers and social scientists calling upon it to rein in its excessive assumptions and claims. Many of these philosophers and social scientists have operated out of a quite different epistemology and worldview. As the twentieth century got underway, however, more and more scientists 'from within' added a chorus of their own. Without necessarily jettisoning the objectivism inherent in positivism, these insiders have challenged its claims to objectivity, precision and certitude, leading to an understanding of scientific knowledge whose claims are far more modest. This is a less arrogant form of positivism. It is one that talks of probability rather than certainty, claims a certain level of objectivity rather than absolute objectivity, and seeks to approximate the truth rather than aspiring to grasp it in its totality or essence.

This more or less attenuated form of positivism is known today as post-positivism.[3]

POST-POSITIVISM

Early inroads into the absoluteness and dogmatism of positivist science were made by a pair of eminent physicists, Werner Heisenberg (1901–76) and Niels Bohr (1885–1962).

Heisenberg, a German scientist, is one of the founders of 'quantum theory'. He articulates an 'uncertainty principle' which well and truly calls into question positivist science's claims to certitude and objectivity. According to Heisenberg's principle, it is impossible to determine both the position and momentum of a subatomic particle (an electron, for instance) with any real accuracy. Not only does this preclude the ability to predict a future state with certainty but it suggests that the observed particle is altered in the very act of its being observed, thus challenging the notion that observer and observed are independent. This principle has the effect of turning the laws of physics into relative statements and to some degree into subjective perceptions rather than an expression of objective certainties.

Bohr, a Dane, received the 1922 Nobel Prize in Physics for his work on the structure of the atom. Like Heisenberg, Bohr is concerned with uncertainty but he has a different view about the nature of the uncertainty in question. Heisenberg's argument is epistemological: in pointing to science's inability to determine subatomic dynamics with accuracy, he locates this limitation in the very way in which we humans know what we know. For Bohr, however, the limitation is ontological rather than epistemological: it is due not to how humans *know* but to how subatomic particles *are*. In fine, these particles need to be seen as a kind of reality different from the reality we are used to dealing with. In thinking or talking about them, we need a new set of concepts. We cannot simply take classical concepts like position and momentum and apply them with accuracy to particles. The traditional concepts may, of course, be the best we have, and we may have no alternative but to make do with them. Yet, we should not succumb too easily to the tyranny of prevailing concepts. Bohr urges us to complement their use with other kinds of description that offer a different frame for our considerations. However successful we may be in doing that, the essentially ambiguous character of human knowledge, including scientific knowledge, cannot be side-stepped, as Bohr's whole discussion underlines very cogently.

The impact of Heisenberg's and Bohr's thought has been far-reaching. These scientists sound a note of uncertainty within what has been a very self-confident philosophy of positivist science. That note comes to echo even more loudly as other thinkers begin to address similar issues within science.

One of the factors prompting this concern with epistemology and the philosophy of science has been the recognition that a contradiction exists in scientific practice. There is a chasm between what science purports to do and what it actually does. For all the positivist concern that statements be verified by observation before being accepted as meaningful, a host of elaborate scientific theories have emerged whose development clearly requires the acceptance of much more than direct conclusions from sense-data. Many of the so-called 'facts' that serve as elements of these theories are not directly observed at all. Instead, they have been quite purposefully contrived and introduced as mere heuristic and explanatory devices. This is true of alleged 'entities' such as particles, waves and fields. Scientists act as if these exist and function in the way they postulate and, in terms of their purposes, this may prove an effective way to proceed. In this situation, it is very easy to go on to reify[4] these presumptions. Yet, by positivism's own criteria, such reification is unjustified.

What is emerging in this line of thought is the picture of scientists actively constructing scientific knowledge rather than passively noting laws that are found in nature. This has clear implications for the status that scientific knowledge deserves to have ascribed to it. Many thinkers—philosophers or scientists, or both—have not been slow to point out these implications.

POPPER'S PRINCIPLE OF FALSIFICATION

Sir Karl Popper (1902–94) was born in Vienna. In the 1930s, like so many other figures we are considering here, he was forced by Nazism's advent to power to quit his native land. After a brief period in England, he spent the years of World War II in New Zealand, returning to England in 1946 and serving as a professor at the London School of Economics from 1949 to 1969.

Popper is interested in the philosophical and political implications of genuinely scientific work. He contrasts scientific work with what is done in the 'pseudo-sciences' and tries to draw a clear line of demarcation between the two. His early ideas are found in *The Logic of Scientific Discovery* and *The Open Society and Its Enemies*. Later works include *Objective Knowledge: An Evolutionary Approach* and *The Self and Its Brain*, the latter coauthored with J.C. Eccles.

Despite early association with the Vienna Circle, Popper offers a view of human knowledge very different from that of logical positivism. Not for him any limiting of valid knowledge to statements capable of empirical verification. How, then, does he see scientific knowledge being established? We find a clue to that in the title of yet another of his books, *Conjectures and Refutations: The Growth of Scientific Knowledge*. Instead of scientists proceeding by way of observation and experimentation, thereby pinpointing scientific laws evident in nature itself, Popper sees them engaging in a continual process of conjecture and falsification. An advance in science is not a matter of scientists making a discovery and then proving it to be right. It is a matter of scientists making a guess and then finding themselves unable to prove the guess wrong, despite strenuous efforts to do so.

In putting this position forward, Popper is taking issue with the scientific method as it has been traditionally understood. In fact, he is challenging one of its pivotal notions. He is confronting head on the role that scientific method ascribes to induction. Induction is the process whereby a general law is established by accumulating particular instances. For example, because scientists find time and time again that water boils at 100°C, at least under certain definable conditions, they have felt confident in ascribing to this 'fact' the status of a universal law of physics. Not everyone has shared their confidence. Eighteenth-century philosopher David Hume characterised that confidence as a matter of psychology but not an outcome of logic. We might boil water a thousand times and find in every case that it boils at 100°C; but in Hume's view this provides no *logical* justification for the belief that it must always boil at 100°C. To assume that it must is to assume a world in which the regularities we perceive today will remain unchanged in the future. That is an assumption, not an empirically established truth. A number of later philosophers, Bertrand Russell and C.D. Broad among them, side with Hume in this, seeing induction as very much the weak link in the chain of empiricist science. Scientists may be as empirical as they like in their observations and experiments; yet they must reckon with the consideration—an unpalatable consideration, perhaps—that a non-empirical logical principle remains intrinsic to scientific method.

Popper's solution to this impasse is to substitute falsification for verification at the heart of scientific method. No matter how many examples we muster in support of a general principle, we are unable, logically, to prove it true in absolute terms; yet it takes only one example at variance with a general law to prove, logically and in absolute terms, that it is false. So Popper believes that, in engaging in observation and experiment, scientists are called upon not to prove a theory (they can never do that) but to try to prove it wrong.

For the Baconian understanding of science as an inductive process Popper has substituted the idea of science as hypothetico-deductive. Scientific method is like this: (a) scientific theories are proposed hypothetically; (b) propositions are deduced from these theories; and (c) the propositions are then tested, that is, every effort is made to prove them false. It is this falsifiability that sets scientific claims apart from non-scientific or pseudo-scientific claims. A theory or hypothesis not open to refutation by observation and experiment cannot be regarded as scientific. With this goal of falsification in view, Popper recommends that all scientific theories be presented as clearly as possible so as to lay them wide open to refutation.

It is only when propositions deduced from scientific theory have survived every attempt to refute them that the theory can be provisionally accepted as true. Here the operative word is 'provisionally'. The conviction that no theory can ever be definitively accepted as true lies at the heart of Popper's philosophy. As he put it (1959, p. 280), 'every scientific statement must remain *tentative for ever*'.

All this evinces a very different picture of science, and of the scientist, from the one we find at large among the positivists.

First, in the search for scientific truth, there is a place for guesswork, intuition, the following up of 'hunches'. Not for Popper the image of the scientist as the detached observer of nature. In fact, he does not believe such disinterested observation is possible. Observation takes place within the context of theory and is always shaped by theory. All our observing is done within a horizon of expectations and is therefore necessarily selective.

Second, on Popper's accounting, what is put forward as scientific truth turns out to be, not something shown to be true, but simply something that scientists have so far been unable to prove false. This turns scientific truths into merely provisional statements. 'Our science', warns Popper (1959, p. 278), 'is not knowledge (*epistēmē*): it can never claim to have attained truth, or even a substitute for it, such as probability'.

> Science is not a system of certain, or well-established, statements; nor is it a system which steadily advances towards a state of finality . . .
>
> The old scientific ideal of *epistēmē*—of absolutely certain, demonstrable knowledge—has proved to be an idol . . . It may indeed be corroborated, but every corroboration is relative to other statements which, again, are tentative. Only in our subjective experiences of conviction, in our subjective faith, can we be 'absolutely certain' . . .
>
> Science never pursues the illusory aim of making its answers final, or even probable. Its advance is, rather, towards the infinite yet attainable aim of ever discovering new, deeper, and more general problems, and of subjecting its ever tentative answers to ever renewed and ever more rigorous tests. (Popper 1959, pp. 278, 280, 281)

On that accounting, Olympian dogmatism would seem entirely out of place among Popperian scientists. One would expect of scientists, instead, a large measure of tentativeness, perhaps even a measure of humility.

Where does one find these Popperian scientists? There are humble scientists, to be sure, and scientists often put their hypotheses forward quite tentatively in the first place. Still, on the whole they do seem to be looking for verification rather than falsification, and the observer of the scientific scene is hard put to find any widespread and impassioned effort to prove scientific theories wrong. This is particularly true of the broader, more fundamental, realm of theory. This is rarely called into question. Even in the face of conflicting evidence scientists only too often cling to theory in a quite determined fashion. Obviously, and unsurprisingly, it takes more than falsification to break scientists loose from what they have known and experienced as the very matrix of their thought and practice. Achieving that, some would want to say, takes nothing short of revolution.

KUHN'S 'SCIENTIFIC REVOLUTIONS'

Possibly the most influential book in modern-day philosophy of science is *The Structure of Scientific Revolutions.*

The ideas contained in this book were developed by Thomas Kuhn (1922–96) while he was a graduate student in theoretical physics at Harvard University. What provided the impetus and starting point for this work was an invitation Kuhn received from University President James B. Conant to do some lecturing in science. The course in question was for undergraduates majoring in the humanities and it was put to Kuhn that he should take an historical perspective. So he turned to the history of science to see what lessons it might hold for scientists today.

This is new territory for Kuhn and the lessons he comes to glean from history are not of the kind he has been anticipating. Led back to Aristotle's *Physics,* he is struck forcefully by what he sees as an utter disparity between Aristotelian physics and the physics of Newton. Not a difference of degree but a difference of kind. Not inchoate, less-formed notions in Aristotle that are later to be developed and brought to fruition in Newton. No, these two sets of ideas appear to him so different as to be incomparable. As Kuhn sees it, Aristotle and Newton do not stand at different points on a continuum; they are not even within the same spectrum.

Accordingly, Kuhn concludes, the thought of Newton cannot have grown and developed out of the thought of Aristotle. At some point, the basis and essential elements of Aristotelian physics must have been jettisoned and replaced by a whole new way of seeing things. There has to have been a revolution in scientific thinking.

It is this insight that leads Kuhn to the thesis he develops in *The Structure of Scientific Revolutions.* There, and elsewhere, he takes a much more historical and sociological perspective than philosophers of science before him. He begins by looking directly at scientists and what they do, whether they be scientists of the past or scientists of the present. Where Popper's philosophising and his focus on logic lead him to see scientists and the process of scientific research in terms of what they ought to be rather than what they are, Kuhn's starting point leads him at once to question the alleged objectivity and value-free neutrality of scientific discovery.

What Kuhn never ceases to emphasise is that scientists do their work in and out of a background of theory. This theory comprises a unitary package of beliefs about science and scientific knowledge. It is this set of beliefs that Kuhn calls a *paradigm*. It is an overarching conceptual construct, a particular way in which scientists make sense of the world or some segment of the world.

For scientists in general, the prevailing paradigm is the matrix that shapes the reality to be studied and legitimates the methodology and methods whereby it can be studied. More than that, the prevailing paradigm is quite simply taken for granted within the contemporary scientific ethos. Any challenges that are mounted tend, at the start at least, to be dismissed out of hand. Normal science, Kuhn says, 'often suppresses fundamental novelties because they are necessarily subversive of its basic commitments' (1970, p. 5). Thus, the paradigm establishes the parameters and sets the boundaries for scientific research and, in the ordinary course of events, scientific inquiry is carried out strictly in line with it. At most, scientists will attempt to solve problems in ways that refine the paradigm and extend its scope. Even Popperian science, fiercely focused as it is on refuting the alleged findings of science, takes place in accordance with the dictates of the ruling paradigm. Such science—science in keeping with the paradigm of the day—is what Kuhn is calling 'normal science'. He sees it as a 'sort of puzzle-solving activity in which . . . most physical scientists are normally engaged' (1977, pp. 221–2). As he puts it, 'normal research, even the best of it, is a highly convergent activity based firmly upon a settled consensus acquired from scientific education and reinforced by subsequent life in the profession' (1977, p. 227). Kuhn goes so far as to characterise normal science as 'a complex and consuming mopping up operation' (1977, p. 188). It 'aims to elucidate the scientific tradition in which [the scientist] was raised rather than to change it' (1977, p. 234).

There comes a time, however, when the paradigm proves inadequate. Findings are proposed that cannot be explained within the context of the paradigm that prevails. When anomalies like this arise, 'nature has somehow violated the paradigm-induced expectations that govern normal science' (Kuhn 1970, pp. 52–3). It is a time of crisis. New findings are being put forward in such cogent or widespread fashion, and theories espoused so fervently, that they succeed in calling the paradigm itself into question. The process is often helped on its way by the impact of a revolutionary scientist—usually, Kuhn thinks, a younger person not schooled so long or so deeply in the paradigm guiding current scientific inquiry. Through factors such as these, it comes to be accepted that a whole new way of viewing reality is called for. It is time for a 'paradigm shift'.

In this period of change, what emerges within science is a 'willingness to try anything, the expression of explicit discontent, the recourse to philosophy and to debate over fundamentals' (Kuhn 1970, p. 91). Normal science is being turned on its head and an era of 'extraordinary science' is being ushered in. It is this development that Kuhn styles a *scientific revolution*.

Once one begins to think in this fashion, it is not difficult to find revolutions enough in the history of science. Galileo (and the Leaning Tower of Pisa?) destroying forever the Aristotelian view that bodies fall at a speed proportional to their weight. Copernicus and his heliocentrism prevailing over earth-centred Ptolemeian astronomy. Lavoisier's oxygen theory of combustion replacing Becher's hypothesis of phlogiston. Darwin's theory of natural selection overthrowing forms of scientific theorising that base themselves on a world governed by design. Einstein's theory of relativity shaking the foundations of Newtonian physics. And so on. These are not mere changes *within* science that leave science itself very much as it was. These are changes *of* science. They alter forever the way scientists see the world they are trying to explain. For Kuhn, then, the history of science is not a story of steady advance through adding new data to those already in hand and gradually developing existing theory. Instead, the significant changes in science appear to have occurred through radical shifts in the way scientists view reality.

How have these shifts in perspective come about? Certainly, many non-scientific factors have played a part. Kuhn effectively relates the 'doing' of science to the broader sweep of history and to social factors and social change. Just as effectively, he links scientific effort to the interests, and the psychology, of both the scientific community and individual scientists. Because of this, his influential line of thought constitutes a further loosening of the hold positivism has taken on scientific thought and research. The picture Kuhn paints is not a picture of objective, valid, unchallengeable findings emerging from scientists working with detachment and in a spirit of unalloyed scientific dedication. To the contrary, scientific endeavour, as Kuhn conceives it, is a very human affair. Human interests, human values, human fallibility, human foibles—all play a part.

If one accepts Kuhn's picture of things, it becomes very hard to sustain an image of science as a 'garden enclosed'. Kuhn's arguments make it impossible to elevate the work of the scientist over that of other professionals. Science now appears as run of the mill as any other human activity. Seen in the light of his arguments, how can science remain on the pedestal where the logical positivists have enshrined it? Change in science, it would seem, takes place in very much the same way as it occurs elsewhere—in art, say, or politics. It certainly does not necessarily come about in a disciplined or orderly fashion. Often, it just seems to 'happen', coming about in makeshift and fortuitous ways. In 'anarchic' fashion, perhaps? Could one go so far as to say that? Yes, even that.

FEYERABEND'S 'FAREWELL TO REASON'

It is Paul Feyerabend (1924–94) who describes scientific progress as 'anarchic'. Science, he tells us, 'is an essentially anarchic enterprise' (Feyerabend 1993, p. 9). This is not a criticism. For Feyerabend, working in anarchic fashion is simply the way things have to be. Rather than decrying scientific anarchism, we should embrace it warmly and celebrate it fervently, for it is necessary for the progress of science and the development of culture. Scientific progress may mean different things to different people, but Feyerabend's thesis is '*that anarchism helps to achieve progress in any one of the senses one cares to choose*' (1993, p. 18). He goes on to outline for us 'an anarchistic methodology and a corresponding anarchistic science' (1993, p. 13). Already we may be glimpsing why Feyerabend has so often been referred to as the *enfant terrible* of late twentieth-century philosophy of science.

Feyerabend too was born in Vienna. He originally studied physics but, after working under Popper, he came to the fore as a philosopher of science in the 1960s. He spent several decades in Britain and the United States before becoming professor of the philosophy of science in Zürich, a post he filled for the last fifteen years of his life.

Feyerabend starts off reasonably close to the position of Popper, his one-time mentor and fellow Austrian. However, his forceful style of presentation provokes, even at the start, an accusation that has never been levelled at Popper—the charge of being an enemy of science. If Feyerabend's critics brand him anti-science on the basis of his early thought, they very soon find further and more explosive ammunition in what he goes on to say and write. He moves not only well beyond Popper but even beyond Kuhn. One way in which he does so is in his attitude to 'normal science'. For all his talk of normal science as a 'mopping up operation', and notwithstanding its failure to challenge the ruling paradigm, Kuhn never fails to uphold the importance of its problem-solving function. Feyerabend, on the contrary, is thoroughly suspicious of this unchallenged continuance of normal science, alleging that it is based on indoctrination and constitutes a threat to academic freedom.

While Feyerabend may not be anti-science, he leaves no doubt about how he views the adulation traditionally offered to science.

On the other hand, we can agree that in a world full of scientific products scientists may be given a special status just as henchmen had a special status at times of social disorder or priests had when being a citizen coincided with being a member of a single universal Church. (Feyerabend 1993, p. 250)

In all this, Feyerabend insists that his quarry is positivism, not science as such. What he is questioning radically is the role of reason in science. He titles one of his books *Farewell to Reason*. Not that he is descending into wild irrationalism. He is querying the role of reason *as it is generally understood*. As he goes to some pains to emphasise in his posthumous autobiography, *Killing Time*, he is not denigrating reason as such but only attacking petrified and tyrannical versions of it. Feyerabend's basic position is that, since science cannot be grounded philosophically in any compelling way, scientific findings are no more than beliefs and we should not privilege them over other kinds of belief—even Voodoo! Voodoo, in fact, 'has a firm though still not sufficiently understood material basis', writes Feyerabend, as he calls for a 'pluralistic methodology' (1993, pp. 36, 38).

Science, then, is 'much more "sloppy" and "irrational" than its methodological image' and 'the attempt to make science more "rational" and more precise is bound to wipe it out' (Feyerabend 1993, p. 157). In Feyerabend's judgment, 'what appears as "sloppiness", "chaos" or "opportunism" . . . has a most important function in the development of those very theories which we today regard as essential parts of our knowledge of nature' (1993, pp. 157–8). Hence his likening of the scientific anarchist to 'an undercover agent who plays the game of Reason in order to undercut the authority of Reason' (Feyerabend 1993, p. 23). He is influenced here by the Austrian satirists Johann Nestroy and Karl Kraus and by Dadaism, that nihilistic movement earlier this century which stressed the absurd and the unpredictable in artistic creation. Feyerabend stresses the absurd and the unpredictable in scientific knowledge.

Anything goes, then? Feyerabend does boldly say as much. He even describes this as the only principle 'that can be defended under *all* circumstances and in all stages of human development' (Feyerabend 1993, pp. 18–19). Yet he has norms of his own. For one thing, he demands that scientists test out their perceptions. The willingness to do this constitutes the difference between science and non-science (or, in his more forthright terms, between the domains of the respectable thinker and the crank). Adopting a certain point of view means a starting point for research, not some kind of conclusion. Cranks will flatly deny that any issue exists or will be content to defend their position, but the respectable thinker thoroughly tests out the usefulness of the viewpoint, taking full account of factors that seem to favour its opponents. As one would expect from what has been said of Feyerabend already, he does not identify the respectable thinker simply with the person who is faithful to the accepted line in science. One example of this is his refusal to dismiss creationism out of hand as a crank viewpoint and his opposition to its exclusion from school curricula. If people are willing to test out their perceptions and have them tested out by others, they are respectable thinkers, no matter how unconventional their thinking, and they have a place in the generation of human knowledge.

How, then, should scientists test out their perceptions? By *counterinduction*. Counterinductive measures are not Popper-style attempts to falsify theories and hypotheses. 'Methodologists may point to the importance of falsifications', Feyerabend writes scathingly, 'but they blithely use falsified theories' (1993, p. 50). No, we need rules that will 'enable us to choose between theories which we have already tested *and which are falsified*' (Feyerabend 1993, p. 51). Counterinduction is just such a 'measuring-stick'. Rather than an attempt to prove something false, it is a calling of 'commonly-used concepts' into question by developing something with which they can be compared.

> Therefore, the first step in our criticism of customary concepts and customary reactions is to step outside the circle and either to invent a new conceptual system, for example, a new theory, that clashes with the most carefully established observational results and confounds the most plausible theoretical principles, or to import such a system from outside science, from religion, from mythology, from the ideas of incompetents, or the ramblings of madmen. (Feyerabend 1993, pp. 52–3)

Ideas of incompetents? Ramblings of madmen? Obviously, anything does go! Feyerabend's point, of course, is that, if we want to examine something we are using all the time, we cannot discover it from the inside. We need, he tells us, 'an *external* standard of criticism', 'a set of alternative assumptions' (Feyerabend 1993, p. 22). This is his strategy of counterinduction. Counterinduction is 'both a *fact*—science could not exist without it—and a legitimate and much needed *move* in the game of science' (Feyerabend 1993, p. 53).

Behind this stance is Feyerabend's recognition that scientific thinking, like all human thought, is historically conditioned through and through.

> However, the material which a scientist actually has at his disposal, his laws, his experimental results, his mathematical techniques, his epistemological prejudices, his attitude towards the absurd consequences of the theories which he accepts, is indeterminate in many ways, ambiguous, *and never fully separated from the historical background*. (Feyerabend 1993, p. 51)

Ideas being historically conditioned and never absolute, Paul Feyerabend believes in pushing them to their extremes. In *Three Dialogues on Knowledge*, a series of dialogues based on the Socratic model, he reveals that, when he comes across unusual ideas, he tries them out. His way of trying them out is to push them to the limit. 'There is', he tells us (1991, p. 50), 'not a single idea, no matter how absurd and repulsive, that has not a sensible aspect, and there is not a single view, no matter how plausible and humanitarian, that does not encourage and then conceal our stupidity and our criminal tendencies'. Many would be comfortable enough with this thought when it is applied to cultural understandings and socio-political stances. People find it far more challenging when applied, as Feyerabend intends it to be applied, to scientific 'truths'. The point is, of course, that Feyerabend refuses to accept the distinction. For him, scientific truths are no less cultural in character, and no less socio-political in origin, than any other of the beliefs we hold. He tells us, in fact, that 'rationalists clamouring for objectivity and rationality are just trying to sell a tribal creed of their own' (Feyerabend 1987, p. 301).

Feyerabend, along with Popper and Kuhn, has had an impact. Positivism, as we have seen, postulates the objective existence of meaningful reality. It considers such meaningful reality to be value-neutral, ahistorical and cross-cultural. It believes that, if one goes about it in the right way, one can identify such reality with certitude. What people like Popper, Kuhn and Feyerabend have done is to question one or other, or all, of these tenets in quite radical fashion.

In the wake of their considerations, some have come to reject positivism and the objectivism that informs it and to adopt a constructionist view of meaningful reality. Others remain within the positivist camp but temper very significantly the status they ascribe to their findings, the claims they make about them. It is not possible, they have come to recognise, to find some Archimedean point from which realities in the world can be viewed free from any influence of the observer's standpoint. They admit that, no matter how faithfully the scientist adheres to scientific method, research outcomes are neither totally objective nor unquestionably certain. They may claim a higher level of objectivity and certitude for scientific findings than for other opinions and beliefs, but the absoluteness has gone and claims to validity are tentative and qualified.

It is this humbler version of the scientific approach, one that no longer claims an epistemologically or metaphysically privileged position, that has come to be known as post-positivism.

Reporting our research requires us to set forth the research process we have engaged in and to do so faithfully and comprehensively. It is, after all, our account of the research process that establishes the credentials of our research. Why should anyone set store by what we are asserting as a result of our investigation? And what store should anyone set by it? The only satisfactory answer to these questions is, 'Look at the way we have gone about it'. The process itself is our only justification. For that reason, expounding our research process, including its more theoretical moorings (or, if you prefer, the assumptions we bring to our methodology and methods), assumes obvious and crucial importance.

What store should anyone set by our research findings? Even in putting the question, we sense another question coming to the fore—and a prior question, into the bargain. What store are we *asking* people to set by our research findings? After all, we may be presenting our findings as objective truths, claiming validity, perhaps generalisability, on their behalf. In that case, we are calling upon people to accept our findings as established fact, or at least as close to established fact as our research has enabled us to reach. On the other hand, we may be offering our findings as interpretation. It is a certain spin we have put on the data. In that case we are inviting people to weigh our interpretation, judge whether it has been soundly arrived at and is plausible (convincing, even?), and decide whether it has application to their interests and concerns.

In other words, we may be presenting our research in positivist terms or non-positivist terms. Let us say it again: it is a matter of positivism vs non-positivism, not a matter of quantitative vs qualitative. It is possible for a quantitative piece of work to be offered in non-positivist form. On the other hand, there is plenty of scope for qualitative research to be understood positivistically or situated in an overall positivist setting, and, therefore, for even self-professed qualitative researchers to be quite positivist in orientation and purpose. When investigators talk, as they often do, of exploring meanings by way of qualitative methods and then 'confirming' or 'validating' their findings by a quantitative study, they are privileging the latter in a thoroughgoing positivist manner. What turns their study into a positivist piece of work is not the use of quantitative methods but the attribution of objectivity, validity and generalisability to quantitative findings.

Accordingly, our consideration of positivism and post-positivism in this chapter turns out to be relevant enough. Called upon to set forth our research process incisively and unequivocally, we find ourselves unable to do that without, for a start, confronting the objectivist understanding of meaning and the positivist understanding of reality—and declaring our hand.

3

CONSTRUCTIONISM: THE MAKING OF MEANING

What of a truth that is bounded by these mountains and is falsehood to the world that lives beyond?

Michel Eyquem de Montaigne, *Essays*

Constructionism is well removed from the objectivism found in the positivist stance. In some areas it seems to have replaced objectivism as the dominant paradigm. If this is indeed the case, and to the extent to which it is the case, we are witnessing the end of a very long tradition. Objectivism—the notion that truth and meaning reside in their objects independently of any consciousness—has its roots in ancient Greek philosophy, was carried along in Scholastic realism throughout the Middle Ages, and rose to its zenith in the age of the so-called Enlightenment. The belief that there is objective truth and that appropriate methods of inquiry can bring us accurate and certain knowledge of that truth has been the epistemological ground of Western science. While it would be extremely premature to sound the death knell of this centuries-old tradition, foundationalism[5] of this kind has certainly come under heavy attack and constructionism is very much part of the artillery brought against it.

What, then, is constructionism? It is the view that *all knowledge, and therefore all meaningful reality as such, is contingent upon human practices, being constructed in and out of interaction between human beings and their world, and developed and transmitted within an essentially social context.*

THE CONSTRUCTION OF MEANINGFUL REALITY

In the constructionist view, as the word suggests, meaning is not discovered but constructed. Meaning does not inhere in the object, merely waiting for someone to come upon it. As writers like Merleau-Ponty have pointed out very tellingly, the world and objects in the world are indeterminate. They may be pregnant with potential meaning, but actual meaning emerges only when consciousness engages with them. How, such thinkers ask, can there be meaning without a mind?

Accepting that the world we experience, prior to our experience of it, is without meaning does not come easy. What the 'commonsense' view commends to us is that the tree standing before us is a tree. It has all the meaning we ascribe to a tree. It would be a tree, with that same meaning, whether anyone knew of its existence or not. We need to remind ourselves here that it is human beings who have construed it as a tree, given it the name, and attributed to it the associations we make with trees. It may help if we recall the extent to which those associations differ even within the same overall culture. 'Tree' is likely to bear quite different connotations in a logging town, an artists' settlement and a treeless slum.

What constructionism claims is that meanings are constructed by human beings as they engage with the world they are interpreting. Before there were consciousnesses on earth capable of interpreting the world, the world held no meaning at all.

> You may object that you cannot imagine a time when nothing existed in any phenomenal form. Were there not volcanoes, and dust-storms and starlight long before there was any life on Earth? Did not the sun rise in the East and set in the West? Did not water flow downhill, and light travel faster than sound? The answer is that if you had been there, that is indeed the way the phenomena would have appeared to you. But you were not there: no one was. And because no one was there, there was not—at this mindless stage of history—anything that *counted as* a volcano, or a dust-storm, and so on. I am not suggesting that the world had no substance to it whatsoever. We might say, perhaps, that it consisted of 'worldstuff'. But the properties of this worldstuff had yet to be represented by a mind. (Humphrey 1993, p. 17)

From the constructionist viewpoint, therefore, meaning (or truth) cannot be described simply as 'objective'. By the same token, it cannot be described simply as 'subjective'. Some researchers describing themselves as constructionist talk as if meanings are created out of whole cloth and simply imposed upon reality. This is to espouse an out-and-out subjectivism and to reject both the existentialist concept of humans as beings-in-the-world and the phenomenological concept of intentionality. There are strong threads within structuralist, post-structuralist and postmodernist thought espousing a subjectivist epistemology but constructionism is different. According to constructionism, we do not create meaning. We construct meaning. We have something to work with. What we have to work with is the world and objects in the world.

As Heidegger and Merleau-Ponty repeatedly state, the world is 'always already there'. The world and objects in the world may be in themselves meaningless; yet they are our partners in the generation of meaning and need to be taken seriously. It is surely important, and liberating, to distinguish theory consistent with experienced reality from theory that is not. Objectivity and subjectivity need to be brought together and held together indissolubly. Constructionism does precisely that.

In this respect, constructionism mirrors the concept of intentionality. Intentionality is a notion that phenomenology borrowed from Scholastic philosophy and in its turn has shared with other orientations. It was the renowned nineteenth-century psychologist and philosopher Franz Brentano who invoked the Scholastic concept of intentionality. Brentano's student and acknowledged founder of phenomenology Edmund Husserl went on to make it the pivotal concept of his philosophy.

Brentano recalls (1973, p. 88) that, in medieval philosophy, all mental phenomena are described as having 'reference to a content, direction toward an object'. Consciousness, in other words, is always consciousness *of something*. 'In presentation something is presented, in judgment something is affirmed or denied, in love loved, in hate hated, in desire desired and so on.'

It is important to note that 'intentionality' and 'intentional' as used here have nothing to do with purpose or deliberation. The root stem of these words is the Latin *tendere*, which means 'to tend'—in the sense of 'moving towards' or 'directing oneself to'. Here 'in-tending' is not about choosing or planning but about *reaching out into* (just as '*ex*-tending' is about *reaching out from*). Intentionality means referentiality, relatedness, directedness, 'aboutness'.

The basic message of intentionality is straightforward enough. When the mind becomes conscious of something, when it 'knows' something, it reaches out to, and into, that object. In contrast to other epistemologies at large towards the end of the nineteenth century, intentionality posits a quite intimate and very active relationship between the conscious subject and the object of the subject's consciousness. Consciousness is directed towards the object; the object is shaped by consciousness. As Lyotard expresses it:

There is thus no answer to the question whether philosophy must begin with the object (realism) or with the ego (idealism). The very idea of phenomenology puts this question out of play: consciousness is always consciousness of, and there is no object which is not an object for. There is no immanence of the object to consciousness unless one correlatively assigns the object a rational meaning, without which the object would not be an object for. Concept or meaning is not exterior to Being; rather, Being is immediately concept in itself, and the concept is Being for itself. (1991, p. 65)

Later phenomenologists, working within the context of an existentialist philosophy, make the process far less cerebral. Not only is consciousness intentional, but human beings in their totality are intentionally related to their world. Human being means being-in-the-world. In existentialist terms, intentionality is a radical interdependence of subject and world.

Because of the essential relationship that human experience bears to its object, no object can be adequately described in isolation from the conscious being experiencing it, nor can any experience be adequately described in isolation from its object. Experiences do not constitute a sphere of subjective reality separate from, and in contrast to, the objective realm of the external world—as Descartes' famous 'split' between mind and body, and thereby between mind and world, would lead us to imagine. In the way of thinking to which intentionality introduces us, such a dichotomy between the subjective and the objective is untenable. Subject and object, distinguishable as they are, are always united. It is this insight that is captured in the term 'intentionality'.

To embrace the notion of intentionality is to reject objectivism. Equally, it is to reject subjectivism. What intentionality brings to the fore is interaction between subject and object. The image evoked is that of humans engaging with their human world. It is in and out of this interplay that meaning is born.

It may be helpful to consider what literary critic and linguistics exponent Stanley Fish has to say. In a well-known essay (1990), Fish recalls a summer program in which he was teaching two courses. One explored the relationship between linguistics and literary criticism. The other was a course in English religious poetry. The sessions for both courses were held in the same classroom and they followed one after the other.

One morning, when the students in the first course had left the room, Fish looked at a list of names he had written on the blackboard. It was the assignment he had set for the students. The people listed were authors whose works the students were expected to consult before the next class. One of the names listed had a question mark after it, because Fish was not sure whether it was spelled correctly.

Fish went to the board, drew a frame around the names and wrote 'p. 43' above the frame. When the students in the second course filed into the room for their class, what confronted them on the blackboard was what we see in Figure 4.

Figure 4

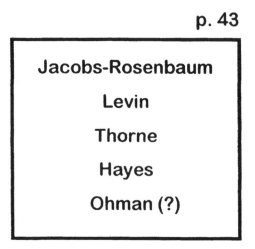

p. 43

Jacobs-Rosenbaum

Levin

Thorne

Hayes

Ohman (?)

Fish began this second class for the day by drawing the students' attention to the list of names. He informed them that it was a religious poem of the kind they had been studying and invited them to interpret it.

The students were equal to the task. The first student to speak commented on the shape of the poem. The poem was a hieroglyph, he surmised, but was it in the shape of an altar or a cross? After this promising start, other students were not slow to follow suit. 'Jacobs' came to be related to Jacob's ladder, an Old Testament allegory for the Christian's ascent into heaven. It is linked in the list to 'Rosenbaum'— *rose tree* in German and surely an allusion to the Virgin Mary, who is often depicted as a rose without thorns and promotes Christians' ascent into heaven through the redemptive work of her son, Jesus. Redemption is effected above all through Christ's suffering and death, symbolised in his being crowned with thorns (corrupted to 'Thorne'?). The reference to Levi (see 'Levin') is not surprising: the tribe of Levi was the priestly tribe and Jesus, after all, is the Great High Priest of the New Testament. 'Ohman' could be given at least three readings (hence the question mark?): it might be 'omen' or 'Oh Man!' or simply 'Amen'. The students also noted that both Old and New Testaments are represented in the poem, three of the names being Jewish, two Gentile, and one ambiguous.

Perhaps this ambiguity is the reason for the question mark after it. And so on.

In the wake of this exercise, Fish asks the question that he uses to shape the title of his essay: How do you recognise a poem when you see one? In this case, the students are not led to recognise the poem as a poem because of particular distinguishing features. The act of recognition comes first. They are told it is a poem. They are invited at the start to address the list on the board with 'poetry-seeing eyes'. Having done that, they are able to detect particular significances in the object as a poem. Fish concludes that reading of any kind is along these same lines, that is, not 'a matter of discerning what is there' but 'of knowing how to *produce* what can thereafter be said to be there' (1990, pp. 182–3).

'Just a moment!', some might want to argue. This list does have a meaning and the members of the first class did, in fact, discern 'what is there'. The list is an assignment.

Fish remains unimpressed. 'Unfortunately, the argument will not hold because the assignment we all see is no less the product of interpretation than the poem into which it was turned. That is, it requires just as much work, and work of the same kind, to see this as an assignment as it does to see it as a poem' (Fish 1990, p. 184).

All right, then. It is not an assignment either. But it *is* a list of names. We can read it as a list of names and that, surely, is to discern 'what is there'. No, not even that, Fish assures us. 'In order to see a list, one must already be equipped with the concepts of seriality, hierarchy, subordination, and so on' (Fish 1990, p. 186). These have to be learned and one cannot see a list without learning them. The meaning of list, as of anything else, is not just 'there'. Instead, making meaning is always an 'ongoing accomplishment'. 'The conclusion, therefore, is that all objects are made and not found and that they are made by the interpretive strategies we set in motion' (Fish 1990, p. 191).

In Fish's story we find human beings engaging with a reality and making sense of it. Obviously, it is possible to make sense of the same reality in quite different ways. Not that we need to be taught that lesson. Moving from one culture to another, as no doubt most of us have done at one time or another, provides evidence enough that strikingly diverse understandings can be formed of the same phenomenon. Yet there are always some who stand ready to dismiss other interpretations as merely quaint viewpoints that throw the 'true' or 'valid' interpretation into clearer relief. What constructionism drives home unambiguously is that there is *no* true or valid interpretation. There are useful interpretations, to be sure, and these stand over against interpretations that appear to serve no useful purpose. There are liberating forms of interpretation too;

they contrast sharply with interpretations that prove oppressive. There are even interpretations that may be judged fulfilling and rewarding—in contradistinction to interpretations that impoverish human existence and stunt human growth. 'Useful', 'liberating', 'fulfilling', 'rewarding' interpretations, yes. 'True' or 'valid' interpretations, no.

There is another lesson that Fish's example drives home, even if Fish does not make it explicit. It is something we have already noted. The object may be meaningless in itself but it has a vital part to play in the generation of meaning. While Fish's students are innovative in making sense of the list of names conceived as a religious poem, the particular names that happen to be on the list play a key role. The students, Fish observes (1990, p. 184), 'would have been able to turn any list of names into the kind of poem we have before us now'. What he does not point out, though he would surely agree, is that they would make different sense of a different list. With different names to engage with, the religious significances they develop would not be the same. It is therefore not a question of conjuring up a series of meanings and just imposing them on the 'poem'. That is subjectivism, not constructionism. The meanings emerge from the students' interaction with the 'poem' and relate to it essentially. The meanings are thus at once objective and subjective, their objectivity and subjectivity being indissolubly bound up with each other. Constructionism teaches us that meaning is always that.

No mere subjectivism here. Constructionism takes the object very seriously. It is open to the world. Theodor Adorno refers to the process involved as 'exact fantasy' (1977, p. 131). Imagination is required, to be sure. There is call for creativity. Yet we are not talking about imagination running wild or untrammelled creativity. There is an 'exactness' involved, for we are talking about imagination being exercised and creativity invoked in a precise interplay with *something*. Susan Buck-Morss (1977, p. 86) finds in Adorno's exact fantasy 'a dialectical concept which acknowledged the mutual mediation of subject and object without allowing either to get the upper hand'. It is, she insists, the attention to the object that 'separated this fantasy from mere dream-like fabrication'.

Bringing objectivity and subjectivity together and holding them together throughout the process is hardly characteristic of qualitative research today. Instead, a rampant subjectivism seems to be abroad. It can be detected in the turning of phenomenology from a study of phenomena as the immediate objects of experience into a study of experiencing individuals. It is equally detectable in the move taking place in some quarters today to supplant ethnography with an 'autoethnography'.

Description of researchers as *bricoleurs* is also a case in point. Denzin and Lincoln (1994) have made 'researcher-as-*bricoleur*' the *leitmotif* of the massive tome they have edited. They devote some columns to it in their opening chapter, refer to it in each of their introductions to the various sections of the book, and return to it in their concluding chapter. Denzin's own chapter 'The art and politics of interpretation' also invokes the notion of the researcher-as-*bricoleur*.

Denzin and Lincoln begin their treatment of the researcher-as-*bricoleur* by citing Lévi-Strauss's *The Savage Mind*. This is to the effect that the *bricoleur* is 'a Jack of all trades, or a kind of professional do-it-yourself person' (Denzin and Lincoln 1994, p. 2). Now the idea of a Jack (or Jill?) of all trades or a do-it-yourself person certainly puts the spotlight on the multiple skills and resourcefulness of the individual concerned. This is precisely what Denzin and Lincoln seek to emphasise from start to finish. *Bricoleurs*, as these authors conceive them, show themselves very inventive in addressing particular tasks. The focus is on an individual's ability to employ a large range of tools and methods, even unconventional ones, and therefore on his or her inventiveness, resourcefulness and imaginativeness. So the researcher-as-*bricoleur* 'is adept at performing a large number of diverse tasks' and 'is knowledgeable about the many interpretive paradigms (feminism, Marxism, cultural studies, constructivism) that can be brought to any particular problem' (Denzin and Lincoln 1994, p. 2).

Given this understanding of *bricoleur*, it is not surprising that Denzin and Lincoln should characterise *bricolage* as 'self-reflexive', a description they draw from Nelson, Treichler and Grossberg (1992, p. 2) writing about cultural studies. When the Jacks and Jills of all trades learn that a job has to be done—they have just finished their carpentry around the door and have painted the ceiling, and now they learn that the toilet is blocked and requires some rather intricate plumbing work—yes, such *bricoleurs* would tend to be self-reflexive. 'Can I do it?' becomes the burning question.

Interestingly, the *bricoleur* described by Denzin and Lincoln is not the *bricoleur* described by Claude Lévi-Strauss, even though he is the principal reference they give for the notion. The words they quote to describe the *bricoleur*, 'a Jack of all trades, or a kind of professional do-it-yourself person', come from a translator's footnote (Lévi-Strauss 1966, p. 17). In that footnote, the sentence cited is preceded by the statement, 'The "bricoleur" has no precise equivalent in English'. And the sentence quoted is not given in full. The rest of the sentence reads: 'but, as the text makes clear, he [the *bricoleur*] is of a different standing from, for instance, the English "odd job man" or handyman'.

What we find in Lévi-Strauss's text, in fact, is a very different under-standing of *bricoleur*. Consequently, the 'analogy' drawn from it (to use Lévi-Strauss's term) carries a very different message. In *The Savage Mind*, the *bricoleur* is not someone able to perform a whole range of specialist functions or even to employ unconventional methods. It is the notion of a person who makes something new out of a range of materials that had previously made up something different. The *bricoleur* is a makeshift artisan, armed with a collection of bits and pieces that were once standard parts of a certain whole but which the *bricoleur*, as *bricoleur*, now reconceives as parts of a new whole. Lévi-Strauss provides an example. The *bricoleur* has a cube-shaped piece of oak. It may once have been part of a wardrobe. Or was it part of a grandfather clock? Whatever its earlier role, the *bricoleur* now has to make it serve a quite different purpose. It may be used as 'a wedge to make up for the inadequate length of a plank of pine' (Lévi-Strauss 1966, p. 18). Or perhaps it 'could be a pedestal—which would allow the grain and polish of the old wood to show to advantage' (1966, pp. 18–19).

Engaged in that kind of project, *bricoleurs* are not at all 'self-reflexive'. To the contrary, they are utterly focused on what they have to work with. The question is not, 'Can I do it? Do I have the skills?'. Rather, the question is, 'What can be made of these items? What do they lend themselves to becoming?'. And answering that depends on the qualities found in the items to hand. It is a matter of what items are there and what are not. It is a matter of the properties each possesses—size, shape, weight, colour, texture, brittleness, and so on. The last thing *bricoleurs* have in mind at this moment is their own self. Imaginativeness and creativity are required, to be sure, but an imaginativeness and creativity to be exercised in relation to *these* objects, *these* materials. An ice cream carton, two buttons, and a coat hanger—I'm supposed to make something of that? Self-reflexive? No, not at all. Nothing is further from self-reflexion than *bricolage*. There the focus is fairly and squarely on the object. True *bricoleurs* are people constantly musing over objects, engaged precisely with what is *not* themselves, in order to see what possibilities the objects have to offer. This is the image of the *bricoleur* to be found in Lévi-Strauss.

> Consider him at work and excited by his project. His first practical step is retrospective. He has to turn back to an already existent set made up of tools and materials, to consider or reconsider what it contains and, finally and above all, to engage in a sort of dialogue with it and, before choosing between them, to index the possible answers which the whole set can offer to his problem. He interrogates all the heterogeneous objects of which his treasury is composed to discover what each of them could 'signify' and so

contribute to the definition of a set which has yet to materialize (Lévi-Strauss 1966, p. 18)

A dialogue with the materials. Interrogating all the heterogeneous objects. Indexing their possible uses. This preoccupation with objects is mirrored in Lévi-Strauss's assertion that the *bricoleur* 'might therefore be said to be constantly on the look out for "messages"' (1966, p. 20).

In their last page of text (1994, p. 584), Denzin and Lincoln come to acknowledge just a little of all this. They state that '*bricoleurs* are more than simply jacks-of-all-trades; they are also inventors'. They write of *bricoleurs* having to 'recycle used fabric', to 'cobble together stories'. Even here, however, the emphasis remains on the *bricoleur's* inventiveness as 'the demand of a restless art'. In this further exposition of the *bricoleur*, there is still no hint of Lévi-Strauss's preoccupation with objects.

Why such preoccupation with objects? Because they are the limiting factor. They are, warns Lévi-Strauss, 'pre-constrained'. The possibilities they bear 'always remain limited by the particular history of each piece and by those of its features which are already determined by the use for which it was originally intended or the modifications it has undergone for other purposes' (Lévi-Strauss 1966, p. 19). The uses to which they might be put must accord with what they are. The ability needed by the *bricoleur* is the ability to 're-vision' these bits and pieces, casting aside the purposes which they once bore and for which they were once designed and divining very different purposes that they may now serve in new settings.

In short, the image of the researcher-as-*bricoleur* highlights the researcher's need to pay sustained attention to the objects of research. This is much more to the fore than the need for versatility or resourcefulness in the use of tools and methods. Research in constructivist vein, research in the mode of the *bricoleur*, requires that we not remain straitjacketed by the conventional meanings we have been taught to associate with the object. Instead, such research invites us to approach the object in a radical spirit of openness to its potential for new or richer meaning. It is an invitation to reinterpretation.

It is precisely this preoccupation with the object that we find in Walter Benjamin and Theodor Adorno. In Benjamin's form of inquiry, Adorno claims (1981, pp. 240–1), 'the subjective intention is seen to be extinguished' and the 'thoughts press close to its object, seek to touch it, smell it, taste it and so thereby transform itself'. Benjamin, in fact, is driven to 'immerse himself without reserve in the world of multiplicity'. Adorno is the same:

> What is ultimately most fascinating in Adorno's *Negative Dialectics* is the incessantly formulated appeal that thought be conscious of its non-sovereignty, of the fact that it must always be molded by material that is by definition heterogeneous to it. This is what Adorno calls the 'mimetic moment' of knowledge, the affinity with the *object*. What interests him most of all is to impose on thought respect for the nuance, the difference, individuation, requiring it to descend to the most minuscule and infinitesimal detail. (Tertulian 1985, p. 95)

A focus of this kind on the object is hardly characteristic of our times. 'No age has been so self-conscious', writes E.M. Cioran. What he calls our 'psychological sense' has 'transformed us into spectators of ourselves'. He finds this reflected in the modern novel, wherein he finds 'a research without points of references, an experiment pursued within an unfailing vacuity'. It does not look outwards to an object. 'The genre, having squandered its substance, no longer has an object.' (Cioran 1976, pp. 139–40).

> To the narrative which suppresses what is narrated, an object, corresponds an *askesis*[6] of the intellect, a meditation *without content* . . . The mind discovers itself reduced to the action by virtue of which it is mind and nothing more. All its activities lead it back to itself, to that stationary development which keeps it from catching on to *things*. (Cioran 1976, p. 141)

Far removed from what Cioran is describing here, constructionism does not suppress the object but focuses on it intently. It is by no means a stationary development. It is meditation *with* content. It well and truly catches on to things.

Constructionism is not subjectivism. It is curiosity, not conceit.

'SOCIAL' CONSTRUCTIONISM

If seeing interpretation as a making of meaning does not condemn us to subjectivism, it does not condemn us to individualism either. We have to reckon with the social origin of meaning and the social character with which it is inevitably stamped.

Fish emphasises that 'all objects are made and not found' but adds at once that 'the means by which they are made are social and conventional'. These means are institutions which 'precede us' and in which 'we are *already* embedded' and 'it is only by inhabiting them, or being inhabited by them, that we have access to the public and conventional senses they make'. Functioning as 'a publicly available system of intelligibility', these institutions are the source of the interpretative strategies whereby we construct meaning (Fish 1990, p. 186).

Where Fish invokes 'a publicly available system of intelligibility', anthropologist Clifford Geertz speaks of 'a system of significant symbols'. Geertz is talking, of course, about culture and he presents the meaningful symbols that constitute culture as an indispensable guide to human behaviour. What, in Geertz's view, would we be without them? Certainly we would not be 'clever savages', as in Golding's *Lord of the Flies*. Nor would we be the 'nature's noblemen' who in Enlightenment thought lurk beneath the trappings of culture. Nor, again, would we be 'intrinsically talented apes who had somehow failed to find themselves', as classical anthropological theory seems to imply. We would be none of these, Geertz insists. Rather, we would be 'unworkable monstrosities' (Geertz 1973, p. 49).

Unworkable? Yes, unworkable. Without culture we could not function. Culture has to do with functioning. As a direct consequence of the way in which we humans have evolved, we depend on culture to direct our behaviour and organise our experience. In the past, Geertz points out, we have tended to see culture as 'complexes of concrete behaviour patterns—customs, usages, traditions, habit clusters'. To view culture primarily in this light is to consider it the outcome of human thought and action. We need to reverse this way of viewing culture. Culture is best seen as the source rather than the result of human thought and behaviour. It is 'a set of control mechanisms—plans, recipes, rules, instructions (what computer engineers call "programs")—for the governing of behavior' (Geertz 1973, p. 44).

In this view of the role of culture, human thought emerges as 'basically both social and public'.

> Thinking consists not of 'happenings in the head' (though happenings there and elsewhere are necessary for it to occur) but of a traffic in what have been called, by G.H. Mead and others, significant symbols—words for the most part but also gestures, drawings, musical sounds, mechanical devices like clocks, or natural objects like jewels—anything, in fact, that is disengaged from its mere actuality and used to impose meaning upon experience. (Geertz 1973, p. 45)

Fish has told us that the institutions constituting our publicly available system of intelligibility precede us. We come to inhabit this pre-existing system and to be inhabited by it. Similarly, in describing culture as a system of significant symbols, Geertz emphasises that, from the point of view of any particular individual, 'such symbols are largely given'. They are already current in the community when the individual is born and they remain in circulation—with some changes, to be sure—after the individual dies (Geertz 1973, p. 45).

Thus, while humans may be described, in constructionist spirit, as engaging with their world and making sense of it, such a description is misleading if it is not set in a genuinely historical and social perspective. It is clearly not the case that individuals encounter phenomena in the world and make sense of them one by one. Instead, we are all born into a world of meaning. We enter a social milieu in which a 'system of intelligibility' prevails. We inherit a 'system of significant symbols'. For each of us, when we first see the world in meaningful fashion, we are inevitably viewing it through lenses bestowed upon us by our culture. Our culture brings things into view for us and endows them with meaning and, by the same token, leads us to ignore other things.

The social constructionism we are talking about here is all-encompassing and we need to be careful not to restrict its ambit. For one thing, it is not to be taken here in an ideational sense only. It is not just our thoughts that are constructed for us. We have to reckon also with the social construction of emotions (Harré 1986). Moreover, constructionism embraces the whole gamut of meaningful reality. All reality, as meaningful reality, is socially constructed.[7] There is no exception.

Not everyone agrees. There are some who take social constructionism to mean that social realities, and only social realities, have a social genesis. Natural or physical realities do not. In other words, they understand social constructionism as denoting 'the construction of social reality' rather than 'the social construction of reality'. The wording used by The Concise Oxford Dictionary of Sociology to describe social constructionism suggests this standpoint. Social constructionists, we are told, 'emphasize the idea that society is actively and creatively produced by human beings', social worlds being 'interpretive nets woven by individuals and groups' (Marshall 1994, p. 484). An even more explicit account is offered by Greenwood:

> Physical and social phenomena . . . differ in one essential respect. Chairs may exist independently of our knowing that they do; our knowledge of the existence of chairs is not constitutive of their existence. In contrast, social phenomena do not exist independently of our knowledge of them . . . Social realities, therefore, are constructed and sustained by the observation of the social rules which obtain in any social situation by all the social interactors involved . . . Social reality is, therefore, a function of shared meanings; it is constructed, sustained and reproduced through social life. (1994, p. 85)

That social realities are socially constructed is something of a truism. The most ardent positivist would find that hard to contradict. What distinguishes constructionism, setting it over against the objectivism inherent in the positivist stance, is its understanding that *all* meaningful reality, precisely as meaningful reality, is socially constructed. The chair may exist as a phenomenal object regardless of whether any consciousness is aware of its existence. It exists *as a chair*, however, only if conscious beings construe it as a chair. As a chair, it too 'is constructed, sustained and reproduced through social life'.

The 'social' in social constructionism is about the mode of meaning generation and not about the kind of object that has meaning. The object involved in the social constructionist understanding of meaning formation need not involve persons at all (and therefore need not be 'social' in that sense). The interaction may be, say, with the natural world—the sunset, the mountains, a tree. Natural these objects may be, but it is our culture (shorthand in most cases today for a very complex mix of many cultures and sub-cultures) that teaches us how to see them—and in some cases *whether* to see them. 'A way of seeing is a way of not seeing', feminist author Ann Oakley sagely advises (1974, p. 27). Accordingly, whether we would describe the object of the interaction as natural or social, the basic generation of meaning is always social, for the meanings with which we are endowed arise in and out of interactive human community.

Accordingly, not only the social scientist but equally the natural scientist has to deal with realities that, as meaningful realities, are socially constructed. They are on an equal footing in this respect. British sociologist Anthony Giddens appears to disagree. He makes the following distinction between the natural world and the social world:

> The difference between the social and natural world is that the latter does not constitute itself as 'meaningful'; the meanings it has are produced by men in the course of their practical life, and as a consequence of their endeavours to understand or explain it for themselves. Social life—of which these endeavours are a part—on the other hand, is *produced* by its component actors precisely in terms of their active constitution and reconstitution of frames of meaning whereby they organize their experiences. (Giddens 1976, p. 79)

What is Giddens postulating here? He is asserting that, while humans do not create the natural world but have to make sense of a 'world always already there' (Heidegger's and Merleau-Ponty's phrase, not Giddens's), the very existence of social phenomena stems from human action. Consequently, the process of bringing these social realities into being is one with the process of interpreting and reinterpreting them. Unlike the natural world, then, social realities are meaningful by virtue of the very act that brings them into existence. Natural realities are not.

Giddens's purpose in making this distinction is to offer a basis for his concept of the 'double hermeneutic' in which social scientists have to engage. Social scientists have the task, first of all, of 'entering and grasping the frames of meaning involved in the production of social life by lay actors' as well as the subsequent task of 'reconstituting these within the new frames of meaning involved in technical conceptual schemes' (Giddens 1976, p. 79). Natural scientists, he believes, do not have the same task to face. They merely construct a 'theoretical meta-language, a network in which the meaning of scientific concepts is tied-in to the meaning of other terms'. That is all they have to worry about. They are faced with a 'single level of hermeneutic problems'. Social scientists are not so lucky. They have two interpretative levels to face. They must contend with a double hermeneutic. 'There is a two-way connection between the language of social science and ordinary language', writes Giddens (1979, p. 12). 'The former cannot ignore the categories used by laymen in the practical organization of social life.'

Natural science, as Giddens sees it, can do what social science cannot do. It is able to ignore the categories used by people in everyday life and avoid or minimise ordinary language, using its own scientific meta-language instead. The natural scientist comes to the task of studying nature with something of a *tabula rasa*.

Blaikie (1993, p. 36) warmly espouses these views of Giddens. He says that the natural scientist studies nature 'as it were, from the outside'. The scientist then has 'to invent concepts and theories to describe and explain'. Contrasting with this, in Blaikie's view, is the study of social phenomena. Here we are talking about 'a social world which people have constructed and which they reproduce through their continuing activities' and which they are 'constantly involved in interpreting'. 'They develop meanings for their activities together', concludes Blaikie. 'In short, the social world is already interpreted before the social scientist arrives.'

How sustainable is this understanding of things?

Our discussion to this point suggests that our knowledge of the natural world is as socially constructed as our knowledge of the social world. The world of meaning into which we are born is a world of trees as much as it is a world of kinship, law, finance or nationalism. Understanding of trees is not something we come to individually 'in the course of our practical life'. As we have already considered, we are taught about trees. We learn that trees are trees and we learn what trees should mean to us. In infancy and childhood we learn the meaning of trees from the culture in which we are reared. Trees are given a name for us and, along with the name, all kinds of understandings and associations. They are a source of livelihood if the setting for our childhood is a logging town. They constitute a focal point of lively aesthetic pleasure if we grow up within an artists' colony. They are the subject of deep reverence, fear perhaps, if we come to adulthood within an animist community. They may have very little meaning at all if we come from a slum neighbourhood in which there are no trees.

So the natural scientist does not come to the study of trees with a clean slate. To be sure, scientists have to lay aside much of the baggage they bring with them so as to study trees in a 'scientific' manner. They come to view trees, or whatever other natural phenomena they happen to be studying, within a particular horizon. But their starting point, inevitably, is the everyday understanding abroad in their culture. Blaikie talks of scientists inventing concepts and theories to understand and explain natural phenomena. In fact, they bring many of the concepts and much of the theory with them to the task. The so-called theoretical metalanguage is not a language existing in itself, distinct from the language spoken in the streets. It is ordinary language adapted to serve a specific purpose. What Blaikie says of the social world is true of the natural world too: people develop meanings together and it is already interpreted before the scientist arrives.

The social world and the natural world are not to be seen, then, as distinct worlds existing side by side. They are one human world. We are born, each of us, into an already interpreted world and it is at once natural and social.

CONFORMISM OR CRITIQUE?

It would seem important to distinguish accounts of constructionism where this social dimension of meaning is at centre stage from those where it is not. Using 'constructionism' for the former and 'constructivism' for the latter has echoes in the literature, even if the terminology is far from consistent. For example, after referring to the objectivist view that the facts of the world exist independently of us as observers, Schwandt (1994, p. 125) states that constructivists 'are deeply committed to the contrary view that what we take to be objective knowledge and truth is the result of perspective'. Constructivists, he adds, 'emphasize the instrumental and practical function of theory construction and knowing'.

This constructivism is primarily an individualistic understanding of the constructionist position and Schwandt contrasts it with a genuinely social constructionism:

> Kenneth and Mary Gergen also challenge the idea of some objective basis for knowledge claims and examine the process of knowledge construction. But, instead of focusing on the matter of individual minds and cognitive processes, they turn their attention outward to the world of intersubjectively shared, social constructions of meaning and knowledge. Acknowledging a debt to the phenomenology of Peter Berger and Alfred Schutz, Kenneth Gergen (1985) labels his approach 'social constructionism' because it more adequately reflects the notion that the world that people create in the process of social exchange is a reality sui generis.
>
> Contrary to the emphasis in radical constructivism, the focus here is not on the meaning-making activity of the individual mind but on the collective generation of meaning as shaped by the conventions of language and other social processes. (1994, p. 127)

It would appear useful, then, to reserve the term *constructivism* for epistemological considerations focusing exclusively on 'the meaning-making activity of the individual mind' and to use *constructionism* where the focus includes 'the collective generation [and transmission] of meaning'.

We might apply this distinction to the views of Giddens and Blaikie which we have just been discussing. In these terms, Giddens and Blaikie seem to have a constructivist view of scientific knowledge of the natural world but a constructionist view of scientific knowledge of the social world. The natural scientist constructs knowledge of the natural world by engaging with it in scientific mode, but the social world is already interpreted 'before the social scientist arrives'. What our considerations to date support is a constructionist view of both.

Whatever the terminology, the distinction itself is an important one. Constructivism taken in this sense points up the unique experience of each of us. It suggests that each one's way of making sense of the world is as valid and worthy of respect as any other, thereby tending to scotch any hint of a critical spirit. On the other hand, social constructionism emphasises the hold our culture has on us: it shapes the way in which we see things (even the way in which we feel things!) and gives us a quite definite view of the world. This shaping of our minds by culture is to be welcomed as what makes us human and endows us with the freedom we enjoy. For all that, there are social constructionists aplenty who recognise that it is limiting as well as liberating and warn that, while welcome, it must also be called into question. On these terms, it can be said that constructivism tends to resist the critical spirit, while constructionism tends to foster it.

Developing a critical spirit *vis-à-vis* our inherited understandings is no mean feat. For a start, there is the phenomenon of *reification* to be reckoned with. We tend to take 'the sense we make of things' to be 'the way things are'. We blithely do that and, just as blithely, hand on our understandings as quite simply 'the truth'. Understandings transmitted in this way and gaining a place in our view of the world take deep root and we find ourselves victims of the 'tyranny of the familiar'. Inherited and prevailing understandings become nothing less than, in William Blake's time-honoured phrase, 'mind-forg'd manacles'.

Another aspect of the process can be described as *sedimentation*. Layers of interpretation get placed one upon another like levels of mineral deposit in the formation of rock. No longer is it a question of existential engagement with realities in the world but of building upon theoretical deposits already in place. In this way we become further and further removed from those realities, our sedimented cultural meanings serving as a barrier between us and them. For this reason, Ortega y Gasset describes inherited and prevailing meanings as 'masks' and 'screens' (1963, pp. 59–63) and warns us that, instead of engaging with the world, we find ourselves 'living on top of a culture that has already become false' (1958, p. 100).

> Culture, the purest product of the live and the genuine, since it comes out of the fact that man feels with an awful anguish and a burning enthusiasm the relentless needs of which his life is made up, ends by becoming a falsification of that life . . .
>
> Thanks to culture, man has gotten away from himself, separated himself from himself; culture intervenes between the real world and his real person. (Ortega y Gasset 1958, pp. 99–101)

Kurt Wolff agrees: our received notions blind us to reality (1989, p. 326). For Gabriel Marcel they are 'closed systems in which thought imprisons us' (1964, p. 35). John Wild, using the same metaphor, speaks of our 'imprisonment in a world of our own construction' (1955, p. 191). As we shall see in the next chapter, it is awareness of this restrictiveness inherent in cultural understandings that drives the phenomenological endeavour to go 'back to the things themselves'.

The critical tradition, encountered today most markedly in what we know as critical theory, is even more suspicious of the constructed meanings that culture bequeaths to us. It emphasises that particular sets of meanings, because they have come into being in and out of the give-and-take of social existence, exist to serve hegemonic interests. Each set of meanings supports particular power structures, resists moves towards greater equity, and harbours oppression, manipulation and other modes of injustice and unfreedom.

Not everyone acknowledges the restrictive and oppressive aspects of our cultural inheritance. Many rest content with celebrating the boon without recognising the burden. For some, in fact, the social origin of our ways of understanding the world and living within it is enough to guarantee their objectivity and validity. Nurse researcher Patricia Benner writes in this vein:

> No higher court for the individual exists than meanings or self-interpretations embedded in language, skills, and practices. No laws, structures, or mechanisms offer higher explanatory principles or greater predictive power than self-interpretations in the form of common meanings, personal concerns, and cultural practices shaped by a particular history. (1985, p. 5)

Such an optimistic reading of culture stands in sharp contrast to the suspicion of culture found in the critical tradition and in large segments of the phenomenological movement. John Brenkman draws our attention to the 'restless consciousness . . . that senses in every work of culture the fact and the effects of social domination' (1987, p. 3). Here Brenkman is expressly reflecting the attitude of Walter Benjamin. Benjamin's own language (1969, p. 256) is even more trenchant: 'There is no document of civilization which is not at the same time a document of barbarism'.

Already we are seeing the bifurcation that occurs within constructionist social science and in research emanating from it. We shall be exploring the interpretivist paradigm in the next two chapters. Notwithstanding the critique immanent in some hermeneutics and central to the traditional phenomenological movement, interpretivism is overwhelmingly oriented towards an uncritical exploration of cultural meaning. In contrast, critical theory, along with many streams of feminist and postmodernist research, invites us to a much more critical stance.

This tension within constructionist research reflects its tortuous history.

The term 'constructionism', particularly 'social constructionism', derives largely from the work of Karl Mannheim (1893–1947) and from Berger and Luckmann's *The Social Construction of Reality* (1967). The ensuing development took the form of a 'sociology of knowledge'. Nevertheless, the idea already had a long history when Mannheim, Berger and Luckmann took it up and can be found, for example, in both Hegel and Marx.

Marx's premise is to the effect that ideology is linked to the economic 'base' of society. Those who own the means of production in any society have the power to effect the kind of consciousness that obtains in that society. In his 1859 *Preface to a Contribution to the Critique of Political Economy*, Marx insists:

> The totality of these relations of production constitutes the economic structure of society—the real foundation, on which legal and political superstructures arise and to which definite forms of social consciousness correspond. The mode of production of material life determines the general character of the social, political, and spiritual processes of life. It is not the consciousness of men that determines their being, but, on the contrary, their social being determines their consciousness. (1961, p. 67)

Social being determines consciousness. Marx's focus on economic power imbues his maxim with a note of radical critique. This critical spirit continues in the phenomenological movement emerging around the turn of the twentieth century. Of this movement Franz Brentano was the precursor, Edmund Husserl the founder, and Martin Heidegger an eminent exponent. Thoroughly imbued with—indeed, predicated upon—the spirit of social constructionism, the phenomenological movement declared itself from the start a philosophy of radical criticism, albeit with none of the economic determinism with which orthodox Marxism is so often charged. Phenomenology became existentialist in purpose and orientation after it was taken up by Ortega y Gasset, a self-professed existentialist (O'Connor 1979, p. 59) and Heidegger, who consistently denied that he was existentialist but presented human beings in existentialist terms for his own purposes. Existential phenomenology, spearheaded in France by Jean-Paul Sartre and Maurice Merleau-Ponty, is militantly anti-objectivist and thoroughly constructionist.

The critical thrust of constructionism was also maintained with vigour in parallel developments on the other side of the Atlantic. The early exponents of American pragmatism—Charles Sanders Peirce, William James and John Dewey—were constructionist and critical. Unfortunately, pragmatism came to be popularised in forms that may have left it constructionist but effectively obscured its critical character. So effectively, and so quickly, was this accomplished that at various points the earlier pragmatists themselves came to be charged with the sins of their followers.

Thus we find Lewis Mumford describing the pragmatism of James and Dewey as an 'attitude of compromise and accommodation'—as 'pathetic' acquiescence, even (1950, pp. 39, 49). Social critic Randolph Bourne, himself a pragmatist and an associate of Dewey, similarly deplores the uncritical character he sees pragmatism assuming in his contemporaries, including his erstwhile mentor. He wants pragmatism's openness, optimism and progressivism to be tested 'inch by inch'. It is not enough, Bourne claims, merely to clarify the values we hold. We 'must rage and struggle until new values come out of the travail' (Bourne 1977, p. 345). In Bourne's view, as Walzer makes clear (1989, p. 58), 'mere eagerness for action and effectiveness, the realist's search for "influence", is a vulgar pragmatism'. Mumford too looks for 'the values that arise out of vision' and deplores the inability of a pragmatism like Dewey's 'to recognize the part that vision must play'. The lack of vision and the consequent lack of values mean 'a maceration of human purposes', Mumford claims (1950, p. 48). 'We are living on fragments of the old cultures, or on abortions of the new.'

Bourne made his comments in the context of the United States' entry into World War I. Much later, during World War II, Frankfurt School theorist Max Horkheimer accused pragmatism of being ineffective and accommodating even *vis-à-vis* the Holocaust. Horkheimer directed this 1944 diatribe at Dewey in particular, as the source of the 'most radical and consistent form of pragmatism' (1974, p. 48). According to Ross Posnock, Horkheimer succeeded in 'creating a rift that has reified into a general assumption among historians that pragmatism and critical theory are irreconcilable' (1991, p. 79).

These charges against pragmatism are harsh and, insofar as they are levelled against the founders of pragmatism, betray a simplistic and distorted reading of pragmatism. Still, it needs to be noted that many followers of Peirce, James and Dewey have themselves been simplistic and distorting in what they put forward in the name of pragmatism. In their case, allegations of conformism and compromise can be said to be well founded. It must also be said that the rhetoric of some of the earlier pragmatists readily lent itself to misinterpretation.

One of the great names in the history of pragmatism is philosopher and social psychologist George Herbert Mead (1863–1931). It is from the thought of Mead that symbolic interactionism was born. Symbolic interactionism is pragmatism in sociological attire. In Mead's thought every person is a social construction. We come to be persons in and out of interaction with our society. The 'Me'—the self as constructed via the 'generalised other'—plays a central role in the process. Mead's social behaviourism embodies a thoroughly social point of view. In the Meadian analysis, human behaviour is social in origin, shaped by social forces, and permeated by the social even in its biological and physical aspects. Consequently, Mead wants us to 'see the world whole'. Our ability to do that is developed socially through 'entering into the most highly organized logical, ethical, and aesthetic attitudes of the community' and coming to recognise 'the most extensive set of interwoven conditions that may determine thought, practice, and our fixation and enjoyment of values' (Mead 1964, p. 337). While Mead's thought is carefully nuanced, it has proved only too easy for his followers to slip from this account of the social genesis of the self to the grateful, unquestioning stance towards culture adopted by most interpretivist researchers today.

Here, then, is the dichotomy we discover within constructionist research. Whatever Mead's own thought, the symbolic interactionism that derives from him envisages a world far removed from that of critical inquirers. The world of the symbolic interactionist, like that of pragmatism as commonly conceived, is a peaceable and certainly growthful world. It is a world of intersubjectivity, interaction, community and communication, in and out of which we come to be persons and to live as persons. As such, it contrasts with the world that the critical theorist addresses. The world of the critical theorist is a battleground of hegemonic interests. In this world there are striking disparities in the distribution of power: some people have dominant power; others have far less power; most have no power at all. This is a world torn apart by dynamics of oppression, manipulation and coercion. Research methodologies basing themselves on the one and the other of these two envisaged worlds will be very different methodologies addressing very different purposes.

It may need to be re-emphasised that the chasm in constructionist thought being pinpointed here is between the critical approach and *popularised* versions of pragmatism. In its origins and its high points, pragmatism has more than enough in common with both phenomenology and critical theory for fruitful dialogue to take place. There are signs that a dialectic of this kind is emerging.

REALISM AND RELATIVISM

Social constructionism is at once realist and relativist.

To say that meaningful reality is socially constructed is not to say that it is not real. As we have noted earlier, constructionism in epistemology is perfectly compatible with a realism in ontology—and in more ways than one.

Stanley Fish underlines the reality of our social constructions when commenting publicly on the so-called Sokal Affair of 1996.[8] It is no contradiction, Fish points out in the *New York Times* (21 May 1996), to say that something is socially constructed and also real. He draws an example from baseball. 'Balls' and 'strikes' are certainly socially constructed. They exist as such because of the rules of the game. Yet they are real. Some people are paid as much as $3.5 million to produce them or prevent their production! They are constructions, and may change in their nature tomorrow if the powers-that-be decide to change the rules, but they are real, nonetheless.

Accordingly, those who contrast 'constructionism' and 'realism' are wide of the mark. Realism should be set, instead, against idealism. Idealism, we have already noted, is the philosophical view that what is real is somehow confined to what is in the mind, that is, it consists only of 'ideas' (to use the word employed by Descartes and his contemporaries). Social constructionism does not confine reality in this way.

Secondly, we should accept that social constructionism is relativist. What is said to be 'the way things are' is really just 'the sense we make of them'. Once this standpoint is embraced, we will obviously hold our understandings much more lightly and tentatively and far less dogmatically, seeing them as historically and culturally effected interpretations rather than eternal truths of some kind. Historical and cross-cultural comparisons should make us very aware that, at different times and in different places, there have been and are very divergent interpretations of the same phenomena.

A certain relativism is in order, therefore. We need to recognise that different people may well inhabit quite different worlds. Their different worlds constitute for them diverse ways of knowing, distinguishable sets of meanings, separate realities.

At the very least, this means that description and narration can no longer be seen as straightforwardly representational of reality. It is not a case of merely mirroring 'what is there'. When we describe something, we are, in the normal course of events,[9] reporting how something is seen and reacted to, and thereby meaningfully constructed, within a given community or set of communities. When we narrate something, even in telling our very own story, it is (again in the normal course of events) the voice of our culture—its many voices, in fact—that is heard in what we say. A consideration of central importance, surely. Yet not all approaches to social inquiry and analysis professing to be constructionist have been equally successful in keeping it in view.

It has become something of a shibboleth for qualitative researchers to claim to be constructionist or constructivist, or both. We need to ensure that this is not just a glib claim, a matter of rhetoric only. If we make such a claim, we should reflect deeply on its significance. What does it mean for our research to be constructionist and constructivist? What implications does being constructionist/constructivist hold?

Important questions these. Being constructionist/constructivist has crucial things to say to us about many dimensions of the research task. It speaks to us about the way in which we do research. It speaks to us about how we should view its data.

We will do well to listen.

4

INTERPRETIVISM: FOR AND AGAINST CULTURE

We pass the word around; we ponder how the case is put by different people; we read the poetry; we meditate over the literature; we play the music; we change our minds; we reach an understanding.

Lewis Thomas, *The Medusa and the Snail*

In the schema presented in the Introduction, the first column is headed 'Epistemology'. Objectivism, which we have related to positivism and post-positivism, and constructionism, which we dealt with in the last chapter, are examples of epistemological positions encountered within the field of social research. As stated already, we shall encounter examples of a more subjectivist epistemology when we come to postmodernism. Now, however, we are returning to our second column, already visited in our discussion of positivism, and will concern ourselves with further theoretical perspectives embedded within research methodologies.

'Theoretical perspective' is being taken here to mean the philosophical stance lying behind a methodology. The theoretical perspective provides a context for the process involved and a basis for its logic and its criteria. Another way to put it is to say that, whenever one examines a particular methodology, one discovers a complexus of assumptions buried within it. It is these assumptions that constitute one's theoretical perspective and they largely have to do with the world that the methodology envisages. Different ways of viewing the world shape different ways of researching the world.

The theoretical perspective considered in this chapter—interpretivism—emerged in contradistinction to positivism in attempts to understand and explain human and social reality. As Thomas Schwandt puts it (1994, p. 125), 'interpretivism was conceived in reaction to the effort to develop a natural science of the social. Its foil was largely logical empiricist methodology and the bid to apply that framework to human inquiry'.

A positivist approach would follow the methods of the natural sciences and, by way of allegedly value-free, detached observation, seek to identify universal features of humanhood, society and history that offer explanation and hence control and predictability. The interpretivist approach, to the contrary, *looks for culturally derived and historically situated interpretations of the social life-world.*

ROOTS OF INTERPRETIVISM

Interpretivism is often linked to the thought of Max Weber (1864–1920), who suggests that in the human sciences we are concerned with *Verstehen* (understanding). This has been taken to mean that Weber is contrasting the interpretative approach (*Verstehen*, understanding) needed in the human and social sciences with the explicative approach (*Erklären*, explaining), focused on causality, that is found in the natural sciences. Hence the emphasis on the different methods employed in each, leading to the clear (though arguably exaggerated) distinction found in the textbooks between qualitative research methods and quantitative research methods. However, discussion of whether methods used in the human and social sciences ought to differ from those of the natural sciences predates Weber's concern with the issue.

Wilhelm Dilthey (1833–1911) does, indeed, contrast *Verstehen* and *Erklären*. He proposes that natural reality and social reality are in themselves different kinds of reality and their investigation therefore requires different methods.

Neo-Kantian philosophers Wilhelm Windelband (1848–1915) and Heinrich Rickert (1863–1936), while rejecting the notion that there is some kind of real distinction between natural reality and social reality, accept that there is a logical distinction, one posited by the mind, between the two. One implication this bears is that, in studying one and the other, we have different purposes in view. In the case of nature, science is looking for consistencies, regularities, the 'law' (*nomos*) that obtains. In the case of human affairs—in historical studies, for instance—we are concerned with the individual (*idios*) case. So Windelband talks of natural science seeking what is *nomothetic* and the human and social sciences seeking what is *idiographic*.

For his part, Rickert talks of a *generalising* method (in the natural sciences) over against an *individualising* method (in the human and social sciences). Thus, a distinction is made between the natural sciences, which seek to establish general laws, and the cultural sciences, which isolate individual phenomena in order to trace their unique development.

What about Weber, then? On the one hand, he agrees with Windelband and Rickert in rejecting Dilthey's real distinction between natural reality and social reality and positing only a logical distinction between them. On the other hand, Weber does not feel that this necessitates the use of different methods in researching these two realms of being.

As Weber sees it, both the natural sciences and the human and social sciences may be concerned at any given time with either the nomothetic or the idiographic. Uniqueness and historicity are manifest in nature as well as humanity, while general covering laws may explain human behaviour as well as natural phenomena. Sociology can be found to engage in empirical research to discover what regularly occurs, while biology or astronomy may sometimes study unique aspects of particular phenomena. Weber holds, then, that the one scientific method should apply to these two forms of science and should cater for both nomothetic and idiographic inquiry.

Admittedly, the natural sciences are primarily concerned with the nomothetic and the human or social sciences primarily with the idiographic. This establishes a different orientation in the one area and the other. Our interest in the social world tends to focus on exactly those aspects that are unique, individual and qualitative, whereas our interest in the natural world focuses on more abstract phenomena, that is, those exhibiting quantifiable, empirical regularities. This, however, is a matter of interest rather than something the nature of the science in question specifically calls for. For his part, Weber looks for empirical validation of any claims made in the social arena and spends the best part of a lifetime attempting to elaborate a methodology that will enable him to verify claims in this way.

To be sure, Weber's *Verstehen* sociology locates the study of society in the context of human beings acting and interacting.

> Interpretative sociology considers the individual and his action as the basic unit, as its 'atom' . . . In this approach the individual is also the upper limit and the sole carrier of meaningful conduct . . . In general, for sociology, such concepts as 'state', 'association', 'feudalism', and the like, designate certain categories of human interaction. Hence it is the task of sociology to

reduce these concepts to 'understandable' action, that is without exception, to the actions of participating men. (Weber 1970, p. 55)

Here Weber is expressing the need to focus social inquiry on the meanings and values of acting persons and therefore on their subjective 'meaning-complex of action'. Nevertheless, he defines sociology as 'a science which attempts the interpretive understanding of social action in order thereby to arrive at a causal explanation of its course and effects' (1968, p. 3). Sociology's 'concepts and generalizations are fashioned on the premise that it can claim to make a contribution to the causal explanation of some historically and culturally important phenomenon' (Weber 1962, p. 51).

Causal! This hardly squares with the position of those who claim to stand in the line of Weber's *Verstehen* but take it to have no interest in causality and contrast it with the *Erklären* approach that does. 'Interpretivism', says Silverman (1990, p. 126), 'rests on the emphatic denial that we can understand cultural phenomena in causal terms'. If that is the case, the interpretivism Silverman is speaking of is far removed from Weber's. Weber certainly *is* interested in causes. He wants to explain as well as understand. He writes (1962, pp. 35, 40) of 'explanatory understanding' and a 'correct causal interpretation of a concrete course of behavior'. Nowak, in fact, goes so far as to claim that, for Weber, '*Verstehen* is a method of explaining and of explaining only' (in Weiss 1986, p. 68).

Going so far may be going too far, all the same, and, in citing Nowak, Weiss feels the need for further distinction. 'Perhaps a better way of saying this would be that *Verstehen* is "for the purpose of explanation"' (Weiss 1986, p. 68). Certainly, Weiss's account accords better with Weber's own definition of sociology. For Weber, as far as human affairs are concerned, any understanding of causation comes through an interpretative understanding of social action and involves an explanation of relevant antecedent phenomena as meaning-complexes. This role ascribed to *Verstehen* implies a difference in outcome in comparison with the natural sciences. As Weber sees it, the causation that the social scientist seeks to clarify is at best 'adequate' rather than 'necessary'. He is ready to 'consider an interpretation of a sequence of events to be *causally adequate*, if on the basis of past experience it appears probable that it will always occur in the same way' (1962, p. 39).

As already suggested, it is Weber's contention that, in any scientific study of society, *Verstehen* has to be substantiated by empirical evidence. He has a passion for empirical knowledge and stresses the need for scientifically valid historical and social data. Weber's philosophy, Lewis assures us, is 'an empiricist venture'.

It was as strictly an empirical sociology as academic philosophy was speculative. For it attempted to establish a science of social fact, and to use an
appropriate methodology devised for historico-political material rather than
for the natural sciences, a methodology which would describe and classify
historical and social facts schematically and deduce experimentally the
laws-system of society. (Lewis 1975, p. 39)

Weber finds the centrepiece of this 'appropriate methodology' in what
he calls the *ideal type*. This is his principal diagnostic tool, a heuristic
device for the precise purpose of amassing empirical data. It seeks to
subject social behaviour, for all its subjective dimension, to the scientific
need for the empirical verification of all knowledge.

Using the word 'tool' to describe Weber's ideal type points up the
important fact that it is something the social scientist makes up. It is
not something found through an analysis of what is real. Weber (1949,
pp. 90–4) calls his ideal types conceptual or mental constructs. They
involve imagination, he tells us, and they are utopian in nature. What
the ideal type embodies is the 'pure case', with no admixture of fortuitous
and confusing features. As such, it never exists in reality, but can serve
as a useful model to guide the social inquirer in addressing real-life cases
and discerning where and to what extent the real deviates from the
ideal. It reveals, Weber tells us (1970, p. 323), what is 'possible and
"adequate"'.

Weber sets strict limits to the use of his ideal types. He believes that
ideal-type methodology is applicable only to social behaviour that can
be described as 'rational goal-oriented conduct' and not to 'rational
value-oriented conduct', 'affectual conduct', or 'traditionalist conduct'.
What is being studied by way of the ideal type is the outcome of persons
acting under a common motivation and choosing suitable means to
the ends they have in view. It is only in regard to such rational
goal-oriented conduct that we can take stock of empirical data according
to preconceived rational criteria implicitly accepted by both actor and
observer.

Alfred Schutz (1899–1959) is very taken with Weber's ideal-type
methodology. Schutz attempts to ground it philosophically and develop
it further by way of his own 'second-order' constructs, which he refers
to as 'puppets' or *homunculi* (1973, p. 255). Like Weber, and the similarly
minded scholars who preceded him from Dilthey on, Schutz strives
to harmonise the idiographic with the nomothetic and make possible
a study of human affairs that can be said to be rigorously scientific. It
was this very concern that launched the *Verstehen* approach in the first
place.

In more recent times, interpretivism seems to have largely cut itself loose from these traditional moorings. While continuing to trace its lineage back to Weber and his call for 'understanding' and 'interpretation', the *Verstehen* approach has not maintained his passion for empirical verification or his concern to explain in causal terms. In most instances, it has accepted what Weber refused to accept, that is, that the human and social sciences require methods essentially different from those of the natural sciences. It is usually not easy to discern the basis for this demand of different methods. Often without thematising the issue, interpretative researchers seem to evince either Dilthey's hard and fast distinction between the subject matter of these two areas of science or at least Windelband's and Rickert's 'distinction of reason' along with the nomothetic/idiographic divide to which these distinctions lead. Blaikie, for one, writes of the 'fundamental difference between the subject matters of the natural and social sciences' (1993, p. 36). Hence the widespread espousal of quantitative research methods in the one and very different qualitative research methods commonly found in the other.

For all that, studies of the natural world and the social world have come closer together. This has been largely due to the development pointed up in Chapter 2, namely, the recognition by many thinkers that positivist science's age-old claims to certitude and objectivity cannot be sustained and that the findings of natural science are themselves social constructions and human interpretations, albeit a particular form of such constructions and interpretations.

What we understand today as the *Verstehen* or interpretivist approach to human inquiry has appeared historically in many guises. It will be useful to consider three historical streams that have borne it along. In their historical order of appearance, these are hermeneutics, phenomenology, and symbolic interactionism. It will suit our purposes to reverse the order.

We will consider symbolic interactionism and phenomenology in the remainder of this chapter. These contrast with each other quite sharply in their attitude towards culture as our inherited meaning system. Symbolic interactionism explores the understandings abroad in culture as the meaningful matrix that guides our lives. Phenomenology, however, treats culture with a good measure of caution and suspicion. Our culture may be enabling but, paradoxically, it is also crippling. While it offers us entrée to a comprehensive set of meanings, it shuts us off from an abundant font of untapped significance.

For culture and against culture, then. Two very different traditions. As researchers, we learn from both.

Symbolic interactionism

Symbolic interactionism offers what is very much an American perspective on life, society and the world. As already noted when discussing constructionism, it stems from the thought of pragmatist philosopher and social psychologist George Herbert Mead. Mead's teaching, which extended over a period of almost 40 years, principally at the University of Chicago, is encapsulated in a posthumous work, *Mind, Self and Society* (1934). This book was compiled by grateful students from papers Mead had left and lecture notes they had accumulated. It is to one student in particular, Herbert Blumer, that most credit must go for the impact Mead's thought has had in the realm of sociology.

In a much-cited formulation, Blumer (1969, p. 2) enunciates three basic interactionist assumptions:

- 'that human beings act toward things on the basis of the meanings that these things have for them';
- 'that the meaning of such things is derived from, and arises out of, the social interaction that one has with one's fellows';
- 'that these meanings are handled in, and modified through, an interpretive process used by the person in dealing with the things he encounters'.

To do them justice, these tenets need to be set against the backdrop of pragmatist philosophy, for the pragmatism informing Mead's social psychology and Blumer's sociology remains a significant dimension of symbolic interactionism today.

Pragmatist philosophy

Within pragmatism, the quintessentially American philosophy, we find diverse streams. There are, one has to say, many pragmatisms. For all that, pragmatist approaches display a number of common characteristics, even if attempts to articulate these characteristics, as in Rescher's generalised account here, tend to reflect a popularised view of pragmatism rather than the careful nuances of its founders:

> The characteristic idea of philosophical pragmatism is that efficacy in practical application—the issue of 'which works out most effectively'—somehow provides a standard for the determination of truth in the case of

statements, rightness in the case of actions, and value in the case of appraisals. (1995, p. 710)

Pragmatism derives, in the first instance, from the work of Charles Sanders Peirce. In launching his pragmatism, Peirce was seeking a critical philosophy. He insisted (1931–58, vol. 5, p. 9) that 'pragmatism is not a Weltanschauung but it is a method of reflexion having for its purpose to render ideas clear'.[10] Peirce went on to develop his own version of phenomenology—'phaneroscopy' he came to call it in the end—independently of the acknowledged founder of phenomenology, Edmund Husserl. Peirce looked to determine the elemental categories present to the mind in their 'Firstness' or qualitative immediacy. In doing so, Peirce was, to a significant degree, paralleling the phenomenologists' efforts to delineate phenomena encountered in immediate experience (Spiegelberg 1981).

Peirce's work remained largely unknown, and certainly unacknowledged, until pragmatism became popular through the work of William James some years later. John Dewey had already been involved with pragmatism for many years and it was the James/Dewey version that now came to the fore. Peirce, unhappy with the turn pragmatism had taken, began to call his own approach 'pragmaticism' instead. This, he hoped, would prove sufficiently ugly a term to discourage any would-be kidnappers!

What had happened to the pragmatism launched by Peirce that led him to disown it? Well, for one thing, it was far less critical. As we have already seen in discussing constructionism, some have gone so far as to accuse James's and Dewey's versions of pragmatism of being totally uncritical. While, in the case of James and Dewey, this appears to rest on a gross misreading, the allegation can certainly be sustained when levelled at the pragmatism that developed later. Pragmatism did become essentially an uncritical exploration of cultural ideas and values in terms of their practical outcomes. Even in James and Dewey, the authentic meaning of ideas and values is linked to their outcomes and therefore to the practices in which they are embedded. Pragmatism, says William James (1950, p. 15), is the 'attitude of looking away from first things, principles, "categories", supposed necessities; and of looking towards last things, fruits, consequences, facts'.

> When it is maintained that conceptualization is purposive [Peirce], or that thought is teleological [James], or that ideas are instruments [Dewey], the methodological principle these doctrines suggest is that the analysis of meanings (of signs, i.e., ideas, concepts, statements) is an analysis of certain kinds of action in certain contexts . . . For the pragmatist, therefore, meaning has reference, if sometimes only remotely so, to the ordinary situations and conditions in which actions occur. (Thayer 1968, p. 429)

In this understanding of things, experience and culture come to be almost interchangeable terms. Seeking the meaning of experience becomes an exploration of culture. Dewey once remarked that he would have avoided many misunderstandings if he had used the word 'culture' instead of 'experience' (in Thayer 1968, p. 173, n.28).

The view of culture and society that pragmatism came to adopt is essentially optimistic and progressivist. The pragmatist world is a world to be explored and made the most of, not a world to be subjected to radical criticism. Horkheimer describes pragmatists as 'liberal, tolerant, optimistic' and believes, in fact, that pragmatists cannot deal with the possibility that, at a given historical moment, 'truth might . . . turn out to be completely shocking to humanity' (1974, p. 51). 'Increasingly', writes Horowitz (1966, p. 29), 'pragmatism came to stand for acquiescence in the social order'. Mary Rogers describes what emerged as a 'pragmatic-naturalist philosophy which focuses on the nature and genesis of a shared world, intersubjectivity, and communication' (1981, p. 140).

This, to be sure, is the focus found in the work of Dewey's associate, George Herbert Mead, through whose thought pragmatism enters sociology in the form of symbolic interactionism.

FROM MEAD TO ETHNOGRAPHY

As we have noted, Mead attributes our very personhood to social forces that shape us and our behaviour. 'A person', Mead says (1934, p. 162), 'is a personality because he belongs to a community, because he takes over the institutions of that community into his own conduct'. This certainly puts the spotlight on the practices found in any given culture as the very source of personhood. For Mead (1934, p. 7), 'the whole (society) is prior to the part (the individual)'. We owe to society our very being as conscious and self-conscious entities, for that being arises from a process of symbolic interaction—interaction, that is to say, by way of significant gestures.

> Only in terms of gestures as significant symbols is the existence of mind or intelligence possible; for only in terms of gestures which are significant symbols can thinking—which is simply an internalized or implicit conversation of the individual with himself by means of such gestures—take place. (Mead 1934, p. 47)

To 'enter the attitudes of the community' and 'take over the institutions of the community', as Mead argues we inevitably do in our emergence into personhood, we must be able to *take the role of others*. We have to see ourselves as social objects and we can only do that through adopting the standpoint of others. The process begins in childhood, Mead teaches us. It starts with early imitative acts and proceeds via play (in which children act out the role of others) and games (in which children have to put themselves in the place of others and think about how others think and act). With games the child starts to think in terms of the 'generalised other'. Later this generalised other will be related to broader social institutions.

Here we find emerging a central notion of symbolic interactionism: the putting of oneself in the place of the other. Coser stresses this point:

> Mead must be credited alongside Cooley and other pragmatists with having been instrumental in stressing the need for always considering situations from the point of view of the actor. For him, just as for Weber, when the sociologist refers to meaning, it is to the subjective meaning actors impute to their actions. (1971, p. 340)

In symbolic interactionism as a theoretical perspective informing methodologies for social research, this notion remains pivotal, as numerous commentators attest:

> Methodologically, the implication of the symbolic interactionist perspective is that the actor's view of actions, objects, and society has to be studied seriously. The situation must be seen as the actor sees it, the meanings of objects and acts must be determined in terms of the actor's meanings, and the organization of a course of action must be understood as the actor organizes it. The role of the actor in the situation would have to be taken by the observer in order to see the social world from his perspective. (Psathas 1973, pp. 6–7)

> Some interpretive sociologists—those identified as 'symbolic interactionists' for example—are content to operate with a relatively naïve set of assumptions about how we come to know about social phenomena. They are prepared to accept the meanings that the actors attribute to social phenomena at face value, and proceed to erect their systematic interpretations on these foundations. This implies that the sociological observer must exercise sufficient discipline on himself to ensure that it is indeed the *actors'* meanings that are recorded in his notebook and not merely his own. (Mitchell 1977, pp. 115–16)

> Methodologically, symbolic interactionism directs the investigator to take, to the best of his ability, the standpoint of those studied. (Denzin 1978, p. 99)

This role taking is an *interaction*. It is *symbolic* interaction, for it is possible only because of the 'significant symbols'—that is, language and other symbolic tools—that we humans share and through which we communicate. Only through dialogue can one become aware of the perceptions, feelings and attitudes of others and interpret their meanings and intent. Hence the term 'symbolic interactionism' (though it is a term that Mead himself never used).

Given the emphasis on putting oneself in the place of the other and seeing things from the perspective of others, it is not surprising that symbolic interactionism should take to its bosom the research methodology developed within cultural anthropology, that is, ethnography. American cultural anthropology was shaped most decisively by Franz Boas, whose experience in studying Arctic Eskimos is said to have turned him from a scientist's view of cognition to an historian's view of culture. Cultures, as Boas comes to see them, are irreducible and incomparable. Through Boas's influence, cultural relativism succeeded in dominating American anthropology, accompanied by a strong rejection of all ethnocentrism (Bloch 1983, pp. 124–8). Culture is not to be called into question; it is not to be criticised, least of all by someone from another culture. Instead, one is to observe it as closely as possible, attempt to take the place of those within the culture, and search out the insider's perspective. Herein lies the origin of ethnography, born to anthropology but adopted (and adapted) by sociology.

For ethnography, then, as for the symbolic interactionism that now commonly forms its matrix, the notion of taking the place of the other is central.

> . . . ethnography is a form of research in which the social settings to be studied, however familiar to the researcher, must be treated as anthropologically strange; and the task is to document the culture—the perspectives and practices—of the people in these settings. The aim is to 'get inside' the way each group of people sees the world. (Hammersley 1985, p. 152)

INTERACTIONIST RESEARCH

Ethnography undertaken from an interactionist perspective has been framed schematically in many ways.

One form in which it has emerged has been the *dramaturgical approach* associated especially with Erving Goffman. Research done in this vein draws on the familiar analogy between social life and the theatre. Actors on a stage form a cast. The cast teams with producer, director, choreographer, stage hands, and the like, to present a theatrical production. It is possible to view people interacting in a life situation (family, social club) or work setting (courtroom, operating theatre) in much the same light. In these settings we find people speaking, dressing and generally comporting themselves in certain ways; we find them displaying certain instruments or items of property; we find them moving, as it were, between 'front-stage' and 'back-stage'—all of this to convince others as to who they purport to be and what they purport to be doing. In this figurative sense, they have an audience and seek to influence the audience by way of roles and scripts and stage props. Who would deny that there are rituals in social life, some quite overt and others subtly disguised, which are very meaningful forms of interaction? Dramaturgy as a form of interactionist research identifies such rituals, examines their rubrical directives, and attempts to delineate their meanings and outcomes.

Game theory is not dissimilar. It analyses social interaction using the everyday concept of the game. The rules of a game define a team of players, specify a set of permissible manoeuvres, and construct a context ('match', 'set', 'bout', 'event' . . .) within which players can play. Viewing social life as a game, one can divide the broad array of social interactions into various events. Within the setting of a particular event, one can go on to distinguish the rules of the game. It is these rules that set boundaries and parameters, appoint players, govern what players are permitted and required to do, and determine the prize for success or the 'wooden spoon' for failure.

Another interactionist strategy takes the form of *negotiated-order theory*. There are many accounts of society that present social settings as definitively structured and offering social actors very clear-cut roles. Negotiated-order theory disputes this view. In this stream of interactionist inquiry, to the contrary, societal arrangements and procedures are considered to be constantly reworked by those who live and work within them. Work settings in which, sometimes on a day-to-day basis, tasks are reassigned, roles exchanged, responsibilities shouldered, and partnerships formed, typify this view of things. In such settings—and, indeed, quite broadly within society as a whole—there is an ongoing, albeit often tacit, process of negotiation and adjustment of action. Analysing this process in specific social situations has proved a useful avenue for interactionist inquiry. Anselm Strauss and his associates have been to the fore in exploring its potential.

Yet another form of interactionist inquiry has to do with the study of deviance. *Labelling theory* models itself on the everyday ways in which we categorise people and things. Society is quick to style certain individuals and groups 'deviant'. However, according to labelling theorists such as Howard Becker in his 1963 book *Outsiders*, while this says much about the society in question, it says little about the behaviour of the deviants. Deviance, from this perspective, is simply behaviour that people so label. Thus, in studying deviants, one is studying only those who have been labelled by society as having engaged in deviant behaviour. This being the case, searching for causes of deviant behaviour by, say, analysing the heredity and environment of so-called deviants, would appear a futile and misguided enterprise. Instead, symbolic interactionism directs us to a study of the labelling process itself. Why is it, we should ask ourselves, that society wants to exclude some members from full and free participation in its life? And what are the mechanisms it uses to do so? Symbolic interactionism's involvement in research of this kind has brought it an enviable reputation for being on the side of the 'underdog'.

Symbolic interactionism has also spawned the research methodology known as *grounded theory*. Grounded theory can be viewed as a specific form of ethnographic inquiry that, through a series of carefully planned steps, develops theoretical ideas. Throughout the process, it seeks to ensure that the theory emerging arises from the data and not from some other source. It is a process of inductive theory building based squarely on observation of the data themselves. Barney Glaser and Anselm Strauss launched this approach in *The Discovery of Grounded Theory* in 1967 and it has subsequently undergone a number of modifications and refinements and been issued in a number of variant forms.

For qualitative research, symbolic interactionism is a diversified and enriching matrix. Several streams have flowed from its headwaters in the thought of Mead. One stream has been the Chicago School with its emphasis on the origin and development of meaning. Another has been the Iowa School, which moved to a much more empirical and quantitative orientation. Then there are the role-theory interactionists, who tend to make social structures far more pivotal to their interactionism. Whatever the stream, the theoretical perspective of symbolic interactionism has clearly proved useful in identifying research questions and framing research processes for several generations of researchers.

PHENOMENOLOGY

Phenomenology, in itself, is a simple enough concept. The phenomenological movement was launched under the battle cry of 'Back to the things themselves!'. The 'things themselves', as phenomenologists understand the phrase, are phenomena that present themselves immediately to us as conscious human beings. Phenomenology suggests that, if we lay aside, as best we can, the prevailing understandings of those phenomena and revisit our immediate experience of them, possibilities for new meaning emerge for us or we witness at least an authentication and enhancement of former meaning (Crotty 1996a).

This line of thought presumes that there *are* 'things themselves' to visit in our experience, that is, objects to which our understandings relate. That there are indeed such objects is what the notion of intentionality proclaims and it lies at the heart of phenomenology. Husserl (1931, p. 245) describes intentionality as 'a concept which at the threshold of phenomenology is quite indispensable as a starting-point and basis'. Natanson (1973, p. 103) calls it 'the axis of phenomenology'.

We have been introduced to intentionality in considering constructionism. It denotes the essential relationship between conscious subjects and their objects. Consciousness is always consciousness *of* something. An object is always an object *for* someone. The object, in other words, cannot be adequately described apart from the subject, nor can the subject be adequately described apart from the object. From a more existentialist viewpoint, intentionality bespeaks the relationship between us as human beings and our world. We are beings-in-the-world. Because of this, we cannot be described apart from our world, just as our world—always a human world—cannot be described apart from us.

We might recall at this point the distinction we made between constructivism and constructionism. Constructivism describes the individual human subject engaging with objects in the world and making sense of them. Constructionism, to the contrary, denies that this is what actually happens, at least in the first instance. Instead, each of us is introduced directly to a whole world of meaning. The *mélange* of cultures and sub-cultures into which we are born provides us with meanings. These meanings we are taught and we learn in a complex and subtle process of enculturation. They establish a tight grip upon us and, by and large, shape our thinking and behaviour throughout our lives.

Our cultural heritage can therefore be seen as pre-empting the task of meaning making so that, for the most part, we simply do not do what constructivism describes us as doing. Phenomenology, however, invites us to do it. It requires us to engage with phenomena in our world and make sense of them directly and immediately. What about the understandings we are already saddled with? These we have to 'bracket' to the best of our ability and let the experience of phenomena speak to us at first hand (Crotty 1996b). Thus, we find phenomenologists talking about 'primordial phenomena', the 'immediate, original data of our consciousness', the 'phenomena in their unmediated and originary manifestation to consciousness'. Big words, some of them, but they refer to *what we directly experience*; that is, the objects of our experience before we start thinking about them, interpreting them or attributing any meaning to them. These are the *things themselves*.

That phenomenology requires us to place our usual understandings in abeyance and have a fresh look at things has been driven home to us by phenomenologist after phenomenologist.

- Phenomenology invites us to 'set aside all previous habits of thought, see through and break down the mental barriers which these habits have set along the horizons of our thinking . . . to learn to see what stands before our eyes' (Husserl 1931, p. 43).
- Phenomenology is 'a return to the unadulterated phenomena' and an 'unusually obstinate attempt to look at the phenomena and to remain faithful to them before even thinking of them' (Spiegelberg 1982, pp. 680, 717).
- Phenomenology 'exhorts a pristine acquaintance with phenomena unadulterated by preconceptions: it encourages the inquirer to sustain an intuitive grasp of what is there by "opening his eyes", "keeping them open", "looking and listening", "not getting blinded"' (Heron 1992, p. 164).
- 'Phenomenology asks us not to take our received notions for granted but . . . to call into question our whole culture, our manner of seeing the world and being in the world in the way we have learned it growing up' (Wolff 1984, p. 192).
- 'It is the task of phenomenology . . . to make us conscious of what the world was like before we learned how to see it' (Marton 1986, p. 40).
- Phenomenology is an 'attempt to recover a fresh perception of existence, one unprejudiced by acculturation' (Sadler 1969, p. 377).

In this same vein, Merleau-Ponty tells us (1962, p. xiv) that 'in order to see the world and grasp it as paradoxical, we must break with our familiar acceptance of it'. The outcome, he assures us, is 'nothing but the unmotivated upsurge of the world'. It is as if Merleau-Ponty sees the world as a seething cauldron of potential meaning that is held down by our received notions. Once phenomenology 'slackens the intentional threads which attach us to the world', we experience the upsurge and can 'watch the forms of transcendence fly up like sparks from a fire' (1962, p. xiii). Merleau-Ponty employs yet another metaphor—the blossoming of wild flowers. Our phenomenological endeavour to break with inherited understandings 'awakens a wild-flowering world and mind'. 'This renewal of the world', Merleau-Ponty assures us (1964, p. 181), 'is also mind's renewal, a rediscovery of that brute mind which, untamed by any culture, is asked to create culture anew'.

Lying behind this attempt to put our culturally derived meanings in abeyance and renew culture in this radical fashion is a deeply rooted suspicion of culture and the understandings it imposes on us. 'Phenom-enology is much more than a suspension of assumptions. The phenomenological reduction is a change of attitude that throws suspicion on everyday experiences' (Armstrong 1976, p. 252).

Why be suspicious of culture? Surely we owe it our very humanness. Phenomenologists are happy to acknowledge that debt. They recognise that it is culture that allows us to emerge from our immediate environ-ment and reflect upon it. They agree that it is because of culture—our symbols, our meaning systems—that we know our past and can plan our future. Yes, our culture is liberating. However, as we have already noted, in agreeing that culture is liberating, phenomenologists remain very aware that it is also limiting. It sets us free but at the same time it sets boundaries. It makes us human but in and through *this* particular culture, *this* special system of significant symbols, *these* meanings. This is circumscribing. In imposing these meanings, it is excluding others. And we should never lose sight of the fact that the particular set of meanings it imposes has come into being to serve particular interests and will harbour its own forms of oppression, manipulation and other forms of injustice.

Another way to look at this matter is to underline the difference between a reality and any concept we might have of it. Because we are the kind of beings we are, we rely on concepts. We have a need to define and classify. Unfortunately, our definitions and classifications displace what they stand for in our experience of them so that, rather than concepts pointing us to realities, realities are relegated to being mere exemplifications of concepts. Yet a concept is never able to exhaust the richness of a phenomenon. As many philosophers and social scien-tists have pointed out, there is always so much that the concept fails to express. It leaves so much behind. Adorno, for one, is most conscious of this. His reflections, Tertulian tells us (1985, p. 95), 'always gravitate around the ineluctable gap between the concept's inherent abstraction and the rich density of the web of phenomena'. Following Benjamin, Adorno wants attention paid to 'everything that has slipped through the conventional conceptual net' (1981, p. 240). John Dewey too talks of what is 'left over', seeing it 'excluded by definition from full reality' (1929, p. 48).

The need we experience to define and classify proves to be a two-edged sword, therefore. Giving ourselves over to it, Cioran emphasises (1976, p. 222), dries us out and renders us barren. 'Our inmost aridity results from our allegiance to the rule of the *definite*, from our plea in bar of imprecision, that innate chaos which by renewing our deliriums keeps us from sterility.'

There is still more. Not only is our symbol system limited and limiting; it is also a barrier. It stands *for* things but it also comes to stand *between* things and us, that is, between us and our immediate experience of objects. It tends to substitute itself for what we actually see, hear, feel, smell, taste or even imagine. We have already seen a number of thinkers describing cultural understandings as nothing less than masks, screens or blindfolds. Heidegger goes so far as to describe them as a seduction and a dictatorship (1962, pp. 164, 213).

Phenomenology is about saying 'No!' to the meaning system bequeathed to us. It is about setting that meaning system aside. Far from inviting us to explore our everyday meanings as they stand, it calls upon us to put them in abeyance and open ourselves to the phenomena in their stark immediacy to see what emerges for us. True enough, the phenomena in their stark immediacy—the 'things themselves'—will prove elusive. In describing what comes into view within immediate experience (or even in thinking about what comes into view), we necessarily draw on language, on culture. For that reason, we end, not with a presuppositionless description of phenomena, but with a reinter-pretation. It will be as much a construction as the sense we have laid aside, but as reinterpretation—as new meaning, or fuller meaning, or renewed meaning—it is precisely what we as phenomenologists are after.

To take a fresh look at phenomena is, of course, to call into question the current meanings we attribute to phenomena. Phenomenology, it is often said, calls into question what is taken for granted. It is critique and grounds a critical methodology. This has been said many times over from the very beginning of the phenomenological movement:

> . . . the science having the unique function of effecting the criticism of all others and, at the same time, of itself is none other than phenomenology. (Husserl 1970a, vol. 1, p. 45)

> Phenomenology is a reflective enterprise, and in its reflection it is critical. (Larrabee 1990, p. 201)

> Phenomenological philosophy is first of all philosophical criticism . . . I disengage from a claim in order to criticise it . . . in the systematically adopted attitude of disengagement. (Zaner 1970, pp. 79–80)

> The value of phenomenology from a critical point of view is evident. The programme of reflecting upon all knowledge and experience, with the ideal of the 'self-givenness' in experience of what is meant, may well have an emancipating effect. (Farber 1991, p. 234)

From what we have considered to this point, two clear characteristics of phenomenology emerge. First of all, it has a note of *objectivity* about it. It is in search of objects of experience rather than being content with a description of the experiencing subject. Second, it is an exercise in *critique*. It calls into question what we take for granted.

In both respects it contrasts sharply with what is usually presented today as phenomenology, at least in the English-speaking world. Here phenomenology is generally seen as a study of people's subjective and everyday experiences. For a start, researchers claiming to be phenomenological talk of studying experience from the 'point of view' or 'perspective' of the subject. What these researchers are interested in is 'everyday' experience, experience as people understand it in everyday terms. If they talk at all of 'phenomenon', it is either used interchangeably with 'experience' or presented as an essence distilled from everyday accounts of experience, a total picture synthesised from partial accounts.

The phenomenological method as understood by these researchers is geared towards collecting and analysing data in ways that do not prejudice their subjective character. It puts in place a number of procedures to prevent, or at least minimise, the imposition of the researcher's presuppositions and constructions on the data. For a start, in most cases the researcher's own knowledge and presuppositions are said to be 'bracketed' so as not to taint the data. ('Bracketing' is a term introduced by Husserl and used by later representatives of the phenomenological movement, but here it is being used in an essentially different sense.) To ensure that the subjective character of the experiences is not prejudiced, these researchers tend to gather data by way of unstructured interviews in which only open-ended questions, if any, are asked. The researchers also want to make sure that the themes pinpointed in the data do, in fact, arise out of the data and are not imposed on them. So they talk of 'intuiting' the data and invite others (often including the subjects) to support their claim that the themes they point to are genuinely to be found in the data.

What has emerged here under the rubric of 'phenomenology' is a quite single-minded effort to identify, understand, describe and maintain the subjective experiences of the respondents. It is self-professedly *subjectivist* in approach (in the sense of being in search of people's subjective experience) and expressly *uncritical*.

In this attempt to understand and describe people's subjective experience, there is much talk of *putting oneself in the place of the other*. This is sometimes styled 'the great phenomenological principle'. Even so, the emphasis typically remains on common understandings and the meanings of common practices, so that phenomenological research of this kind emerges as an exploration, via personal experiences, of prevailing cultural understandings.

This is a new understanding of phenomenology and one may well ask how it came to be. As argued elsewhere (Crotty 1995, 1996a), it is very much a North American development. When phenomenology arrived on the shores of that continent, it was slow to receive any kind of welcome at all. In the end, within philosophy and to some extent and for some time within sociology, it gained a measure of acceptance and a number of adherents, but overall the indigenous forms of philosophy (pragmatism) and sociology (symbolic interactionism) won out. In psychology there was even less acceptance. In the 1960s, when phenomenologists like van Kaam and Giorgi and Colaizzi began expounding their stepwise methodologies for phenomenological research, humanistic psychology was already at centre stage and not about to surrender its hold on the audience. What seems to have happened is that, instead of being genuinely transplanted west of the Atlantic, phenomenology was grafted onto local stock. It was not permitted to set down its own roots. Consequently, its fruit embodies the American intellectual tradition far more than any features of its parent plant. It has been assimilated to that tradition. Its 'foreignness' has been removed. It has been translated into something familiar.

For one thing, we have noted how central to symbolic interactionism is the notion of 'taking the place of the other'. It is not central to phenomenology. One can read Spiegelberg's massive history of the phenomenological movement (1982) from cover to cover but the so-called 'great phenomenological principle' is not to be found there. Why should it be there? The phenomenology of the phenomenological movement is a first-person exercise. Each of us must explore our own experience, not the experience of others, for no one can take that step 'back to the things themselves' on our behalf.

In all this transformation the vocabulary of phenomenology remains. There is still talk of 'experience' and 'phenomenon', of 'reduction' and 'bracketing'—of 'intentionality', even; yet the meaning of these terms is no longer the meaning they have borne within the phenomenological movement from which they have been taken.[11]

Does it matter that this new understanding of phenomenology has arisen? It would seem to matter a great deal. Not because a different methodology has emerged laying claim to the name of phenomenology. The phenomenological movement emanating from Husserl has no monopoly on that word. The word was used in different senses long before Husserl borrowed it from Brentano. It is used in different senses today. There is no place here for any kind of purism or the mounting of a defence of some alleged orthodoxy. Still, it is legitimate enough to lament what has been lost in the process. What has been lost is the objective character and critical spirit, so strong in the phenomenological tradition.

When the focus on the object is lost, inquiry readily becomes very subjectivist—even, at times, narcissistic. And, when the critical spirit is lost, there is at best a failure to capture new or fuller meanings or a loss of opportunities to renew the understandings that already possess us. At worst, it means that oppression, exploitation and unfreedom are permitted to persist without question. To use Walzer's words, 'the maxim holds here as elsewhere: Criticize the world; it needs it!' (1989, p. x) Walzer is not speaking of phenomenology. If he were, he might need to say that the maxim holds here *more* than elsewhere. As critique of the very notions to be used in any further critique, phenomenology is first critique, most basic critique, a radical and necessary element in all human inquiry.

To refer to phenomenology as 'first' critique is already to acknowledge that it is not the only critique. Husserl often states that he is concerned with 'beginnings', and phenomenology may be viewed as essentially a starting point. One may wish to argue that it is a most valuable starting point—an essential starting point, even—but it is by no means the be-all and end-all of social inquiry.

Nor is the initial attempt to contemplate the immediate phenomenon the last. The sociologist will lay the phenomenological mantle aside and move far afield, but needs to return to the starting point time and again. What phenomenology offers social inquiry is not only a beginning rooted in immediate social experience but also a methodology that requires a return to that experience at many points along the way. It is both starting point and touchstone.

Merleau-Ponty sounds this note for us. He warns us that, instead of attempting to establish in positivist fashion the things that 'build up the shape of the world', we need to recognise our *experience* 'as the source which stares us in the face and as the ultimate court of appeal in our knowledge of these things' (1962, p. 23). For Merleau-Ponty, the phenomenological return to experience is philosophy—not philosophy as a particular body of knowledge but philosophy as a vigilance that never lets us forget the origin of all our knowledge. Philosophy of this kind, he insists, is necessary to sociology 'as a constant reminder of its tasks'. Through it 'the sociologist returns to the living sources of his knowledge' (Merleau-Ponty 1964, p. 110).

What, then, is the world as the phenomenologist sees it? Certainly a bountiful world, a world teeming with potential meaning.

Our experience is no less than an existential encounter with a world which has a potentially infinite horizon. This human world is not predetermined, as common sense or physicalist language would indicate; it is a world that is open for the discovery and creation of ever-new directions for encounter, and hence open to the emergence of as yet undiscovered significance. (Sadler 1969, p. 20)

Yet the phenomenologist's world is also a world in which our received notions—the systems of significant symbols that make us human—are seen to hide that potential meaning from us and hold us back from bringing it to birth. Phenomenologists chafe under what they see to be a tyrannous culture. They long to smash the fetters and engage with the world in new ways to construct new understandings.

Research, for phenomenologists, is this very attempt to break free and see the world afresh.

5

INTERPRETIVISM:
THE WAY OF HERMENEUTICS

Ye that are of good understanding, note the doctrine that is
hidden under the veil of the strange verses!

Dante Alighieri, *The Divine Comedy*

The term 'hermeneutics' came into modern use in the seventeenth
century in the context of biblical studies. Hermeneutics was, and is, the
science of biblical interpretation. It provides guidelines for scholars as
they engage in the task of interpreting Scripture. The actual explanation
of what a biblical text means is known as exegesis. Behind all exegetical
activity, governing how it is carried out, lies a complexus of theories,
principles, rules and methods. That complexus came to be known as
hermeneutics. In broad terms, it could be said that hermeneutics is to
exegesis what grammar is to language or logic is to reasoning.

Since then, the word has migrated into many areas of scholarship. Not
only has hermeneutics been brought to bear on texts other than the
Scriptures, but it has been brought to bear on unwritten sources also—
human practices, human events, human situations—in an attempt to
'read' these in ways that bring understanding. This outcome squares with
the centrality of language in any concept of human being. We are
essentially languaged beings. Language is pivotal to, and shapes, the
situations in which we find ourselves enmeshed, the events that befall
us, the practices we carry out and, in and through all this, the understandings we are able to reach.

An older, more traditional view of language has it representing and
articulating our concepts of reality, which in their turn reproduce or

reflect reality. As the medieval philosophers would have it, the way things are (*ordo essendi*) shapes the way we perceive things (*ordo cogitandi*) and this gets expressed in the way we speak (*ordo loquendi*). Especially since the 'linguistic turn' in philosophy and social science, this has been more or less reversed. It is now language, the way we speak, that is considered to shape what things we see and how we see them, and it is these things shaped for us by language that constitute reality for us. Thus, the *ordo loquendi* constitutes the *ordo cogitandi* and, as far as meaningful reality is concerned, even the *ordo essendi*. Looked at in this light, the realities we have referred to above—our situations, events, practices and meanings—are constituted by language. To bring to bear upon them forms of interpretation that emerged in the first instance as ways of understanding language is not so peculiar after all.

> Ricoeur's famous phrase 'the symbol gives rise to thought' expresses the basic premise of hermeneutics: that the symbols of myth, religion, art and ideology all carry messages which may be uncovered by philosophical interpretation. Hermeneutics is defined accordingly as a method for deciphering indirect meaning, a reflective practice of unmasking hidden meanings beneath apparent ones. While this method had originally been used by theologians to investigate the inner meanings of sacred texts, it was radically redeployed by modern thinkers like Dilthey, Heidegger, Gadamer and Ricoeur to embrace man's general being in the world as an agent of language. (Kearney 1991, p. 277)

Etymologically 'hermeneutics' derives from the Greek word ἑρμηνεύειν (*hermeneuein*), which means 'to interpret' or 'to understand'. Underpinning this meaning in ancient Greek usage are the notions of 'saying', 'explaining' and 'translating', which already suggests the idea of addressing something that is in some way strange, separated in time or place, or outside of one's experience, with the purpose of rendering it familiar, present and intelligible (Palmer 1969, pp. 12–14).

There is an obvious link between *hermeneuein* and the god Hermes. Hermes is the fleet-footed divine messenger (he has wings on his feet!). As a messenger, he is bearer of knowledge and understanding. His task is to explain to humans the decisions of the gods. Whether *hermeneuein* derives from Hermes or the other way round is not certain.

HISTORICAL ORIGINS

While the word is only about two-and-a-half centuries old, hermeneutics as a disciplined approach to interpretation can be traced back to the ancient Greeks studying literature and to biblical exegesis in the Judeo-Christian tradition.

The Greeks took texts to be wholes rather than merely a juxtaposition of unorganised parts. Because of this, they expected that grammar and style, and even ideas, would be consistent in any particular text and throughout the writings of any one author or school. On this basis, they proceeded to codify principles of grammar and style and to identify the logic found in particular authors and schools. These principles and emphases, which the Greeks used to correct, confirm or authenticate various passages and even whole texts, can be said to constitute their hermeneutics, even if the word itself was not to emerge for some 2000 years. Whatever of the word, the relating of part to whole and whole to part discernible in the interpretative practices of the ancient Greeks would become an enduring theme within hermeneutics.

Another tradition stemmed from Jewish hermeneutical practices. In interpreting its sacred Scriptures, Rabbinic Judaism had different procedures for dealing with narrative texts and legal texts. *Haggadah* ('story') sought to draw moral lessons from narratives. Here a number of hermeneutical devices were employed. Some of these made it possible to bring separate texts together. Others either creatively embellished the existing narrative text or added anecdotes to it. *Halakhah* ('procedure') was the way in which legal texts were read. This had its own hermeneutical devices. The text was regarded as a divine code of behaviour and the devices enabled it to be mined for deeper significances. Sometimes *haggadah* and *halakhah* were combined in a form of literature known as *targum* ('translation'), which itself required hermeneutical principles for its interpretation.

The first Christians inherited Jewish ways of interpreting. However, a significant development occurred in the second century. Drawing on the writings of Philo Judaeus, this move combined the approach deriving from Judaism with another approach that found its source in Greek practice. According to Philo, while interpreters are to look for a spiritual sense in the text, they must find a basis for this spiritual sense in the literal sense that the text bears.

Philo's thought on the matter was very influential. Two conflicting schools developed, however, and became locked in bitter controversy. One, headed by Origen, was centred at Alexandria. The other school was centred at Antioch and found its main representative in the person of Theodore of Mopsuestia. While both schools accepted the twofold sense to be found in texts, a literal meaning and a spiritual meaning, Alexandria emphasised the spiritual meaning far more than Antioch did. The Alexandrian school saw texts as allegorical, drawing from them meanings that were at once moral and mystical. Antioch, to the contrary, gave more prominence to the literal meaning of texts. It looked very much to what the author intended and what the written words conveyed grammatically. These different hermeneutical approaches led to significantly different theologies. Where Alexandria saw Jesus as a divine being who took on human form, Antioch saw Jesus as a human elevated to divine status.

St Augustine, in Platonic mode, situated true understanding in what he termed 'eternal reasons'. These are essentially divine; but Augustine believed them to be discernible in nature and in texts. Not surprisingly, Augustine agreed that primacy should be accorded to the spiritual sense in the interpretation of religious texts.

Such privileging of the spiritual sense led to a proliferation of interpretations bearing little relationship to the literal meaning of texts. In response, the Church began to exercise stronger control of scriptural interpretation. It came to be accepted that discerning the true meaning of sacred texts requires guidance. There are certain assumptions one needs to bring to the task of interpretation and these derive not from something inherent in the text but from religious tradition.

Tradition is, of course, a pivotal notion within Catholicism. Although contemporary Catholic theology, in the wake of Vatican II, tends to meld Scripture and Tradition in a way that contrasts with their earlier articulation as twin sources of faith, the faith tradition has always shaped biblical interpretation for Catholics in quite decisive ways. On the other hand, with the Protestant Reformation and its emphasis on 'Scripture alone', interpretative practices arose that sought to apply biblical data to present-day situations rather than reading them in ways that square with historical traditions. Both orientations—looking back to tradition and looking outward to the contemporary world—have echoes in the hermeneutics we find today within philosophy and the human sciences.

THE HERMENEUTIC MODE OF UNDERSTANDING

What, one might ask, are the characteristic ways in which hermeneutic theories differ from other approaches to meaning and understanding?

For a start, it can be said that, in one way or another, hermeneutics views texts as strange and far off. It is because of this alienation or 'distantiation' that the interpretative task is deemed to be problematic. Even so, talk of alien or distant texts needs to be tempered since, paradoxically, hermeneutics also assumes an affinity of some kind between text and reader—a commonality that provides a basis for the interpretation that is to emerge. Texts are not just antique or foreign curiosities. They are means of transmitting meaning—experience, beliefs, values—from one person or community to another. Hermeneutics assumes a link between the two that makes the exercise feasible.

Understanding interpretation in this fashion has immediate implications. For a start, hermeneutics obviously grounds the meaning of texts in more than their sheerly semantic significance. Account tends to be taken, for example, of features such as the intentions and histories of authors, the relationship between author and interpreter, or the particular relevance of texts for readers.

Secondly, to emphasise that hermeneutics is a sharing of meaning between communities or persons is already to indicate that it is no mere academic exercise. It has practical purposes in view. The origins of hermeneutics already suggest this, for religious hermeneutics has always been more than just a disciplined attempt to identify textual meaning and intent; it is very much a form of inquiry into how texts can and should be *applied*. The same is true of the long tradition of legal hermeneutics. It is equally true of modern hermeneutics: determination of meaning is a matter of practical judgment and common sense, not just abstract theorising.

Even more importantly, to see hermeneutics as a sharing of meaning between communities or individuals is to situate hermeneutics within history and within culture.

> It has now become a commonplace to say that 'we all interpret'. However, hermeneutics—the critical theory of interpretation—is the only current in western thought that has made this issue its own, notwithstanding its presence in both Marxism and that so-called science of phenomena, phenomenology. Through hermeneutics, interpretation has become part of our cultural self-understanding that only as historically and culturally located beings can we articulate ourselves in relation to others and the world in general. (Rundell 1995, p. 10)

Included in much hermeneutic theory is the prospect of gaining an understanding of the text that is deeper or goes further than the author's own understanding. This aim derives from the view that in large measure authors' meanings and intentions remain implicit and go unrecognised by the authors themselves. Because in the writing of the text so much is simply taken for granted, skilled hermeneutic inquiry has the potential to uncover meanings and intentions that are, in this sense, hidden in the text. Interpreters may end up with an explicit awareness of meanings, and especially assumptions, that the authors themselves would have been unable to articulate.

An even more consistent theme in the literature of hermeneutics is the notion of the 'hermeneutic circle'. One form in which the hermeneutic circle is encountered is the claim that, in order to understand something, one needs to begin with ideas, and to use terms, that presuppose a rudimentary understanding of what one is trying to understand. Understanding turns out to be a development of what is already understood, with the more developed understanding returning to illuminate and enlarge one's starting point.

Another way to conceptualise the hermeneutic circle is to talk of understanding the whole through grasping its parts, and comprehending the meaning of parts through divining the whole.

> Our knowledge claims in regard to the meaning of a whole text or of the meaning structure of some society will be supported by evidence supplied by our knowledge of the meaning of particular sentences or acts. On the other hand, our knowledge claims in regard to the meanings of those individual elements will be supported by and justified in terms of our knowledge of the meaning of the entire structure. This is the classical form of the hermeneutic circle as developed in the nineteenth century. (Okrent 1988, p. 161)

Some have seen this attention to the whole as characteristic of the human sciences in particular. They accept that one can satisfactorily understand the natural world simply by understanding the parts that make it up. In the case of the human sciences, however, this simply will not do. To understand a text bearing upon human affairs or a culture that guides human lives, one needs to be able to move dialectically between part and whole, in the mode of the hermeneutic circle. This has been put forward in support of a claim we have considered already (and called into question)—that the human sciences and the natural sciences have quite different subject matters and that the understanding (*Verstehen*) exercised in the human sciences is not required in the natural sciences. In dealing with interpretivism in Chapter 4, we found this claim propounded by Wilhelm Dilthey.

Modern hermeneutics

Dilthey is of central importance in the history of modern hermeneutics. He was not the first modern hermeneuticist, however. Around the turn of the nineteenth century and in the early years of that century, it was Friedrich Ast (1778–1841) and Friedrich Schleiermacher (1768–1834) who extended hermeneutics beyond the realm of biblical exegesis. Schleiermacher, much more than Ast, strove to develop a general hermeneutics that would illuminate all human understanding and not just offer principles and rules for interpreting particular texts. He can be seen as the founder of modern hermeneutics.

SCHLEIERMACHER: GRAMMAR AND PSYCHOLOGY

Schleiermacher, a German Protestant theologian, was a professor at Halle from 1804 to 1807 and at Berlin from 1810.

For Schleiermacher, reading a text is very much like listening to someone speak. Speakers use words to express their thoughts and listeners are able to understand because they share the language that a speaker employs. They know the words, phrases and sentences that they are hearing and they understand the grammatical rules. On this basis, they are able to put themselves in the place of the speaker and recognise what the speaker is intending to convey. There is place, then, for a kind of empathy in the speaker–listener interchange and Schleiermacher extends this to the interpretation of texts.

Already we can see the twofold dimension that Schleiermacher posits in all hermeneutics. Hermeneutics is at once grammatical and psychological. Attention to the grammatical aspect situates the text within its literary context, at the same time reshaping that literary setting by the interpretation it makes of the text. On the more psychological side, the hermeneuticist is able to divine and elucidate not only the intentions of the author but even the author's assumptions.

DILTHEY'S 'OBJECTIVE MIND'

Schleiermacher's biographer, Wilhelm Dilthey, is hailed as one of the most eminent philosophers of the late nineteenth century. For many years a professor at the University of Berlin, he continued his influential work after his retirement by gathering disciples around him in the final years of his life. What he emphasised to these followers was the twofold message he had preached throughout his teaching years: *life* and *history*, both inextricably intertwined.

From the positivists Dilthey had learned to eschew metaphysics, to regard all previous philosophy as partial only, and to base his own philosophy 'on total, full experience, without truncations: therefore, on entire and complete reality' (in Marías 1967, p. 379). In citing Dilthey to this effect, Marías tells us that, for Dilthey, philosophy 'is the science of the real; that is, of all the real *without* truncations' (1967, p. 383). For all that, Dilthey is no positivist, at least not in the sense in which positivism has come to be defined in our time. He believes firmly that human understanding can never exhaust the real and that in the real there will always remain something unknowable and ineffable. To be sure, we all have a *Weltanschauung*, a worldview that guides our actions; however this is grounded not in the intellect but in life.

The life Dilthey is referring to is, above all and before all, *historical* life. Dilthey is most aware of what he calls the rise of historical consciousness. He never loses sight of the historical character of the world and of ourselves within the world. Few have stressed the essentially historical character of human existence as forcefully as he does. The historicism[12] we find today in so much of human and social science stems in no small measure from Dilthey. With the keenest of insights, he recognises what Marías calls 'the peculiar ephemerality of the historical event'—that all people live within history and nothing, therefore, is definitive. History, Dilthey tells us, is 'an immense field of ruins' (in Marías 1967, p. 380). Gadamer, as we shall see, wants to reclaim the classical as 'preservation amid the ruins of time' (1989, p. 289). Dilthey will have none of that.

Dilthey's emphasis on the historical character of life and the humanness of science (his interest is in the *Geisteswissenschaften*—the 'sciences of the spirit') leads him, as we have seen already, to distinguish sharply between natural reality and social phenomena. Unlike the phenomena encountered in nature, social phenomena are seen to stem from the subjectivity of human consciousness. Accordingly, Dilthey believes, study of the one and of the other calls for different methods. Even in the field of human and social science, however, he continues to seek objective knowledge. What he wants to elaborate is a methodology for gaining objective knowledge that escapes the reductionism and mechanism of natural science and remedies its failure to take account of the historical embeddedness of life.

For Dilthey, there are universal spiritual forms shaping the particular events one encounters in social experience. The texts humans write, the speech they utter, the art they create and the actions they perform are all expressions of meaning. Inquiring into that meaning is much more like interpreting a discourse or a poem than investigating a matter of natural reality through an experiment in, say, physics or chemistry. Scientific experiments seek to know and explain (*Erkennen* or *Erklären*). Inquiry into human affairs seeks to understand (*Verstehen*). This distinction, as we have seen earlier, is often attributed to Weber. Whether that can justly be done at all is a moot point. If it is done, it calls at the very least for a number of important qualifications. We should also note Paul Ricoeur's spirited attempt to supplant Dilthey's dichotomy with a dialectical form of integration. Ricoeur (1976, p. 87) offers the notion of a 'hermeneutical arc' that moves from existential understanding to explanation and from explanation to existential understanding.

The early Dilthey invoked the notion of empathy as Schleiermacher had done. True enough, people's perspectives, beliefs and values differ from age to age and culture to culture. Still, Dilthey felt at this time, we are all human beings and therefore able to understand—and, as it were, relive—what has happened in the past or in another place. This assumption on Dilthey's part came under heavy fire at the time and he revised his views in the light of the criticism he was receiving. We find him adopting a far more historicist position, accepting that people's speech, writings, art and behaviour are very much the product of their times. The historically derived worldview of authors constrains what they are able to produce and cannot be discounted in hermeneutical endeavours.

Dilthey comes to acknowledge, in fact, that the author's historical and social context is the prime source of understanding. The human context is an objectification or externalisation—an 'expression' (*Ausdruck*), Dilthey also calls it—of human consciousness. He terms this the 'objective mind' and acknowledging it transforms his approach to hermeneutics. The psychological focus found in his work to date gives way to a much more sociological pursuit. Empathy is replaced by cultural analysis. Dilthey moves from personal identification with individuals to an examination of socially derived systems of meaning. On the track of people's 'lived experience' (*Erlebnis*) as fiercely as ever, he now accepts that their lived experience is incarnate in language, literature, behaviour, art, religion, law—in short, in their every cultural institution and structure.

Gaining hermeneutical understanding of these objectifications, externalisations, or expressions of life involves a hermeneutic circle. The interpreter moves from the text to the historical and social circumstances of the author, attempting to reconstruct the world in which the text came to be and to situate the text within it—and back again.

In according a place in hermeneutics, as in all human understanding, to the interpreter's lived experience, Dilthey has not abandoned his quest for an objective knowledge of the human world. True, the objectivity of this kind of knowledge will always differ from the scientific objectivity claimed, say, in the findings of physics and chemistry. Nevertheless, Dilthey believes, objectivity and validity can be increasingly achieved as more comes to be learned about the author and the author's world, and as the interpreter's own beliefs and values are given less play.

HEIDEGGER'S PHENOMENOLOGICAL HERMENEUTICS

The phenomenological hermeneutics of Martin Heidegger can, with even greater validity, be seen as a hermeneutical phenomenology. It is clearly the phenomenological dimension that is to the fore in his *Being and Time* (1962). For Heidegger, hermeneutics is the revelatory aspect of 'phenomenological seeing' whereby existential structures and then Being itself come into view.

Hermeneutics, Heidegger tells us, 'was familiar to me from my theological studies' (1971, pp. 10–11). Characteristically, Heidegger takes this word and gives it fresh meaning. In his hands it comes to represent the phenomenological project he has embarked upon.

> . . . the meaning of phenomenological description as a method lies in *interpretation*. The λόγος of the phenomenology of Dasein has the character of a ἑρμηνεύειν . . .[13] Philosophy is universal phenomenological ontology, and takes its departure from the hermeneutic of Dasein, which, as an analytic of *existence* has made fast the guiding-line for all philosophical inquiry at the point where it *arises* and to which it *returns*. (Heidegger 1962, pp. 61–2)

This passage reflects Heidegger's lifetime focus on ontology, the study of being. For him, philosophy *is* ontology. Heidegger's interest in ontology began as early as 1907 when he was given a doctoral dissertation to peruse. The dissertation, written by Franz Brentano, was entitled *Von der mannigfachen Bedeutung des Seienden nach Aristoteles* ('On the Manifold Meanings of Being in Aristotle'). This volume caught the imagination of the eighteen-year-old Heidegger and launched him on a never-ending search for the meaning of being.

The passage just cited also reflects Heidegger's adoption of phenomenology as the way into ontology. There is, as he sees it, no other way. If, for Heidegger, philosophy is ontology, ontology, by the same token, is phenomenology.

> Phenomenology is our way of access to what is to be the theme of ontology, and it is our way of giving it demonstrative precision. *Only as phenomenology is ontology possible.* (Heidegger 1962, p. 60)

Let us recall what we have discussed already regarding phenomenology. It is an attempt to return to the primordial contents of consciousness, that is, to the objects that present themselves in our very experience of them prior to our making any sense of them at all. Sense has been made of them, of course. Our culture gives us a ready-made understanding of them. So we need to lay that understanding aside as best we can. Or, in Heidegger's terms, we must rid ourselves of our tendency to immediately interpret.

> The achieving of phenomenological access to the entities which we encounter, consists rather in thrusting aside our interpretative tendencies, which keep thrusting themselves upon us and running along with us, and which

conceal not only the phenomenon of such 'concern', but even more those entities themselves *as* encountered of their own accord *in* our concern with them. (Heidegger 1962, p. 96)

Heidegger does not embark, therefore, on any exploration of culturally derived meanings. Indeed, he is most dismissive of these meanings as the seductive and dictatorial voice of *das Man*—the 'they', the anonymous One (Crotty 1997). What Heidegger embarks upon instead is a phenomenology of human being, or Dasein, to use the word that he consistently uses.

Heidegger's phenomenology of Dasein brings him, in the first instance, to his starting point on the journey towards Being, that is, the shadowy pre-understanding of Being that we all possess and which he calls the 'forestructure' of Being. Reaching that pre-understanding is already a phenomenology. Its further unfolding, together with the manifestation of Being itself and the unveiling of other phenomena in the light of Being, remains a phenomenological process throughout.

To talk of manifestation and unveiling is to talk in hermeneutical vein. And to talk of hermeneutics is to invoke the notions of interpretation and description. Heidegger is bringing together in a unitary way not only ontology and phenomenology but, through hermeneutics with its connotations of dialectics or rhetoric, the element of language as well. For Heidegger, Richardson tells us (1963, p. 631), hermeneutics and phenomenology become one: 'If "hermeneutics" retains a nuance of its own, this is the connotation of language'.

For Heidegger, therefore, hermeneutics is not a body of principles or rules for interpreting texts, as it was for the earlier philologists. Nor is it a methodology for the human sciences, as Dilthey understood it to be. Heidegger's hermeneutics refers 'to his phenomenological explication of human existing itself' (Palmer 1969, p. 42). Heidegger's hermeneutics starts with a phenomenological return to our being, which presents itself to us initially in a nebulous and undeveloped fashion, and then seeks to unfold that pre-understanding, make explicit what is implicit, and grasp the meaning of Being itself.

In a passage quoted above, Heidegger, in talking of the 'hermeneutic of Dasein', states that it makes fast the guiding-line for all philosophical inquiry 'at the point where it *arises* and to which it *returns*'. Here Heidegger is describing his hermeneutical phenomenology as a circular movement. In our quest for Being, we begin with and from a pre-understanding of Being. The task is to unfold this rudimentary understanding and render explicit and thematic what is at first implicit and unthematised. This explication leads us first to a grasping of 'existentials'—structures of being that make human existence and behaviour possible—and on to a grasping of Being itself. This more enlightened understanding of Being then returns to enrich our existence in the world.

What Heidegger is alluding to here is his version of the 'hermeneutic circle' (see Figure 5). We must, he tells us, 'leap into the "circle", primordially and wholly' (1962, p. 363). As we have already seen, the term 'hermeneutic circle' has a long history, but Heidegger fills the term with meaning of his own. 'This circle of understanding', he tells us (1962, p. 195), 'is not an orbit in which any random kind of knowledge may move; it is the expression of the existential forestructure of Dasein itself'.

Figure 5

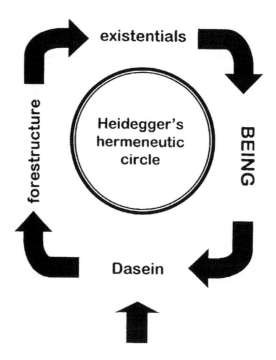

In his later works Heidegger is preoccupied with the second part of the circle. Instead of addressing Dasein as the entrée to Being, he concerns himself directly with Being. The phenomenology of Dasein found in *Being and Time* is replaced by a hermeneutic dialogue with the pre-Socratic Greeks and with poets such as Hölderlin.

There is, Heidegger believes, an originality about the thought of the early Greeks. They were in touch with Being in a way that has been subsequently lost. We need, he tells us, to make 'a painstaking effort to think through still more primally what was primally thought' (1977, p. 303). In this shift in approach—the move from an analytic of Dasein to a running conversation with the early Greek thinkers—there is a new emphasis on history. Some commentators have accused *Being and Time* of being ahistorical. The same charge cannot be levelled at the later works. As the 1930s moved on, Heidegger focused more and more on the 'history of Being'. He wrote of the 'Event' (*Ereignis*) wherein Being is unfolded within historical epochs, both giving itself to thought and withholding itself from thought.

From this perspective, the earliest Greek thought is a 'self-blossoming emergence' (Heidegger 1959, p. 14). It is primordial thought and its primal character needs to be recaptured. There at the dawn of Western civilisation it is a new beginning. As Heidegger puts it, 'the beginning, conceived primally, is Being itself' (*Der Anfang—anfänglich begriffen—ist das Seyn selbst* [1989, p. 58]). Hence his call to think through even more primally what is primally thought.

Heidegger also directs us to poetry, telling us that 'our existence is fundamentally poetic' (1949, p. 283). Poetry can lead us to the place where Being reveals itself. It provides the 'clearing' where Being is illuminated. Thoughtful poetising 'is in truth the topology of Being', a topology 'which tells Being the whereabouts of its actual presence' (Heidegger 1975, p. 12). The essence of poetry is 'the establishing of being by means of the word' (Heidegger 1949, p. 282) and the poet 'reaches out with poetic thought into the foundation and the midst of Being' (Heidegger 1949, p. 289).

In this conversation of the later Heidegger with the Greeks and the poets (and in Hölderlin he finds a poet who is himself taken up with early Greek thought) is a new form of the hermeneutic circle. As Caputo underlines, it is a circling process between Being and beings. This is at once an unconcealing and a concealing. It is a 'coming over' of Being into beings and therefore a revelation of Being. Yet it is also the 'arrival' of beings and this means a concealing of Being. In this process, called by Heidegger the *Austrag*, 'Being and beings are borne or carried outside of one another yet at the same time borne toward one another' (Caputo 1982, p. 148).

> Now *aus-tragen* is the literal translation of the Latin *dif-ferre*, *dif-ferens*, to carry away from, to bear outside of. Hence the *Austrag* is the dif-fering in the difference between Being and beings, that which makes the difference between them, that which opens up the difference, holding them apart and sending them to each other in the appropriate manner, so that Being revealingly conceals itself in beings. (Caputo 1982, pp. 151–2)

As in *Being and Time*, here too hermeneutics means for Heidegger an unveiling of Being. It still means radical ontology. A profound change has occurred, however. Heidegger now sees the history of the West as the history of Being and is preoccupied with the Event that gives Being. All along he has charged Western thought with *Seinsvergessenheit*, 'oblivion of Being'. Early on in his work, this was a reproach that we are preoccupied with beings to the neglect of Being. Now Heidegger changes tack. Western thought may be mindful enough of Being after its own fashion, but it has utterly ignored what opens up the difference between Being and beings. This is what *Seinsvergessenheit* means in the later Heidegger. He is telling us that the focus should lie with the Event rather than with the outcome of the Event. As Caputo explains (1982, pp. 2–4), we need 'to think the sending and not to be taken in by what is sent, to think the giving and not to lose oneself in the gift'. In English we say 'There is Being', but the equivalent in German is 'It gives (*es gibt*) Being'. Heidegger wants us to take a 'step back' and think the 'It' which Western metaphysics has traditionally left behind (Caputo 1982, p. 149).

According to the later Heidegger, then, 'Being is "granted" to us in an experience that we must make every effort to render faithfully' (Caputo 1982, p. 11). His own sustained attempt to render this experience faithfully constitutes the core of Heidegger's hermeneutics.

GADAMER'S HISTORICAL HERMENEUTICS

Hans-Georg Gadamer (1900–) distances himself from both Schleiermacher and Dilthey and draws on his teacher, Heidegger, in his own fashion and for his own purposes.

Gadamer sees us as thoroughly historical—as, indeed, 'historically effected' consciousnesses. It is because of this historicality that we are able to link with the tradition of the past and interpret what has been handed on.

> Gadamer thus argues initially that 'hermeneutics must start from the position that a person seeking to understand something has a bond to the subject matter that comes into language through [tradition]'. (Rundell 1995, p. 32)

What Rundell is suggesting to us here is that there are two pivotal aspects of Gadamer's thought. First, we stand in a tradition. Second, all tradition is wedded to language. Language is at the core of understanding, for 'the essence of tradition is to exist in the medium of language' and '*the fusion of horizons that takes place in the understanding is actually the achievement of language*' (Gadamer 1989, pp. 378, 389).

For Gadamer, then, hermeneutical understanding is historical understanding. His is an historical hermeneutics that mediates past and present. It brings together the horizon of the past and the horizon of the present. As we have just seen, he describes this process as a fusion of horizons. This proves to be a key concept in his hermeneutics and he believes that an historical mediation of this kind between past and present underlies all historical activity as its 'effective substratum'. '*Understanding is to be thought of less as a subjective act than as participating in an event of tradition*, a process of transmission in which past and present are constantly mediated' (Gadamer 1989, p. 290).

In this fusion of horizons, the first pole is the *past*. Gadamer's historical hermeneutics has to do with the past. 'Hermeneutical experience is concerned with *tradition*', says Gadamer (1989, p. 358). 'This is what is to be experienced.' He goes on to tell us (1989, p. 361) that the highest type of hermeneutical experience is 'the openness to tradition characteristic of historically effected consciousness'.

The second pole is the *present*, the horizon of the interpreter. Not that we need consciously to bring the two poles together. They are 'always already' there. 'Working out the historical horizon of a text', Gadamer tells us (1989, p. 577), 'is always already a fusion of horizons'. Thus, 'the horizon of the present cannot be formed without the past. There is no more an isolated horizon of the present in itself than there are historical horizons which have to be acquired' (Gadamer 1989, p. 306).

We need to look more closely at how Gadamer understands this 'fusion of horizons':

- The fusion of horizons shows 'how historically effected consciousness operates' and is, in fact, the 'realization' of 'the historically experienced consciousness that, by renouncing the chimera of perfect enlightenment, is open to the experience of history' (1989, pp. 341, 377–8).
- A fusion of horizons is required because the historical life of a tradition 'depends on being constantly assimilated and interpreted', so that every interpretation 'has to adapt itself to the hermeneutical situation to which it belongs' (1989, p. 397).
- The fusion of horizons is such that, 'as the historical horizon is projected, it is simultaneously superseded' (1989, p. 307).
- The fusion of horizons is the means whereby 'we regain the concepts of a historical past in such a way that they also include our own comprehension of them' (1989, p. 374).
- The fusion of horizons is such that 'the interpreter's own horizon is decisive, yet not as a personal standpoint that he maintains or enforces, but more as an opinion and a possibility that one brings into

play and puts at risk, and that helps one truly to make one's own what the text says' (1989, p. 388).

- The fusion of horizons relates to 'the unity of meaning' in a work of art. The very point of historically effected consciousness is 'to think the work and its effect as a unity of meaning' (1989, p. 576). The fusion of horizons constitutes 'the form in which this unity actualizes itself, which does not allow the interpreter to speak of an original meaning of the work without acknowledging that, in understanding it, the interpreter's own meaning enters in as well'. (p. 576).

In this last citation, you will notice, Gadamer is referring to works of art. Artworks figure prominently in his thought. They are for him the exemplar *par excellence* of what is handed down in tradition. Thus, Gadamer begins his major work *Truth and Method* with a treatise on aesthetics, which opens with a section on 'the significance of the humanist tradition' and concludes by linking aesthetics and history. We must acknowledge, he says 'that the work of art possesses truth'. This is an acknowledgment that 'places not only the phenomenon of art but also that of history in a new light' (Gadamer 1989, pp. 41–2). Artworks 'are contemporaneous with every age' and 'we have the task of interpreting the work of art in terms of time' (Gadamer 1989, pp. 120–1).

Gadamer's interest lies in historical works of art. We cannot really judge contemporary works, he feels, for any such judgment 'is desperately uncertain for the scholarly consciousness'.

> Obviously we approach such creations with unverifiable prejudices, presuppositions that have too great an influence over us for us to know about them; these can give contemporary creations an extra resonance that does not correspond to their true content and significance. Only when all their relations to the present time have faded away can their real nature appear, so that the understanding of what is said in them can claim to be authoritative and universal. (1989, p. 297)

Temporal distance thus performs a filtering function. It excludes 'fresh sources of error' and offers 'new sources of understanding' (Gadamer 1989, p. 298). Itself subject to 'constant movement and extension', the filtering process 'not only lets local and limited prejudices die away, but allows those that bring about genuine understanding to emerge clearly as such' (Gadamer 1989, p. 298).

The 'prejudices' that Gadamer is referring to are the inherited notions derived from one's culture. Prejudices in this sense play a central role in Gadamer's analysis. They are far more important in that analysis than any individual actions we might carry out. Not only is Gadamer not really interested in contemporary artworks, as we have just seen, but, for all his talk about our 'judgment' on works of art, he is not interested in individual judgments either. His concern lies with prejudices, and he strives mightily to redeem the notion of prejudice from the dismissiveness with which it is regularly greeted in current thought. He has already told us that understanding is not so much a subjective act as a placing of ourselves within a tradition. Now he warns us against the privatising of history. Our inherited prejudices stem from 'the great realities of society and state' and are immeasurably more important than the individual judgments recorded in self-awareness.

> Self-reflection and autobiography—Dilthey's starting points—are not primary and are therefore not an adequate basis for the hermeneutical problem, because through them history is made private once more. In fact history does not belong to us; we belong to it. Long before we understand ourselves through the process of self-examination, we understand ourselves in a self-evident way in the family, society, and state in which we live. The focus of subjectivity is a distorting mirror. The self-awareness of the individual is only a flickering in the closed circuits of historical life. *That is why the prejudices of the individual, far more than his judgments, constitute the historical reality of his being.* (Gadamer 1989, pp. 276–7)

A distorting mirror? Only a flickering in the closed circuits of historical life? Gadamer offers little comfort here to the many researchers who are eager to inquire into 'private' history. They focus quite intensely on 'self-awareness', 'autobiography', 'self-examination and 'self-reflection' and, curiously, a number of them invoke Gadamer's support in doing so. But he is obviously not on their side.

For Gadamer, the starting point is not the autonomous individual self so lionised in current versions of humanism. His starting point is the tradition in which we stand and which we are meant to serve. *History does not belong to us. We belong to history!* We find this stance confirmed as Gadamer looks for models for his historical hermeneutics. He finds the models he is after in theological hermeneutics and legal hermeneutics. According to Gadamer, we are to consider the cultural tradition in the same light as the exegete considers the Scriptures and the jurist considers the law, that is, as a 'given'. In the case of sacred texts and the law, the interpretative efforts of exegetes or jurists are obviously not to be seen in the light of 'an appropriation as taking possession' of the texts or a 'form of domination' of the texts. Like the exegete and the jurist, we too must see our hermeneutical endeavours as 'subordinating ourselves to the text's claim to dominate our minds' and as a 'service of what is considered valid' (Gadamer 1989, p. 311).

Most forms of the tradition, 'constantly assimilated and interpreted' though they may be (Gadamer 1989, p. 397), still have to prove themselves worthy of such obeisance and service. They do so through the unity and coherence they display. For Gadamer, the cultural tradition is a universe of meaning. The meaningfulness of transmitted texts is determined by the tradition as a whole, just as the tradition as a whole is a unity comprising the meaning of the texts transmitted within it. Gadamer insists that we read the tradition in this way:

> Thus the movement of understanding is constantly from the whole to the part and back to the whole. Our task is to expand the unity of the understood meaning centrifugally. The harmony of all the details with the whole is the criterion of correct understanding. The failure to achieve this harmony means that understanding has failed. (1989, p. 291)

This is Gadamer's great hermeneutic rule. We are to extend the unity of understanding in ever-widening circles by moving from whole to part and from part to whole. Brenkman, for one (1987, pp. 26–44), finds this principle problematic. Gadamer imposes it as a methodological tool (it is our 'task'); yet he wants to claim that our experience of the tradition as an organic unity is premethodological. Is Gadamer wanting to have it both ways, then? Brenkman's criticism is not without foundation. Is the unity, which Gadamer values so highly, inherent in the tradition, as he claims? Or is it imparted to the tradition by the way in which he insists that we read it?

Moreover, there are forms of the tradition that escape the need even for this kind of validation. These are 'classical' forms. The classical, Gadamer tells us, 'epitomizes a general characteristic of historical being: preservation amid the ruins of time' (1989, p. 289). In confronting other forms of the tradition, we need to overcome the barrier of distance. Not so with the classical. 'What we call "classical"', Gadamer tells us, 'does not first require the overcoming of historical distance, for in its own constant mediation it overcomes this distance by itself' (1989, p. 290).

> The 'classical' is something raised above the vicissitudes of changing times and changing tastes. It is immediately accessible . . . when we call something classical, there is a consciousness of something enduring, of significance that cannot be lost and that is independent of all the circumstances of time—a kind of timeless present that is contemporaneous with every other present. (Gadamer, 1989, p. 288)

What is one to make of this? Gadamer uses religious and legal hermeneutics as models and calls on hermeneuticists to 'serve the validity of meaning'. This validity is taken, without further ado, to be found in all classical works. It is also found in any other forms of the tradition that pass Gadamer's unity-and-coherence test. As Brenkman points out, this approach ignores the social site of the work's genesis and the social site of its reception and takes no account of the hegemony and oppression inherent in both of them. This is an essentially conservative position and has drawn the fire of more critically minded analysts. Jürgen Habermas, for example, finds Gadamer's embrace of tradition particularly problematic and he has engaged in debate with him over many years on this and other issues.

This dialogue has led Habermas to a 'critical hermeneutics'. Joined by Apel and others, Habermas is insistent that no hermeneutics can prescind from the setting in which understanding occurs. At once social, historical and discursive, this setting is the battleground of many interests and no analyst or researcher can afford to ignore it, as the discussion in the next two chapters will highlight.

HERMENEUTICS, READING THEORY AND LITERARY CRITICISM

Hermeneutics is invoked in many fields of inquiry relating to the act of reading. These include literary criticism and reading comprehension theory. As Stanley Straw asserts, 'hermeneutics . . . is an activity related to all criticism in its attempt to make meaning out of the act of reading' (1990b, p. 75). Not everybody agrees. Hirsch, for example, makes a sharp distinction between hermeneutics and literary criticism based on a 'rigid separation of meaning and significance' (1967, p. 142).

Even among those who accord hermeneutics a rightful place in reading theory and literary criticism, there have been, and are, many conflicting viewpoints. In the main, these have to do with the respective place and status to be accorded in interpretation to author, text and reader. One might, in fact, conceive of interpretation theory as a continuum that privileges author or text at one end and reader at the other.

If we do conceive interpretation theory as a continuum of that kind, at what point on the spectrum would we place someone like novelist and critic Umberto Eco? While it would be difficult to position him with any kind of precision, he would have to be seen as standing at some distance from either extreme. On any accounting, he would not be up at the end that privileges the reader. For several decades now, Eco believes, the role ascribed to the reader in the task of interpretation has been exaggerated. In reaction to this, he draws attention (1992, pp. 64–6) to the importance of the *intentio operis* (literally, the 'intention of the work', that is, the purpose expressed in and by the text itself) over against the *intentio lectoris* (the 'intention of the reader', that is, the personal purpose that the reader brings to the reading or infuses into the reading). This reflects a time-honoured Scholastic distinction between *intentio operis* and *intentio operantis*. The former is a purpose intrinsic to the action being done, while the latter is a purpose brought to the action by the agent. In the context of hermeneutics, Eco uses this distinction to resist the prevailing trend to privilege the reader. Overemphasising the reader's role leads to what he dubs 'overinterpretation'. It opens the floodgates to an undifferentiated torrent of interpretations. Eco refers (1992, p. 34) to 'the idea of the continuous slippage of meaning' found in many postmodernist concepts of criticism.

Not that Eco is overlooking the extent to which textual meanings can be indeterminate. Nor is he denying the reader a genuinely critical role in interpretation. His approach allows for many diverse interpretations to emerge. Yet he does want to set some limits. A message, Eco says (1992, p. 43), 'can mean many things but there are senses it would be preposterous to accept'.

What Eco is attempting to establish is a 'dialectical link' between *intentio operis* and *intentio lectoris*. The reader, he feels, ought to have some ideas regarding the purpose of the work in question. The text, surely, is *about* something. Glimpsing this 'aboutness' provides readers with a sense of direction. How will readers know whether their assumptions about the *intentio operis* are justified? Rather like the ancient Greeks referred to earlier, and like Gadamer with his hermeneutic rule, Eco believes that texts have a certain unity and coherence. One may have confidence in one's 'sense of aboutness' if it holds up throughout the entire work. If it does not hold up, one needs to think again. Thus, 'the internal textual coherence controls the otherwise uncontrollable drives of the reader' (Eco 1992, p. 65).

Eco's standpoint has many critics. Some find him too liberal. Others find him too restricting.

First of all, there are those who welcome Eco's emphasis on purposes but feel he does not go far enough. It is not enough, they suggest, to invoke *intentio operis*. *Intentio auctoris*—authorial intent—must be identified and taken into account. The attitude of such critics tends to be straightforward, if nothing else. 'A text means what its author intended it to mean', write Knapp and Michaels (1985, p. 469). This, of course, is a very traditional approach to reading.

There are others, however, for whom Eco's viewpoint is far too restrictive. For a start, they question his assumption that all texts have sufficient unity and coherence to ground the intention he looks to establish. Moreover, they fear, to limit authentic interpretation to what is considered *intentio operis* or *intentio auctoris* means in practice to subject the interpreter to 'canonical' or 'classical' readings of the text and preclude other ways of interpreting it. This, in their view, is impoverishing.

One thinks, for instance, of feminist author Adrienne Rich's celebrated call to 're-vision' texts (1990, pp. 483–4). She defines re-vision as 'the act of looking back, of seeing with fresh eyes, of entering an old text from a new critical direction'. Re-vision means a radical feminist critique of literature, which will use literature as a clue to how women have been living and how women can 'begin to see and name—and therefore live—afresh'. 'We need', says Rich, 'to know the writing of the past, and know it differently than we have ever known it; not to pass on a tradition but to break its hold on us'. In a feminist hermeneutic of this kind, for all its lack of focus on authorial or textual intent, there is surely both authenticity of interpretation and richness of meaning. Who would deny that?

These viewpoints—seeing interpretation as essentially an identification of authorial intent, or looking instead to an intention intrinsic to the text as such, or making the reader pivotal in the generation of meaning—are embodied, with their many variants, in the history of both literary criticism and reading comprehension theory. Tracing 'the history of conceptualizations of reading', Straw and Sadowy (1990, p. 22) point to a movement 'from a *transmission* notion of reading (roughly, from 1800 to 1890), to a *translation* notion of reading (roughly, 1890 to the late 1970s), to an *interactive* notion of reading (a notion predominant now within the reading establishment)'. The authors detect a further movement over the past few years to '*transactional* and *constructionist* notions of reading' (1990, p. 22).

Straw uses the same terms, and identifies the same phases, to characterise changes that have occurred historically within literary theory in North America. In the 'transmission' period, the emphasis was on the author's intentions. 'Positivist/expressive realism notions of literary theory and criticism held English studies in a choke-hold well into the twentieth century', writes Straw (1990a, p. 53); '*reading the text* was the same as *reading the author*'. The 'transmission' period was followed by a 'translation' period after World War I. Formalist approaches to texts emerged—in the shape of Russian Formalism in continental Europe and New Criticism in Anglo-American circles. This move replaced nineteenth-century deification of the author with a twentieth-century reification of the text. The New Critics 'insisted on the presence within the work of everything necessary for its analysis; and they called for an end to any concern by critics and teachers of English with matters outside the work itself—the life of the author, the history of his times, or the social and economic implications of the literary work' (Guerin et al. 1979, p. 75).

The 'translation' phase did not last. In Europe, first of all, and then in the Anglo-American world, it gave way to an 'interaction' period. A systems approach began to be applied to literature, as elsewhere, and this 'culminated in what has been called "Structuralism in Literature"' (Straw 1990a, p. 58). Structuralist thought, growing out of the linguistic principles of Saussure, came to be applied to many diverse fields. In literary criticism it led to a proliferation of highly nuanced approaches that, for all their diversity, share a belief 'that structures can be used systematically to reach an interpretation of any particular text' (Straw 1990a, p. 61).

What they also share (and even share with their allegedly anti-structuralist opponents) is an understanding that literary criticism is interactionist in nature. In the earlier phases, to be sure, interpretation had been seen as a matter of communication. This remains the case in the interactive phase, even if it is now seen as essentially *inter*communication—not one-way transmission of a message from author to reader but interplay between author and reader via the text.

Important as it is, the understanding of reading and criticism as interaction does not signal an end to development, or even a slowing of development. Thinking in relation to interpretation of texts has already moved on from its interactive phase. It has moved 'beyond communication', Straw tells us. What has emerged is a *transactional* understanding of reading and interpretation.

> In contrast to conceptualizations of reading built on the communication model, transactional models suggest that reading is a more generative act than the receipt or processing of information or communication. From the transactional view, meaning is not a representation of the intent of the author; it is not present in the text; rather, it is constructed by the reader *during* the act of reading. The reader draws on a number of knowledge sources in order to create or construct meaning. (Straw 1990b, p. 68)

This, we will note, relates closely to our earlier considerations under the rubric of constructivism. Straw goes on to say of texts what others, like Merleau-Ponty, have said of the world and objects in the world, namely, that their meaning is indeterminate. Given such indeterminacy, 'transactional theories suggest that meaning is created by the active negotiation between readers and the text they are reading'. What is happening is a 'generating of meaning in response to text'. Recognition of this transactional dimension is found in reception theorists in

Germany, post-structuralists in France, and reader-response critics in the Anglophone countries (Straw 1990b, p. 73).

While different periods emphasise particular ways of understanding the act of reading or analysing the process of textual criticism and tend to portray each of them in exclusivist fashion, perhaps we should just acknowledge that there are different ways of reading and interpreting. Each way has something to offer researchers as they gather their data and especially as they interpret the data they have gathered. Approaches that privilege author, or text, or reader, need not be seen as either watertight compartments or incompatible options.

Some scholars, as we have seen, inveigh against giving weight to authorial intent or to textual form and content. They do so on the ground that this inhibits the freedom of the interpreter. They want to see the interpreter left free to engage uninhibitedly with the text and able to construct meaning without restraint. Yet, if we are talking about freedom, it is surely a gross limitation on interpreters to regard as null and void any readings that look to the author's personality, or the author's life and times, or the author's stated or implied intentions. It is equally a gross limitation on interpreters to dismiss interpretations that draw directly on features of the text as such. Interpreters would seem to be most free when they are left at liberty to read and interpret in a wide variety of ways.

A first way to approach texts might be described as *empathic*. This is an approach characterised by openness and receptivity. Here we do more than extract useful information from our reading. The author is speaking to us and we are listening. We try to enter into the mind and personage of the author, seeking to see things from the author's perspective. We attempt to understand the author's standpoint. It may not be our standpoint; yet we are curious to know how the author arrived at it and what forms its basis.

There can also be an *interactive* approach to texts. Now we are not just listening to the author. We are conversing. We have a kind of running conversation with the author in which our responses engage with what the author has to say. Dialogue of this kind can have a most formative and growthful impact on ideas we brought to the interchange. Here, in fact, our reading can become quite critical. It can be reading 'against the grain'.

Then there is the *transactional* mode of reading. What happens in this mode is much more than refinement, enhancement or enlargement of what we bring to our engagement with the text. Out of the engagement comes something quite new. The insights that emerge were never in the mind of the author. They are not in the author's text. They were not with us as we picked up the text to read it. They have come into being in and out of our engagement with it.

These are all possible ways of reading. There are others beside. And we are free to engage in any or all of them. These various modes prove suggestive and evocative as we recognise research data as text—and, even before that, as we take human situations and interactions as text. In this hermeneutical setting, ways of reading are transfigured as ways of researching.

Hermeneutics as it appears in reading theory and literary criticism seems much more run of the mill than the hermeneutics we encounter in Schleiermacher, Dilthey, Heidegger, Gadamer and Ricoeur. In reading theory and literary criticism, it seems little more than a synonym for interpretation. Nor does hermeneutics seem much more than a synonym for interpretation in many contemporary instances where the term is invoked to describe the research process engaged in.

In the more philosophical and especially the more historical usage of the term, there is a certain mystique to be reckoned with. Whether we are speaking of Dilthey's universal spiritual forms that shape social events within human history, or of Heidegger's search for the Event that gives Being, or of Gadamer's fusion of horizons between past and present, there seems to be a grandeur and profundity, a certain aura, about what is going on. Hermeneutics in this vein, it would seem, is not just any old attempt at interpretation.

It would not be right to put too firm a wedge between these two forms. After all, literary critics are not at all averse to citing Heidegger and Gadamer. Nevertheless, the mystique just referred to is hardly mirrored in social research that employs, say, observation and interviewing and analyses its data by allowing major themes to emerge in quite straight-forward ways. Historical research that looks to interpret tradition, the classics, and the canon of literature and art we have inherited (or, indeed, historical research that looks to break with the traditional, the classical and the canonical) would seem to square much better with the hermeneutics stretching from Schleiermacher to Ricoeur.

Horses for courses, then. Researchers looking to get a handle on people's perceptions, attitudes and feelings—or wanting to call these into question as endemic to a hegemonic society and inherited from a culture shaped by class, racial and sexual dominance—may be best placed to find useful insights if they look to the hermeneutics of the reading theorists and the literary critics. On the other hand, in research that echoes with profoundly spiritual, religious, historical or ontological overtones, especially where we are linked to other interpretative communities in ways that both bring us close and place us at a distance, it may be profitable to seek guidance in the philosophico-historical rendering of hermeneutics.

Either way, our debt to the hermeneutic tradition is large.

6

CRITICAL INQUIRY:
THE MARXIST HERITAGE

Suit the action to the word,
the word to the action.

William Shakespeare, *Hamlet*

In discussing interpretivism in the previous two chapters, the issue of critical inquiry has already emerged for us. By and large, interpretivism is an uncritical form of study. Phenomenology, to be sure, at least in its more authentic guise, is self-professedly critical. Still, not all phenomenologists have recognised the critical character of their enterprise or exploited it to the full. As Brenkman is able to claim (1987, p. 5), the critical challenge mounted by the Frankfurt School 'has also figured— sometimes as negative counterpoint, sometimes as shared project—in the phenomenological tradition'. Similarly, while Paul Ricoeur can point to a critical *demystifying* hermeneutics (as in Marx, Nietzsche and Freud), he also acknowledges that for some (Rudolf Bultmann, for instance), hermeneutics is merely *demythologising*. In the former, the text is considered to represent false reality and efforts are made to remove the masks and illusions and gain new interpretation. Thus, Ricoeur expressly links demystification with 'suspicion' and 'disillusionment' (1974, p. 408) and states that demystification 'recognizes myth as myth but with the purpose of renouncing it' (1974, p. 335). In the case of demythologisation, however, the text is reverenced and its hidden meaning caringly sought after. As Ricoeur points out, 'demythologization is distinguished from demystification by the fact that it is moved by the will to better comprehend the text' (1974, p. 389).

In large part, therefore, the critical inquiry that forms the subject matter of this chapter stands in stark contrast to what we have been considering under the heading of interpretivism. It is a contrast between a research that seeks merely to understand and a research that challenges . . . between a research that reads the situation in terms of interaction and community and a research that reads it in terms of conflict and oppression . . . between a research that accepts the *status quo* and a research that seeks to bring about change.

There have always been social critics, of course. From Socrates on, and no doubt earlier still, society has not lacked members ready to call it into question. While the role of the social critic may have come to the fore in modern times and its importance may have been heightened, Walzer is right to argue (1989, p. 4) that the modern social critic is 'not the first'. It is sometimes claimed that criticism as a self-consciously chosen role is a recent phenomenon; that, unlike the social criticism of earlier times, today's version is levelled at the social order itself, at institutions and structures and not merely at individual behaviour; and that the social critic today is alienated and isolated to an extent not experienced by counterparts in other eras. Walzer does not accept any part of this argument. He insists that, in the first two of these respects, today's critics are little different from those encountered in the recorded history of the past and that, in regard to the third, the very opposite is the case.

All the same, today's critical enterprise is carried out in a very different world. In speaking of critique, we are not referring to violent revolution, let us remember. Unlike Mao Zedong in his famous dictum, we are not talking about the power that comes out of the barrel of a gun. We are talking of the power of *ideas* and it is certainly conceivable that critical thought today has more potency. This is the case that John Ralston Saul argues. As Saul sees it, critical thought is now being put forward in a world whose ruling elites carry greater burdens of knowledge than ever before and have a greater dependence on those burdens of knowledge than ever before. The knowledge that the elites control may be their strength but it also constitutes their vulnerability. Saul says of the elites that the 'possession, use and control of knowledge have become their central theme—the theme song of their expertise'. He believes that 'their power depends not on the effect with which they use that knowledge but on the effectiveness with which they control its use' (1992, p. 8).

When we look around at the influence and strength of money, of armies, of legal officials, or indeed at the ease with which writers are silenced through censorship, violence and imprisonment, it seems that the word is a fragile blossom. But one step back from this immediacy is enough to reveal the power of language. Nothing frightens those in authority so much as criticism . . .

Language—not money or force—provides legitimacy. So long as military, political, religious or financial systems do not control language, the public's imagination can move about freely with its own ideas. Uncontrolled words are consistently more dangerous to established authority than armed forces. (Saul 1992, p. 8)

Another difference is that social critics today rarely stand alone. In an age of popular mobilisation, democratic and totalitarian politics, state-sponsored schooling and mass communication, it is, Walzer suggests, 'more likely that wherever they go, they go in crowds'. Indeed, the people themselves are frequently the critical subjects, so that 'the critic participates in an enterprise that is no longer his alone; he agitates, teaches, counsels, challenges, protests *from within*'. Such critics 'need to find a place to stand, close to but not engulfed by their company' (Walzer 1989, pp. 24–6).

This dilemma of standing close but not being engulfed is shared by the critics whom Walzer makes the subject of his study. These are Julien Benda with his crusade against 'intellectual treason'; pragmatist Randolph Bourne pleading for cosmopolitanism in the face of a concerted move towards a uniform Americanism; existential phenomenologist Martin Buber seeking a true Zion ('We have full independence, a state, and all that pertains to it, but where is the nation in the state? And where is that nation's spirit?'); founder of the Italian communist party, Antonio Gramsci, and his *Prison Notebooks*; Ignazio Silone abandoning communist party activism for the writing of novels about peasants and villages; George Orwell, creator of *1984* and internal critic of English socialism; Algerian-born existentialist novelist Albert Camus, for whom the Algerian issue proves a nemesis; another existentialist, pioneer feminist Simone de Beauvoir, with her ambiguous feminist goal of women's 'more and more profound assimilation into our once masculine society'; Frankfurt School member Herbert Marcuse, critic of the 'one-dimensional man'; Michel Foucault and his institutional genealogies; and finally Breyten Breytenbach, the 'critic in exile'.

These are all, Walzer says, 'men and women of the left' (1989, p. 26), even if they 'don't often match the stereotype of a leftist social critic' (p. 225). This is not to say, however, that they are all Marxists, or neo-Marxists, or post-Marxists. It is customary today to see the towering figure of Karl Marx casting his shadow over all inquiry that describes itself as critical. In social science literature, without a doubt, the neo-Marxist (post-Marxist?) Frankfurt School is now accorded a monopoly on the descriptor 'critical theory'. For all that, it needs to be remembered that social critics emerge from a multitude of background orientations. In going on to discuss the seminal work of Marx and to explore the remarkable history and invaluable contributions of the Frankfurt School membership, we should keep in mind that critical inquiry is not co-extensive with either of these, or with both of them together.

KARL MARX

Despite the *caveat* that has just been entered, Karl Marx (1818–83) must be recognised as one of the principal moulders of modern thought. Certainly, he more than anyone else has inspired and laid the foundation for the critical inquiry that obtains today.

> Marx was unlike Comte or Mill or any other representative thinker of his age. He alone did what they all set out to do but failed to accomplish: he fused philosophy, history, and economics into a grandiose synthesis. The fusion may have been imperfect; it may have left some important problems unsolved or half-solved; here and there it may actually have misled his followers into an acceptance of thought patterns stemming from the 'bourgeois revolution' and not really relevant to the theory and practice of socialism. All these and other valid arguments can be urged against the man and his creation. No matter—there he stands, a colossus in the midst of ordinary mortals. The critic of literature takes for granted the disparity between Shakespeare and the minor Elizabethans. The historian of socialism who has taken the measure of Marx need not trouble himself unduly over his rivals. (Lichtheim 1968, p. 185)

Describing Marx as someone who succeeded in synthesising philosophy, history and economics suggests the consummate academic, a thinker withdrawn from the ordinary day-to-day pursuits of humanity. Nothing could be further from the truth. Marx was a person of action and his thought was focused on real-life women and men, society as it is experienced, and not on mere abstractions.

That he was a genuine activist cannot be doubted. In 1842, after an abortive attempt to lecture at the University of Bonn following the gaining of his doctorate, Marx became editor—and a crusading editor at that, author of many a trenchant editorial—of *Rheinische Zeitung* (*The Rhineland Gazette*) in Cologne. One year later, however, the radical stance adopted by this newspaper under Marx's editorship led to his dismissal and to the paper itself being banned. He moved to Paris where he came into contact with German workers and French socialists and became a communist. 'What Marx came to know in Paris', writes Ernst

Fischer (1973, p. 19), 'was the proletariat'. He continued to criticise the Prussian government and in 1845 it prevailed upon the French authorities to expel him. This time he found refuge in Brussels where he published his first economic essay, *The Poverty of Philosophy: A Reply to Proudhon's Philosophy of Poverty*.

At the end of 1847, Marx attended the Second Congress of the League of Communists in London and was commissioned to draft *The Communist Manifesto*. This was completed in January 1848 with the assistance of his friend and sponsor Friedrich Engels, whom he had met during his time in Paris. A month later the February Revolution took place in Paris. Marx, who was accused of being involved in preparations for armed uprisings in both Brussels and Cologne, was expelled by the Belgian authorities and returned to Paris. Almost immediately he moved back to Cologne to organise the publication of *Neue Rheinische Zeitung* (*The New Rhineland Gazette*) and became its first editor. A short-lived editorship, as it turned out. First, the paper was temporarily suppressed during a declared state of emergency a few months after the first issue. Then Marx was accused of sedition and incitement to armed rebellion. Acquitted by a Cologne jury early in 1849, he was declared a stateless person and had a deportation order served on him in May of that year. Printed in red, the final issue of *Neue Rheinische Zeitung* appeared two days later. Marx (together with his family, for he had married in 1843 and by now had several sons and daughters) was once more on the move. He returned briefly to Paris but in August 1849 went to England to begin what was to prove a very long exile. He died there in 1883.

The image many have of Marx during those 35 years in England is of a scholar living in poverty and busily at work in the Reading Room of the British Museum, writing hundreds of articles and creating his best-known work, *Das Kapital*. It is again the image of the stereotypical academic, far removed from the action for change so evident in Marx's earlier years. The history of these years hardly bears this out. Marx did write *Das Kapital* (and much besides) during this period. Volume I appeared in 1867, the other two volumes being published posthumously under the editorship of Engels. And Marx did live in poverty. His wife suffered a series of nervous breakdowns and several of his children died very young—as a result, some suggest, of malnutrition and lack of proper care. But he was no armchair strategist. His activism never abated.

Hardly had he arrived in London when he found himself heavily involved in arranging support for German refugees there. A year later he was chairing weekly meetings of the London chapter of the League of Communists. In 1852 he played a key role in developing and establishing a new German workers association in London. Over this time he kept in touch with people pressing for change in a number of countries, including Hungary and, of course, his native Germany where a long-time acquaintance and founder of the General Workingmen's Association, Ferdinand Lassalle, was busily engaged in socialist pursuits. Marx met with Lassalle in Berlin in 1861 but became increasingly critical of his views and his mode of political agitation.

In 1864 the First International was founded in London and Marx was elected a member of the General Council as the representative for Germany. At the Fourth Congress of the International in Basle, he clashed bitterly with Russian anarchist Mikhail Bakunin. Marx's communism won out over Bakunin's anarchism and Bakunin was expelled from the International in 1872 at its fifth (and final) congress at The Hague, in which Marx took a very active part.

In his graveside address, when Marx was buried in Highgate Cemetery on 17 March 1883, Engels declared him to be, above all else, a 'revolutionist'. As Engels went on to say, fighting was Marx's element and he fought with a passion, a tenacity and a success that few could rival.

It is not surprising, then, to find that Marx the philosopher takes a very activist view of philosophy. 'The philosophers have only *interpreted* the world in different ways', he wrote in his *Theses on Feuerbach*; 'the point is to change it'. His starting point for such action for change is not abstract ideas about the world but concrete social reality. 'All social life is essentially *practical*' and the mysteries that we discover in it and that have the propensity to lead us towards mysticism 'find their rational solution in human practice and in the comprehension of this practice' (Marx 1961, p. 84).

> In direct contrast to German philosophy, which descends from heaven to earth, here we ascend from earth to heaven. That is to say, we do not set out from what men say, imagine, or conceive, nor from what has been said, thought, imagined or conceived of men, in order to arrive at men in the flesh. We begin with real, active men, and from their real-life process show the development of the ideological reflexes and echoes of this life-process. The phantoms of the human brain also are necessary sublimates of men's material life-process, which can be empirically established and which is bound to material preconditions . . . Life is not determined by consciousness, but consciousness by life. (Marx 1961, p. 90)

In his earlier years, Marx was a member of the Young Hegelians, the more radical followers of the late idealist philosopher G.W.F. Hegel. Given the words just cited, we will not be surprised to learn that he comes to find Hegel too abstract. He accuses Hegel of being overly preoccupied with ideas, thereby turning the world, and history, on its head. He wants history to walk on its feet instead. 'The Hegelian philosophy of history', he tells us, 'is concerned, not with real, nor even with political, interests, but with pure thoughts'. It is 'a *speculative*, esoteric history' (1961, p. 72).

While attempting to turn Hegelianism right side up, Marx retains its central notion: that the succession of societal forms and regimes we find in history also represents stages in our human self-understanding. In doing this, he also retains, and valorises, Hegel's concept of the 'dialectic'. The notion of the dialectic is integral to Marx's view of history. His social philosophy has come to be known as both 'dialectic materialism' and 'historical materialism'.

To recognise the dialectic is to recognise that realities are never isolated entities standing in a linear, causal relationship to one another. Dialectically, reality can only be understood as multifaceted interaction. This is to paint a picture of reality, and therefore of thought, as inevitably the bearer of contradiction, forever in conflict with itself. Thus, when Marx points up distinguishable periods in human history, for example 'ancient society', 'feudal society' and 'bourgeois (or capitalist) society', each of these periods ('a society at a definite stage of historical development, a society with a unique and distinctive character') is to be seen as essentially at war with itself (1961, p. 156).

This inner contradiction, this perennial antagonism within every form of society, comes to be encapsulated in the term 'class struggle'. In capitalist society Marx perceives a basic conflict between capital and labour, between the bourgeoisie and the proletariat, and he believes there are analogues of this conflict in all earlier forms of society. Part 1 of *The Communist Manifesto* begins with the words, 'The history of all hitherto existing society is the history of class struggles' (Marx and Engels 1937, p. 10). Thus, the class struggle of today mirrors the conflict in ancient times between free persons and slaves. Equally, it mirrors the conflict in feudal times between aristocracy or landed gentry, on the one hand, and the enserfed peasants, on the other. These are not to be seen merely as destructive conflicts. Hegel's dialectic holds not only the notion of thesis and antithesis standing over against each other but also the notion of their interaction leading to a synthesis. Marx draws on these Hegelian notions to show how the conflict in ancient times between the free and the enslaved led to the development of feudal society. Similarly, the conflict in feudal times between the landed gentry and the serfs led to the development of capitalist society. And, in apocalyptic vein, he holds out the assured hope that the conflict today between the bourgeoisie and the proletariat will lead to the development of a socialist, then communist, world, a classless society born of an emancipatory process and offering true freedom to all.

Driving this dialectical and, in his view, ultimately liberating process is what Marx conceives as the *relations of production*. Production is central to his analysis. The action of human beings on the world lies at the heart of history. It is through such action that we become fully human. Speaking of the way in which humans produce their means of subsistence, Marx states that this production 'is already a definite form of activity of these individuals, a definite way of expressing their life, a definite *mode of life*'. 'What human beings are, therefore, depends on the material conditions of their production' (Marx 1961, pp. 69–70).

It is obvious enough that the means of production that people create for themselves and have available to them differ from era to era. Marx places at the very centre of his exposition something that is not quite so obvious: that the social *relations* created by the means of production ('forces of production', Marx likes to term the latter) also differ from era to era. Marx stresses that the hand mill presupposes a division of labour different from that of the steam mill: 'The hand mill will give you a society with the feudal lord, the steam mill a society with the industrial capitalist' (Marx 1961, pp. 106–8). In other words, 'a determinate mode of production, or industrial stage, is always bound up with a determinate mode of cooperation, or social stage' (Marx 1961, p. 77).

The relationship between the forces of production and the corresponding social relations of production is an uneasy one. Over time new productive forces emerge and the social relations of production have to change in order to accommodate them. When this happens, society's basic economic equilibrium is shattered and a different form of social relations of production must be established. In ancient times, following the move from what Marx considers to be a primordial form of communal living, the economy is characterised by landed property. At least at the start, this is communal or State property and it is essentially linked to the use of slaves. In Rome, as Marx points out (1961, p. 128), slavery 'remained the basis of the whole productive system'. Yet slavery as practised in antiquity has inherent limitations. Maintaining it proves unworkable as new material conditions of production arise. The use of slave labour in that form comes to be a barrier to the effective deployment of the different instruments of production that come to hand. So slave labour gives way to serf labour. This has to happen because of the very nature of feudal property; that is, estates property, which has replaced the more communal forms of property of earlier times.

> Like tribal and communal property it is also based on a community, but the directly producing class which confronts it is not, as in the case of the ancient community, the slaves, but the enserfed small peasantry . . . This feudal structure was, just as much as the communal property of antiquity, an association against a subject producing class, but the form of association and the relation to the direct producers were different because of the different conditions of production. (Marx 1961, p. 129)

Similarly, feudalism gives way to capitalism because of changes in the forces of production and the inability of the existing relations of production to cater for them. As Marx and Engels underline, 'the feudal relations of property became no longer compatible with the already developed productive forces'. Instead, they proved to be 'so many fetters' and therefore 'were burst asunder' (Marx and Engels 1969, p. 113).

For Marx, then, the 'multitude of productive forces accessible to men determines the nature of society' (Marx and Engels 1969, p. 31). It is easy to see why he has been regarded as an economic determinist. To be sure, there are other forces at work in the shaping of any society but, at rock bottom, the economic forces are the ones that count. (Equally, there are many groupings in society other than the two classes he highlights but, at rock bottom, the bourgeoisie and the proletariat are the ones that count.) Marx speaks of these other forces, for example legal and political forces, as 'superstructures' built on the economic structure as their 'real foundation' (1961, p. 67). Marx is not dismissing the importance of the superstructure. For example, he is ready to affirm that effective action for change stems from awareness of the conflict between productive forces and the social relations of production and that such awareness can occur only at an ideological—that is, a legal, political or religious—level (Marx and Engels 1969, p. 62). It remains his contention, however, that what goes on at this superstructural level derives its effectiveness from the economic forces at work (p. 33).

This contention takes the form, particularly, of asserting that economic forces determine how we think. In talking of economic forces being the real foundation for legal and political superstructures, Marx adds that there are 'definite forms of social consciousness' corresponding to the economic structure. In words we have noted already, Marx (1961, p. 67) is ready to claim, 'It is not the consciousness of men that determines their being, but, on the contrary, their social being determines their consciousness'. The social being he refers to is, before all and above all, economic being. This means that those who hold economic hegemony are able to shape the perceptions and viewpoints of those who do not.

The ideas of the ruling class are, in every age, the ruling ideas: i.e. the class which is the dominant *material* force in society is at the same time its dominant *intellectual* force. The class which has the means of material production at its disposal, has control at the same time over the means of mental production, so that in consequence the ideas of those who lack the means of mental production are, in general, subject to it . . . The individuals composing the ruling class . . . rule also as thinkers, as producers of ideas, and regulate the production and distribution of the ideas of their age. Consequently, their ideas are the ruling ideas of the age. (Marx 1961, p. 93)

Marx is describing an oppression that touches the entire gamut of human life and human affairs. It does not have to do just with work. It permeates the totality of the worker's existence. It even includes, as we have just seen, a shaping of the way in which people think, the begetting of a 'false consciousness' and the imposition of a corresponding 'ideology' or system of beliefs and values, which is not seen for what it is but is taken to represent the way things really are. That all this should breed a deep-seated alienation on the part of workers goes without saying and Marx, at least in his early writings, dwelled on this notion of proletarian alienation at considerable length, painting a picture of it that is rich and multifaceted.

Alienation translates the German *Entfremdung*, which signifies 'the activity or process by which someone becomes a stranger to himself' (Aron 1965, p. 147). In keeping with the primacy he accords to the economic, it is economic alienation that Marx sees as the root of any other form that alienation may take. In the economic alienation inherent in the capitalist relations of production, work no longer belongs to the worker. This is, for Marx, an inestimable loss, for he views human beings as productive by their very nature. Our labour—our productivity—is our 'species-life'. Along with 'social life' and 'sensuous life', it characterises us as human beings. The capitalist system, however, succeeds in making workers strangers to their own work. What ought to be an expression of their very being becomes merely instrumental, a means of subsistence. This 'alienation of labour' has the effect 'that the work is *external* to the worker, that it is not part of his nature, that consequently he does not fulfil himself in his work' (Marx 1961, pp. 176–7). This has broad and long-term implications. Marx finds himself forced to ask, 'What is the significance, in the development of humanity, of this reduction of the greater part of mankind to mere abstract labour?' (pp. 176–7).

The alienation Marx is describing here is a 'self-alienation'. He adds to this yet another form of alienation, the 'alienation of the thing'. The alienation of the thing lies in 'the relationship of the worker to the *product of labour* as an alien object which dominates him'. More broadly, this is 'a relationship to the sensuous external world, to natural objects, as an alien and hostile world'. (Marx 1963, p. 125). And there is still more. It is not just an alien and hostile natural world that stands over against the workers. There are also 'alien and hostile men' (Marx 1961, p. 177).

> A direct consequence of the alienation of man from the product of his labour, from his life activity and from his species-life, is that *man is alienated* from other *men*. When man confronts himself, he also confronts other *men*. What is true of man's relationship to his work, to the product of his work and to himself is also true of his relationship to other men, to their labour and to the objects of their labour. (Marx 1963, p. 129)

This is 'an inhuman situation'. Indeed, 'in the fully developed proletariat, everything human is taken away, even the *appearance* of humanity' (Marx 1961, pp. 236–7). 'All is under the sway of inhuman power' (Marx 1964, p. 156).

Is there any way out? Yes, there is. It is the way of revolution. The proletariat 'is forced, by an ineluctable, irremediable, and imperious *distress*—by practical *necessity*—to revolt against this inhumanity'. It 'can and must emancipate itself' (Marx 1961, p. 237). Note that Marx is not talking about others emancipating the proletariat. It must emancipate itself. This is a theme that Marxist writers, much later, will throw into bold relief. Brazilian educationalist Paulo Freire is one important figure who does that, as we shall see. Another strand in Marx's thought that Freire exploits is his insistence that the proletariat, in triumphing, does not simply substitute itself for the oppressors in place. 'It is only victorious by abolishing itself as well as its opposite', writes Marx (1961, p. 237). The proletariat 'can only emancipate itself by destroying the conditions of its existence' and it 'can only destroy its own conditions of existence by destroying all the inhuman conditions of existence of present-day society' (Marx 1961, p. 237).

In this way alienation is overcome. '*Every* emancipation is a *restoration* of the human world and of human relationships to *man himself*' (Marx 1961, pp. 236–41).

MARXISM AFTER MARX

On Marx's death it was left to Friedrich Engels to take things forward. From papers left by Marx he compiled and published the two further volumes of *Das Kapital*. Among those papers he found Marx's *Theses on Feuerbach*, written in 1845. He published this work in edited form in

1888. We owe many other Marxian texts to Engels's research and editorial efforts. These tasks undoubtedly enabled Engels to exercise significant influence over the subsequent reception and interpretation of Marx's thought. Commentators have questioned whether—or, rather, to what extent—his influence has contributed to, and detracted from, a genuine understanding of what Marx taught. Some suggest that a number of emphases found in Marxist theory are due to the cultural atmosphere abroad in Europe in the late ninetfenth century (especially the demand for philosophical grounding of concepts), rather than to any predilection for theory of that kind on the part of Marx himself.

Over these last decades of the century, both before and in the wake of Marx's death, the newborn discipline of sociology pondered the implications of his teachings hard and long. Among the sociologists paying close attention to Marxist concepts were Ferdinand Tönnies, Émile Durkheim and Georg Simmel. Max Weber, in particular, was deeply influenced by Marx's thought, as is readily acknowledged by Weberian scholars. After referring to the role played by Nietzsche in Weber's development, Donald MacRae writes (1974, p. 52): 'As for Marx, one of the most frequently recurrent questions set students of sociology in Britain and America is the request to discuss the proposition that "Weber's sociology is a debate with the ghost of Karl Marx"'.

Weber, of course, differs markedly from Marx on many issues. For him, the bourgeoisie and the proletariat are not the only groupings in society that count. Nor is Weber ready to accord to economic interests the well-nigh exclusive hegemony that Marx attributes to them. In this respect, MacRae quotes Weber to the effect that 'ideals *and* material interests directly govern men's concepts' (1974, p. 58). For all the differences, however, Weber remains heavily indebted to Marx.

> For Weber, Marx was a quarry of ideas and facts . . . Weber's debt here is
> not one of generalised judgement but it is considerable . . . it is the Marx
> of ideology, prophecy and German social democracy who counts as a major
> object of Weber's public political consciousness. (MacRae 1974, pp. 60–1)

The German social democracy to which MacRae refers found itself in severe crisis around the turn of the twentieth century. For some followers of Marx, orthodox Marxism was now displaying positivist and evolution-ist features and appeared to be cast in excessively Hegelian form. This was seen to be due, at least in part, to the influence of Engels and Karl Kautsky (1854–1938), both of whom had been personally associated with Marx and were involved with the posthumous editing of his work. The 'revisionists'—Marxists who felt that Marxism had gone astray and wished to see it return to a more authentic form—set their sights on

Kautsky. Their own protagonist was Eduard Bernstein (1850–1932), who argued that the trends discernible within Western capitalism were not those predicted by Marx and that Marxist theory needed to be adapted in the light of those trends. The Kautsky–Bernstein dispute ended with the defeat of Bernstein and revisionism generally.

Kautsky was to remain a sign of contradiction. After the Bolshevik revolution in Russia in 1917, he crossed swords with its chief architect, Vladimir Ilyich Lenin (1870–1924). For Kautsky, as for many other orthodox Marxists of that time, the events in Russia failed to signal the victory of a proletarian revolution. What had emerged in that country, he believed, was a dictatorship *over* the proletariat, not a dictatorship *of* the proletariat. This dispute, as Aron points out (1965, pp. 180–1), issued in two streams of Marxist thought. One regarded the Soviet regime as, at least basically, the fulfilment of Marx's vision. The other deemed it a gross distortion of Marxist ideals, insisting that socialist planning and collective ownership must be wedded to political democracy.

This set the scene for vigorous discussion of Marxist ideas and for the emergence of a 'Western Marxism'. The discussion was carried out on many fronts. There was, for instance, the distinctly Hegelian, and therefore heavily dialectical, Marxism of György (Georg) Lukács (1885–1971), for whom the proletariat, object as it is of capitalist exploitation, becomes the subject of history through revolutionary class consciousness. There was the praxis-oriented Marxism of Antonio Gramsci (1891–1937), which moved away from the historical determinism and materialism of the Marxist orthodoxy. Karl Korsch (1886–1961) also made praxis the centrepiece of his approach as he sought to unmask the fetishistic objectification of social relations. And there was Karl Mannheim (1893–1947), whose Marxism served as the matrix for his development of a sociology of knowledge. These were all to the fore in the early 1920s with Lukács in Vienna, Gramsci in Rome, Korsch in Leipzig, and Mannheim in Frankfurt.

Forty years on and Western Marxism has not lost its impetus. In the 1960s and 1970s we find Louis Althusser (1918–90), Algerian-born like Camus, making a sharp distinction between the earlier, humanistic Marx and the later, much more 'scientific' Marx, and attempting to introduce elements of structuralism into Marxism. Such eclecticism was far from new in the history of Marxist thought.

> The most striking fact about the relation between Marxism and philosophy, in the West at least, is how eclectic Marxists have been in their attitude to philosophy. Marxists have usually tried to articulate their ideas through whatever happened to be the current dominant philosophy. The revival of interest in Hegel between the wars, coupled with the influence of Freud,

was decisive for the formulations of the Frankfurt School; the post-war vogue for existentialism led to all sorts of New Left variations on Marxism with a human face, of which Sartre's later work is only the most prominent example; the subsequent prestige of structuralism in the 1960s and 1970s led to the arcanely theoretical Marxism of Althusser and his disciples; while the rational choice of Marxism of more recent years is evidently an effort to come to terms with some of the dominant concepts of the Reagan–Thatcher years. (McLellan 1995b, p. 527)

If we want to characterise Western Marxism, we might do best to underline the emphasis it has placed on culture as distinct from economics. The emphasis has been on the superstructure rather than the economic sub-structure. This has certainly been the case with the group of scholars—formed in Frankfurt, forced into a twenty-year exile from Frankfurt, but triumphantly re-established in Frankfurt—with whom critical social inquiry from a Marxist perspective has been strongly identified for almost three-quarters of a century.

THE INSTITUTE FOR SOCIAL RESEARCH

The Frankfurt School has been mentioned several times already. It has its origins in the Institute for Social Research set up in 1924 under the patronage of Felix Weil. Weil, the son of a multimillionaire and a student of Robert Wildebrandt, a socialist professor of political economy at Tübingen, wanted to establish an institutional context for the discussion of Marxist ideas. He was aided in this project by Kurt Gerlach, a left-wing socialist who had taught at Leipzig before becoming professor of economic science at Aachen. In 1922 Gerlach was invited to take up a professorship at Frankfurt and to work with Weil in establishing the Institute.

As Wiggershaus documents (1994, pp. 17–18), the submission that Weil and Gerlach made to the Prussian Ministry of Science openly described the proposed institute as one that would 'serve first and foremost for the study and broadening of scientific Marxism'. They were more guarded in their approach to the University authorities. Marxism was mentioned only in passing and not in relation to the aims of the Institute. At its official opening on 22 June 1924, however, the inaugural director of the Institute, Carl Grünberg, left no doubt in the minds of his listeners as to its orientation. 'I, too', he declared in his formal address for that occasion, 'am one of the supporters of Marxism'. He went on:

Up till now Marxism, as an economic and sociological system, has been to a great extent neglected at German universities, in considerable contrast with those of other countries—indeed, in practice, it has been reluctantly tolerated at best. In the new research institute, Marxism will from now on have a home. (In Wiggershaus 1994, p. 27)

Even at the start the Marxism envisaged for the Institute was by no means orthodox and, as the Institute got underway, it brought together thinkers who diverged from one another in significant ways. The Institute for Social Research has manifested very markedly the eclecticism already referred to. This is even more true of the broader, vaguer entity which goes by the name of the Frankfurt School and for which the Institute served as the 'organizational seedbed' (Wolin 1992, p. 46). So much so that some commentators question whether the Institute or the School should be regarded as Marxist in any true sense of the word. Zoltán Tar writes of a 'certain cloud of myth, ambiguity and confusion surrounding the Frankfurt School' and argues that the 'notion that the school represents a Marxist orientation in sociology rests only on a superficial acquaintance with the work of Max Horkheimer, Theodor W. Adorno, and other thinkers of the Frankfurt School' (1977, p. 2). Tar describes Horkheimer's views in particular as 'Marx turned upside down' and 'obviously based on a distortion of the Marxian vision' (1977, p. 180). In the end, according to Martin Jay (1973, p. 296), the Institute 'presented a revision of Marxism so substantial that it forfeited the right to be included among its many offshoots'. Mészáros, in fact, regards the School as Weberian rather than Marxist:

> Significantly, however, the impact of the Weberian influence on the Frankfurt School makes itself felt in the complete *reversal* of this sociohistorical concretization of the alienating contradictions of twentieth century capitalism by Lukács and others. Accordingly, not only is the Marxian social agency of the anticipated revolutionary transformation eliminated from the conceptual framework of 'critical theory' but, altogether, the problematic of *'reification'* is deprived of its social ground and redrafted in the abstract and ahistorical Weberian sense of 'rationalization'. (1989, p. 22)

Such judgments notwithstanding, most analysts of Frankfurt School philosophy and social science are content to accept its broadly Marxist character, while recognising that the Marxism in question is no purist form but a neo-Marxism or post-Marxism containing a strong admixture of elements drawn from other sources. Thus, Outhwaite writes (1994, p. 5) of 'the broad Marxist tradition' that 'inspired the original Frankfurt Institute for Social Research'. For all the criticisms of authors like Tar, Jay and Mészáros, Horkheimer himself, who succeeded Grünberg as director of the Institute in 1930, had no doubts about the authenticity of the Institute's Marxism. 'Marxism won its decisive meaning for our thought', he was to write some 40 years later (1973, p. xi). The story he tells is the story of how 'a group of men, interested in social theory and from different scholarly backgrounds, came together with the belief that formulating the negative in the epoch of transition was more meaningful than academic careers' (1973, p. xi). 'What united them', he declares, 'was the critical approach to existing society' (1973, p. xi).

If the School's relationship to Marx is a complex one, its history is complex also. The first members of the Institute for Social Research were either Jews or, as Wiggershaus puts it, 'people who had largely been forced back into an affiliation with Judaism by the Nazis' (1994, p. 4). Identified as both Jewish and Marxist, they had no chance of surviving once Nazism came to power in 1933. Hitler was appointed Chancellor on 30 January 1933, elections for the Eighth Reichstag took place on 5 March, and on 13 March the Institute's premises were searched by the police and closed down. A statement by the Gestapo dated 14 July declared that 'the Institute of Social Research in Frankfurt am Main is hereby seized and confiscated in favour of the Free State of Prussia, as the aforementioned Institute has encouraged activities hostile to the state' (Wiggershaus 1994, p. 128).

Most of the members and associates of the Institute fled abroad. Besides Horkheimer, these included Erich Fromm, Friedrich Pollock, Leo Lowenthal, Herbert Marcuse and Henryk Grossman. Horkheimer, Pollock and Lowenthal found refuge in Geneva in the first instance but this could only be temporary. Horkheimer went to the United States to investigate the prospects there and was offered accommodation for the Institute at Columbia University in New York. One by one, core members of the Institute joined Horkheimer in New York and the Institute resumed its work. Karl Wittfogel had delayed his departure and fell into Nazi hands. After time spent in various concentration camps, he was released and managed to travel, first to England, then to the United States. Theodor Adorno too had remained behind in Germany and was back and forth to England where he was studying at Oxford. Horkheimer finally convinced him to join the Institute in its exile in America and he came to New York in 1938. Walter Benjamin, never a formal member of the Institute, was engaged as a freelance researcher, beginning at the time of the Institute's exile in Switzerland. He resisted all invitations to join the Institute in the United States, preferring to remain in Europe. Escaping Nazism became more and more difficult for him as time went on and in 1940, after being refused entry into Spain via the Pyrenees, he committed suicide in the border town of Port Bou.

This was clearly a time of great trauma for those involved with the Institute for Social Research. While this Institute-in-exile continued its research activities with enthusiasm, it did so in what Wiggershaus describes as 'a kind of "splendid isolation" from its American environment' (1994, p. 2). Connerton (1980, p. 4) agrees: 'They were marginal in exile'. Its seminars were rarely attended by American students and it was abundantly clear that the interests of Institute members and those of their American counterparts were far apart. During this period, as was pointed out in Chapter 3, Horkheimer launched an astonishing attack on American pragmatism in general and John Dewey in particular. Nor was his criticism limited to pragmatism. 'Horkheimer,' states Wiggershaus (1994, p. 248), 'was increasingly impatient in his criticism of the various scientific disciplines, and increasingly severe in his labelling of every theoretical and philosophical tendency which was not critical of society, and which was successful in the USA, as a form of recognition and acceptance of existing conditions'.

Still, there were a number of people associated with Columbia University who purported to be of critical bent and might have been expected to establish ready rapport with the exiled members of the Institute. The so-called 'New York intellectuals' were there, for example —anti-Stalinists grouped around the journal *Partisan Review* and attempting to wed Marxism to a modernist critique of society. But rapport failed to emerge.

> The common ground shared by the *Partisan Review*-Columbia circle and the Frankfurt intellectuals was substantial . . . Given these shared concerns, what is most remarkable about the relationship between the New York liberal intellectuals and the Frankfurt School is its virtual nonexistence. A lack of sympathetic interaction existed despite physical proximity. (Posnock 1991, p. 78)

Posnock is not alone in concluding that the critique instituted by Horkheimer and his colleagues offered too radical a challenge to structures and beliefs cherished by American thinkers at that time for any genuine dialogue to happen.[14]

In addition to that, relations between the Institute and New York's New School for Social Research were awkward, to say the least. The New School had been founded by liberal thinkers in the wake of World War I but had become increasingly conservative. There were now anti-Marxist elements there and these reflected the anti-Communist mood of the times. McCarthyism was some time off, but suspicions were abroad in American society. In July 1940 police visited the Institute for Social Research, asking for information on its staff members and examining materials it had produced.

In 1941 most of the principal members of the Institute moved to Los

Angeles, leaving Lowenthal in charge of what Wiggershaus calls a 'rump' of the Institute in New York, although the New York centre continued to function as the official headquarters. As if the conflicts from external factors were not enough, the Institute now experienced internal conflict 'between Los Angeles and New York, between an interest in large-scale, long-term and theory-oriented research and an interest in quick results and methodologically well grounded research' (Wiggershaus 1994, p. 397). The formal links with Columbia University were cut in 1946.

Despite an unpromising ambience and internal divergences, and with many of the members involved in government service in one way or another, the Institute remained productive through the war years and into the 1950s, even if Wiggershaus describes this period as one of 'productive decay'. Certainly this period was marked by a most fruitful collaboration between Horkheimer and Adorno. They co-authored *Dialectic of Enlightenment*, which was published in 1947. Adorno's *Minima Moralia*, first published in 1951, was written at a time when, as his Dedication acknowledges, circumstances caused his collaboration with Horkheimer to be interrupted. Nevertheless, he insists, a '*dialogue intérieur*' continued between them and, as far as the book is concerned, 'there is not a motif in it that does not belong as much to Horkheimer as to him who found the time to formulate it' (Adorno 1974, p. 18).

In the early 1950s the Institute returned to Germany. Horkheimer had visited Frankfurt in 1948 and 1949. After his second visit, an appeal calling for the Institute to be re-established at the University of Frankfurt and signed by many eminent scholars was published in the *American Sociological Review*. That same year Adorno went to Frankfurt as Horkheimer's deputy. Horkheimer joined him in 1950. Pollock followed. Lowenthal and, significantly for its financial independence, the Institute's patron Felix Weil remained in the United States. So too did Marcuse, who gained professorships at Brandeis (1954) and San Diego (1965) universities, as well as a surprising popularity in the 1960s, especially among activist students. Erich Fromm had moved away early on. This left Horkheimer, Adorno and Pollock. Few as they were, in the persons of these three figures so central to its history and activities, the Institute for Social Research had well and truly returned to life in Frankfurt. Its premises were officially declared open in November 1951. 'Frankfurt School', and 'critical theory' as a catch-all phrase for the social philosophy of the Frankfurt School, were terms still to be coined, but the stage was set for a resumption of the Institute's work on German soil and, in due course, for 'second generation' Frankfurt theorists to arrive on the scene.

CRITICAL THEORY

The philosophical stance of the Frankfurt School might not have been dubbed 'critical theory' until the 1950s but the words themselves had certainly occurred in the writings of the School's principal membership. In 1937, for example, in the Institute's journal *Zeitschrift für Sozialforschung* (to become, from 1940 onwards, *Studies in Philosophy and Social Science*), Horkheimer published a landmark article entitled 'Traditional and critical theory'. It was accompanied by an article by Herbert Marcuse, 'Philosophy and critical theory'.

The term 'critical theory' suggests a coherent body of thought but, given the turbulent history of the Institute and the varied backgrounds, widely different disciplines and strong personalities of its membership, it would be most surprising if a unified approach, and therefore a 'School' in the true sense of the word, had emerged. Wolin writes of 'a number of significant intellectual tensions within the inner circle of the Frankfurt School itself' and of 'various competing epistemological conceptions embraced by the School's individual members' (1992, p. 40). In the judgment of Jürgen Habermas, who joined the Institute in the mid-1950s as Adorno's research assistant, a united approach did not emerge at any stage. 'For me', Wiggershaus records Habermas as stating, 'there was never a consistent theory' (Wiggershaus 1994, p. 2). Wiggershaus himself asserts that 'the terms "Frankfurt School" and "Critical Theory" had never corresponded to a uniform phenomenon' (p. 657).

What did Horkheimer mean by critical theory in his essay of 1937? His disjunction of 'traditional' theory from 'critical' theory in the title of that essay points up the opposition he posits between a theory that merely reflects the current situation and a theory that seeks to change the situation. The need to change the situation was crystal-clear to Horkheimer. 'Benjamin's notion of history as incessant process of ruination and decline, a *Verfallsgeschichte*', writes Wolin (1992, p. 41), 'appears to have exerted a dominant influence on the thinking of Adorno and Horkheimer'. Horkheimer is in pursuit of a theory that is wedded to practice in the service of a more just organisation of life in society. He wants 'a theory which becomes a genuine force, consisting in the self-awareness of the subjects of a great historical revolution'. Traditional theory is not what he is after. It is not wedded to practice. It is not a genuine force. Why not? Because, Horkheimer believes (1982, p. 231), of its 'Cartesian dualism of thought and being'.

Horkheimer's 1937 article reflects the program he had set for himself and the Institute in his inaugural address as its director in January 1931.

In that address Horkheimer recognises the dichotomy in German thought between the vitalism that had become the dominant philosophy—a *Lebensphilosophie* that values the immediacy and flux of direct experience and has no time for empirical data—and a positivist science that reduces valid knowledge to what can be verified statistically, thus robbing experience of its vitality. He seeks a wedding of philosophy and the various forms of science. He wants a social theory that brings together philosophical construct and empirical detail. He has no interest in a social science that remains bogged down in the mire of aimlessly accumulated facts and does no more than mirror the fragmentation characteristic of contemporary society. Nor does he want a philosophy divorced from the lived reality of social life. What he wants to see is philosophy and science informing each other in dialectical fashion. Were that to occur, we would have a social philosophy that stands as a critical theory of society and is able to 'escape the fate of becoming sheer ideology: the intellectual masking of an indigent social reality' (Wolin 1992, p. 50).

This programmatic statement provided direction for the Institute's research activities throughout the 1930s, first in Frankfurt, then in New York. On it was founded an interdisciplinary program wherein philosophical reflection is 'measured against the concreteness of empirical social findings', the outcome being 'the methodological reconstruction of reality as a "concrete totality"' (Wolin 1992, pp. 48–9). One outcome of this research thrust is the Institute's *Studies in Authority and the Family*, which was published in 1936 and contains a significant empirical component.

In the 1940s, however, with Horkheimer's move to California and the forging of his very close partnership with Adorno, there occurred an important turn in his thinking. Wolin reminds us that Adorno became a member of the Institute's inner circle only in 1938:

> But from that time on, the orientation of the Institute as a whole changed decisively. In Adorno, Horkheimer found the gifted philosophical spirit he had long been seeking as a collaborator for his book on 'dialectical logic'. It is not hard to see that Adorno, whose interests were exclusively philosophical and aesthetic, weaned Horkheimer further away from the empirical side of his 1931 program and in the direction of a social philosophy unencumbered by empirical moorings. (1992, p. 60)

The Adorno who allegedly moved Horkheimer from his 'interdisciplinary materialism' to a philosophy of history was born in 1903. He was given the name of Theodor Wiesengrund-Adorno. The hyphenation joins the surname of his father to part of the name of his mother, who was of Corsican descent. During his time in California in the 1940s, he changed his surname to Adorno, Wiesengrund becoming just an initial.

Adorno was a musical composer and musicologist as well as philosopher. Aesthetic considerations were never far from his thought. The ideas expressed in *Dialectic of Enlightenment*, written with Horkheimer between 1941 and 1944, came to maturity in his later works, *Negative Dialectics* (published in 1966) and *Aesthetic Theory* (left unfinished at his death in 1969 but published posthumously).

Already in *Dialectic of Enlightenment* Adorno is railing against the domination exercised by the 'concept'. He and Horkheimer write of the 'rigidity and exclusiveness' that concepts assume (Horkheimer and Adorno 1972, p. 22). The 'universality of ideas as developed by discursive logic' is set in apposition to 'domination in the conceptual sphere' and said to be 'raised up on the basis of actual domination' (p. 14) This is impoverishing as well as oppressive. We substitute concepts for what they represent but no concept can ever capture the richness of the reality. Adorno points out that 'objects do not go into their concepts without leaving a remainder' (1973, p. 5). There is a '"more" which the concept is equally desirous and incapable of being' (1973, p. 162). So we are beset by 'wretched cover concepts that will make the crucial differences vanish' (p. 152). Adorno feels so strongly about this that he does not hesitate to draw a literally shocking analogy. 'If thought is not measured by the extremity that eludes the concept', he warns, 'it is from the outset in the nature of the musical accompaniment with which the SS liked to drown out the screams of its victims' (1973, p. 365).

Yet we need to conceptualise. Part of this need is our urgent desire to make realities our own, to overcome the distance between us as subject and them as object, to reduce 'difference'. This is what Adorno brands identitarian thinking. It is an identity logic. And it stands in the tradition of German idealism, which has untiringly sought to identify subject and object and reduce the irreducible Other. What Adorno wants us to do, to the contrary, is to 'defend the irreducibility of non-conceptual material (of the real in its opacity) against the ravenous power of the concept' (Tertulian 1985, p. 91).

> In truth, all concepts, even the philosophical ones, refer to nonconceptualities, because concepts on their part are moments of the reality that requires their formation, primarily for the control of nature. What conceptualization appears to be from within, to one engaged in it—the predominance of its sphere, without which nothing is known—must not be mistaken for what it is in itself. Such a semblance of being-in-itself is conferred upon it by the motion that exempts it from reality, to which it is harnessed in turn. (Adorno 1973, p. 11)

Adorno wishes to strip conceptualisation of the 'predominance' it has arrogated to itself and restore predominance to the object instead. 'Identitarian thinking is subjectivistic even when it denies being so', claims Adorno, whereas 'the critique of identity is a groping for the preponderance of the object' (1973, p. 183). Adorno's negative dialectics calls upon us to pay attention to the Other and, at all times, to 'release the nonidentical' (1973, p. 6). 'Dialectics', he tells us, 'is the consistent sense of non-identity' (1973, p. 5).

How are we to 'release the non-identical'? How can we maintain 'a consistent sense of non-identity'? How might we 'grope for the preponderance of the object'? Certainly not by looking to traditional philosophy for direction. According to Adorno, the original sin of all philosophy is that it tries to grasp the non-conceptual through conceptual means. He reverses the process (hence his *negative* dialectics): philosophy must 'strive by way of the concept to transcend the concept' and 'thus reach the nonconceptual' (Adorno 1973, pp. 15, 9). Adorno wishes to reach, by way of the concept, a 'sphere beyond control, a sphere tabooed by conceptuality' (1973, p. 14).

In our traditional ways of thinking, we multiply resemblances in order to identify and classify realities and establish a system that will bring things together for us as a manageable totality. This process leads to the loss of many precious differences, even if it offers us the security of making realities 'our own'. Adorno cites Nietzsche's dictum that 'to perceive resemblances everywhere, making everything alike, is a sign of weak eyesight' (1974, p. 74). Adorno's negative dialectics, his nonidentity mode of cognition, does not fall into this trap. 'The matters of true philosophical interest at this point in history', Adorno claims (1973, p. 8), 'are nonconceptuality, individuality, and particularity—things which ever since Plato used to be dismissed as transitory and insignificant'.

Not that Adorno believes we can simply cease to identify and classify. 'To think is to identify', he reminds us (1973, p. 5). Yet, if we cannot resolve the contradiction, we can at least dwell in it dialectically. We can maintain a creative tension between the conceptual and the nonconceptual, the general and the particular. It is 'up to dialectical cognition to pursue the inadequacy of thought and thing, to experience it in the thing' (1973, p. 153).

Adorno practices dialectical (or nonidentical) cognition, which functions by multiplying difference while preserving resemblances rather than assimilating them through identification. Analogy and similitude (as opposed to conceptual definition) characterize this kind of mimetic cognition. It attempts to use concepts non-conceptually, not as instruments that circumscribe but as tentative acts of expression that suggest rather than fix meaning. In turn, this mimetic cognition serves Adorno as a model both for renovated human conduct (which he calls aesthetic or mimetic) and the social and political arrangements that would encourage such conduct. (Posnock 1991, pp. 106–7).

Here Posnock repeatedly uses the word 'mimetic'. This, along with the noun 'mimesis', is prominent in Adorno's vocabulary. Etymologically, mimesis and mimetic mean 'imitation' and 'imitative', respectively. Plato employs the word *mimesis* in attacking poetry and the arts generally. He accuses artists of engaging in trickery because they offer mere replicas of things and not the realities themselves. For him, the prisoners in his allegory of the cave are in the lowest form of being because they see only the shadows or copies of things. Artists make things worse because they produce imitations of imitations. Adorno stands in a tradition, however, that eagerly embraces precisely what Plato scorns. For Adorno, we are essentially imitative beings.

We have already noted the importance of role playing—initially playful and game-based role playing—in Mead's social psychology. Without it, according to Mead, we would not enter into the attitudes of the community and could not achieve personhood. Imitation plays a central role in Adorno's analysis too. In fact, he is ready to privilege mimesis and challenges the primacy that 'bourgeois morality' accords to genuineness and authenticity. In accordance with the dictates of bourgeois morality, the individual is bidden to 'be wholly and entirely what he is'. This morality, in Adorno's judgment, is not true. 'The untruth is located in the substratum of genuineness itself, the individual' (Adorno 1974, p. 152). The call to genuineness is untrue because the image on which it is based—the image of the autonomous, all-responsible individual—is untrue.

To assert this is to fly in the face of contemporary affirmations of the individual self. Adorno wants 'to call for the abolition of the spell of selfhood hitherto promoted by the subject' (1984, p. 195). He denies to the self the defined and abiding character, and the autonomy and authority, that the liberal tradition has emphasised so passionately. The self, he claims to the contrary, owes its very being to society.

Precisely as an absolute, the individual is a mere reflection of property relations. In him the fictitious claim is made that what is biologically one must logically precede the social whole, from which it is only isolated by force, and its contingency is held up as a standard of truth. Not only is the self entwined in society; it owes society its existence in the most literal sense. All its content comes from society, or at any rate from its relation to the object. It grows richer the more freely it develops and reflects this relation, while it is limited, impoverished and reduced by the separation and hardening that it lays claim to as an origin. (Adorno 1974, pp. 153-4)

A few sentences later and Adorno is asserting, 'Genuineness is nothing other than a defiant and obstinate insistence on the monadological form which social oppression imposes on man'. 'Monadological', of course, derives from Leibniz's monads, which for Leibniz are the basic individual substances making up the universe. A monad is seen as entirely self-sufficient and for that reason is often described as 'windowless'. It serves as a metaphor for the self-sufficient, controlling individual which the term 'person' tends to evoke today. This is an image of the person that Adorno regards as 'itself compulsive in nature' (1973, p. 222). He wants to challenge it.

Equally, Adorno wants to challenge the call to authenticity that accompanies this image. Nietzsche reproached Wagner for play acting but, as Adorno sees it, an actor should be reproached not for play acting but for any denial of play acting. To be sure, an inauthenticity wherein something claims to be what it is not deserves to be convicted of lying. Yet, says Adorno (1974, pp. 154-5), 'authenticity itself becomes a lie the moment it becomes authentic, that is, in reflecting on itself, in postulating itself as genuine, in which it already oversteps the identity that it lays claim to in the same breath'. The discovery of genuineness is 'a last bulwark of individualistic ethics' and we should recognise the ungenuineness of the genuine. 'The ungenuineness of the genuine stems from its need to claim, in a society dominated by exchange, to be what it stands for yet is never able to be' (1974, pp. 154-5).

As Adorno would have it, we should warmly embrace mimesis and engage unashamedly in mimetic behaviour. We should dwell in the object of our experience, seeking simply to mimic what we experience as fully as possible rather than believing we can capture what we experience conceptually. Here Adorno borrows from Benjamin the notion of 'constellation'. Instead of building a theoretical system, we delineate a constellation. In the case of a constellation, unlike that of a conceptual system, no claims to fullness or completedness are advanced. Adorno refers to the 'trial arrangement' of constellation (1977, p. 131). It is a temporary structure only, for negative dialectics means thinking in such a way 'that the thought form will no longer turn its objects into immutable ones, into objects that remain the same' (Adorno 1973, p. 154).

By themselves constellations represent from without what the concept has cut away within: the 'more' which the concept is equally desirous and incapable of being . . .

... what is indissoluble in any previous thought context transcends its seclusion in its own, as nonidentical. It communicates with that from which it was separated by the concept ... The inside of nonidentity is its relation to that which it is not, and which its managed, frozen self-identity withholds from it. It only comes to in relinquishing itself, not in hardening ...

Cognition of the object in its constellation is cognition of the process stored in the object. As a constellation, theoretical thought circles the concept it would like to unseal, hoping that it may fly open like the lock of a well-guarded safe-deposit box: in response, not to a single key or a single number, but to a combination of numbers. (Adorno 1973, pp. 162–3)

Mimetic behaviour is, of course, the quintessential behaviour of the aesthete. Art, Adorno tells us, is 'a refuge for mimetic behaviour' and its subject 'takes up varying positions *vis-à-vis* its objective other from which it is always different but never entirely separate' (1984, p. 79). Works of art 'defy every pre-established universality' (1984, p. 123). They 'take an advance on a praxis that has not yet begun' (1984, p. 124). Paradoxically, therefore, rather than art copying reality, Adorno believes that reality should imitate art. 'Works of art represent a class of objects the truth of which can only be imagined as the truth of an inner domain. And imitation is the royal road that leads into this inner domain. (Adorno 1984, p. 183).

In this fashion Adorno (1973, p. 221) calls for non-identity and bids us look for a 'dawning sense of freedom'. This, he tells us, 'feeds upon the memory of the archaic impulse not yet steered by any solid I'. He invites us to 'yield to the object', which 'means to do justice to the object's qualitative moments' (1973, p. 43). And he urges us, as we have seen, to experience the inadequacy of thought and thing 'in the thing' (1973, p. 153). All this sounds quite phenomenological, doesn't it? Adorno's words have the ring of phenomenology's 'Back to the things themselves!'. His insistence (1973, p.11) that all concepts 'refer to nonconceptualities' and that conceptualisation is 'harnessed' to reality is most reminiscent of the phenomenological notion of intentionality.

Mind you, Adorno is very critical of Husserl's transcendental phenomenology and, while sharing some of their concerns, he rejects the existentialism of the existential phenomenologists. Despite that, it may be suggested that what Adorno is proposing, and what he leads Horkheimer to engage in, is a form of phenomenological critique rather than the more directly social critique instituted by the Frankfurt School earlier on. We may recall that, in our discussion in Chapter 4, phenomenology commended itself as 'first critique', propaedeutic to further critique along one or other sociological line. Adorno's thought lends itself to this view of things, that is, to accepting the need for a critique of consciousness that in turn informs a critique of society. 'For Adorno', writes Pauline Johnson (1984, p. 83), 'the subversive character of Marxism in the contemporary situation rests with its ability to provide a critique of the prevailing consciousness which serves to perpetuate the system'.

In this way, Adorno brings social action and non-identity thinking together. As Tertulian makes clear (1985, pp. 90–1), Adorno engages both in 'brutal transitions from the socio-historical to the philosophical level' and in a 'brutal retroversion of philosophical theorems into socio-historical realities'. He points up 'the concept's power to master non-conceptual heterogeneous material' and insists that this power of the concept 'merely prolongs, on the level of thought, domination on the social level'. The battle must be fought on both fronts, then. Adorno calls for 'immanent criticism'. This is a critique from within rather than one that purports to be from without and in it we experience the inadequacy of thought and thing 'in the thing'. Yet it is not to be set over against social action. In this immanent critique we are already looking to society and calling it to account.

> Hence immanent criticism cannot take comfort in its own idea. It can neither be vain enough to believe that it can liberate the mind directly by immersing itself in it, nor naïve enough to believe that unflinching immersion in the object will inevitably lead to truth by virtue of the logic of things if only the subjective knowledge of the false whole is kept from intruding from the outside, as it were, in the determination of the object . . . Dialectics cannot, therefore, permit any insistence on logical neatness to encroach on its right to go from one *genus* to another, to shed light on an object in itself hermetic by casting a glance at society, to present society with the bill which the object does not redeem. (Adorno 1981, p. 33)

Accordingly, we should not take Adorno's invitation to return to the 'archaic impulse not yet steered by any solid I' to be akin to Bergson's vitalism, which looks to intuition as the entrée to the living flow of immediate reality. Rorty writes of 'Bergsonian nostalgia for the rich, whooshy, sensuous flux we bathed in before conceptual thought started to dry us out' (1983, p. 33). Adorno is not inviting us to such intuition or a bathing of that kind. He sees Bergson's philosophy of life as 'a cult of irrational immediacy'. 'Every cognition including Bergson's own needs the rationality he scorns' (Adorno 1973, pp. 8–9). What Jay says of Horkheimer is true of Adorno also: Adorno, like Horkheimer, believes that Bergson and similarly minded philosophers 'had gone too far in emphasising subjectivity and inwardness' and 'had minimized the importance of action in the historical world' (Jay 1973, p. 51).

So Adorno's negative dialectics by no means indicates that he has joined the ranks of the philosophers for whom Marx had such scorn—people content to interpret the world but with no interest in changing it. Freeman-Moir (1992, p. 103) talks of an academic Marxism in which the two revolutionary moments of theory and practice are torn apart. 'Intellectuals are left only with the activity of interpreting the world and the vision of change becomes more and more diluted' (p. 114). As we have seen already, Adorno is not guilty of any such retreat from action for change. If he is concerned with consciousness, it is because, in his view, proletarian consciousness has lost its revolutionary character. If he is concerned with art, it is because, in his view, art has a social role that is at once subversive and redemptive.

> The only philosophy which can be responsibly practised in face of despair is the attempt to contemplate all things as they would present themselves from the standpoint of redemption. Knowledge has no light but that shed on the world by redemption: all else is reconstruction, mere technique. Perspectives must be fashioned that displace and estrange the world, reveal it to be, with its rifts and crevices, as indigent and distorted as it will appear one day in the messianic light. (Adorno 1974, p. 247)

We might note that the picture of Adorno emerging for us here is not the picture that Jürgen Habermas (1929–) paints. In the person of Habermas we encounter the so-called second generation of Frankfurt thinkers and arrive back at our own times. He is one of several scholars who stand forth in clear relief as we begin to look at critical thought since the start of the 1960s. Paulo Freire is another. A third is Louis Althusser.

Althusser's name has already emerged for us. His is a structuralist Marxism and we will leave our consideration of it until the last chapter, where we will be discussing structuralism in the context of post-structuralism and postmodernism. Habermas and Freire we need to deal with now. And we need to sum up what this tradition of critical thought means for research today.

This will preoccupy us in the chapter that follows.

7

CRITICAL INQUIRY: CONTEMPORARY CRITICS & CONTEMPORARY CRITIQUE

So free we seem, so fettered fast we are.

Robert Browning, *Andrea del Sarto*

This chapter links closely to the one we have just left. It will reinforce the continuity between the two if we take up again the matter of Habermas's judgment on Adorno, referred to at the end of Chapter 6.

Habermas, the most illustrious of the second-generation Frankfurt theorists, claims that Adorno, in rejecting identity logic, 'surrendered to an uninhibited scepticism concerning reason' (Habermas 1987, p. 129). Adorno, as Habermas understands him, replaced reason with a mimesis that presents itself as 'the sheer opposite of reason, as impulse' (Habermas 1984, p. 390). This would be an Adorno whose mimesis is romantic irrationalism and who, in consequence, is closing himself off from the possibility of social critique.

This does not square well with Adorno's rejection of Bergson's 'cult of irrational immediacy' and his insistence that any cognition whatsoever requires rationality. Nor, on the face of it, does it square well with Adorno's demand that, in experiencing the inadequacy of thought and thing 'in the thing', we are to 'present society with the bill which the object does not redeem'. Wiggershaus leaves us in no doubt about his view on Adorno's relationship to rationality:

> Adorno's approach in philosophy was similar to that of his writings on sociology, music and literature. He was concerned to produce a philosophy that would increase the rationality of the perceiving subject and make the subject sensitive to the structure of objects. (Wiggershaus 1994, p. 530)

Habermas's reading of Adorno is hardly a generous interpretation, therefore, and this no doubt reflects the strained relations that characterised Habermas's involvement with the Institute for Social Research. In that involvement with the Institute we find a useful setting for our consideration of his ideas.

JÜRGEN HABERMAS AND COMMUNICATIVE REASON

Horkheimer was suspicious of Habermas from the start. He was extremely critical of Habermas's *Students and Politics* research project, a piece of work he undertook with Christoph Oehler and Friedrich Weltz soon after becoming an associate of the Institute in 1956. As Horkheimer saw it, some of the critique Habermas institutes in this work implies that, for a people 'held in the shackles of bourgeois society by a liberal constitution', violence is the only alternative. 'It is simply not possible', Horkheimer wrote to Adorno (in Wiggershaus 1994, p. 554), 'to have admissions of this sort in the research report of an Institute that exists on the public funds of this shackling society'. In the end, the study did not appear in the Institute's own series *Frankfurt Contributions to Sociology* but was brought out by a different publishing house. This, Wiggershaus claims, was very much to the detriment of the Institute.

> The Institute of Social Research, whose identity Horkheimer saw as being threatened by Habermas, remained virtually anonymous in the book, and thus denied itself in the very publication that was to become the most successful empirical study the re-established Institute ever produced. (Wiggershaus 1994, p. 555)

There is something ironic in Horkheimer's reading violence into Habermas's text. As Rundell observes:

> Habermas' work is fuelled by a simple idea. In the context of 'a modernity at variance with itself', he is preoccupied with the public and non-violent strength of the better argument, which he terms rational practical discourse . . .
>
> Habermas' notion of politics, at its most minimal and anthropological, simply means a non-violent inter-subjectivity in the making, where words—more strictly, sentences or speech acts—rather than rituals or weapons, are the form of social intercourse that counts. (1991, p. 133)

Habermas's next project was an analysis of the changes that had taken place within the bourgeois 'public sphere'. This he proposed as his *Habilitation* thesis at Frankfurt. It was rejected. Many authors attribute its rejection to Adorno but, according to Wiggershaus, it was Horkheimer who blocked the way. Adorno, says Wiggershaus (1994, p. 555), was proud of Habermas and wanted to see the thesis proposal accepted. The upshot was that Habermas removed his project from the Institute and completed his thesis under the supervision of Marburg professor Wolfgang Abendroth. While engaged in this post-doctoral work, he became professor of philosophy in Heidelberg.

Horkheimer, and not Adorno, may have been the villain in the piece but the two were closely linked. Habermas may well have felt that Adorno should have done more on his behalf. Indeed, Wiggershaus refers in this connection to 'Horkheimer's hostility and Adorno's weakness' (1994, p. 566). Perhaps we should not be surprised at Habermas being so absolute and trenchant in his criticism of Adorno's negative dialectics.

Be that as it may, the issue of 'reason', so central to negative dialectics, lies also at the heart of Habermas's relationship to the tradition of the Frankfurt School he joined in 1956. That tradition had come to level an increasingly radical challenge to the hegemony that it saw instrumental reason assuming in the development of Western society. Horkheimer and Adorno depict Western society as a social and political economy, at once capitalist and bureaucratic, which reduces all social relations to the level of objectified and commodified administered systems. As they see it, the development of this form of society springs from the Enlightenment's understanding of reason as instrumental rationality. This is an understanding that decisively splits subject from object and looks, above all else, to gain control over nature and render it predictable. On the basis of this understanding, Horkheimer and particularly Adorno make refutation and rejection of identity thinking pivotal to their critique of capitalist society.

Habermas has never shared the radically anti-capitalist stance of Horkheimer and Adorno. Nor does he want to reject reason as wholeheartedly as he believes Adorno has done. Adorno accepts of dialectics that, 'being at once the impression and the critique of the universal delusive context, it must now turn even against itself'; indeed, it 'lies in the definition of negative dialectics that it will not come to rest in itself' (1973, p. 406). Such affirmations lead Habermas to conclude that Adorno has really abandoned immanent critique for 'total' critique, leaving no way out.

> According to Habermas, while Adorno (as well as Horkheimer and Marcuse) generated a critique of modern society from the ground of the deformations and transvaluations of enlightenment thinking, he was, because of his own reading of reason, largely immune to its meaning and grounding in any positive sense whatsoever. (Rundell 1991, p. 135)

The Frankfurt School, Habermas believes, rests its notion of immanent critique on Marx's theory of history. This spurs him to a further elucidation of the Marxian origin of critical theory. He moves beyond the position on Marx and Marxism that he upheld in his first years with the Institute, arguing now that a praxis-oriented philosophy of history cannot be soundly grounded in Marx's theoretical framework. He wants to establish a new basis for such philosophy of history. The immanent critique proposed by the Frankfurt School theoreticians is not up to the task, because 'bourgeois consciousness has become cynical' (Habermas 1979, p. 97). By this he means that people can no longer recognise as their own the truths and values to which immanent critique directs them.

Habermas is seeking to do what he believes the later Frankfurt School has proved unable to do, that is, provide a normative basis for critical theory. To this end, he develops a positive concept of reason in contradistinction to what he regards as an utterly negative concept of reason in Horkheimer and especially Adorno. This he does in *Knowledge and Human Interests*, which he published in 1968, four years after returning to Frankfurt to take up Horkheimer's chair in philosophy and sociology. In this book Habermas revisits Marxian theory and engages in a fresh critique of it. The method of argument Habermas employs is that of an internal investigation of philosophy itself and has some affinity with Adorno's immanent critique.

> Unlike Adorno, however, Habermas uses the method to build up a positive theory by examining earlier positions from within, exposing their limitations, building on their strengths, moving on to later positions and repeating the process in order to arrive at a more comprehensive and satisfactory position. (Roderick 1986, pp. 51–2)

Concluding that Marx's focus on production is an inadequate base on which to ground a socially and historically developing rationality, Habermas posits a distinction between labour as instrumental action and social interaction as communicative action. These two forms of action, together with the exercise of power and domination (an issue that has, of course, preoccupied him from the start), constitute the basis for his well-known threefold typology of human knowledge. In establishing this typology, Habermas is drawing on his central epistemological tenet: that human beings constitute their reality and organise their experience in terms of cognitive (or 'knowledge-guiding') *interests*. Thus, the empirical sciences are led by a technical interest in predicting and controlling objectified processes. This is the realm of instrumental action. Secondly, the historico-hermeneutic sciences—that is, the cultural or human sciences—are guided by a practical interest in achieving intersubjective understanding. This interest is styled 'practical' because of the crucial importance to human beings of securing and developing mutual understanding in the everyday conduct of life. Then there are the critical sciences (Habermas includes here psychoanalysis and the critique of ideology), which are governed by the intent to bring about emancipation from the relations of dependence that ideology in particular has set in place and that come to appear to us as natural. In other words, 'the specific viewpoints from which we can apprehend reality as such in any way whatsoever' are an orientation 'toward technical control', or an orientation 'toward mutual understanding', or an orientation 'toward emancipation' (Habermas 1972, p. 311).

Habermas's treatment of this issue is already set very firmly in the context of language. He has avidly embraced the 'linguistic turn' in philosophy (referred to above in our discussion of hermeneutics). In *On the Logic of the Social Sciences*, first published in 1967, Habermas (1988, p. 117) describes language as 'the web to whose threads subjects cling and through which they develop into subjects in the first place'. He concludes, 'Today the problem of language has taken the place of the traditional problem of consciousness'. A year later, in *Knowledge and Human Interests* (1972, p. 314), he continues this theme: 'What raises us out of nature is the only thing whose nature we can know: language. Through its structure, autonomy and responsibility are posited for us'.

This emphasis on language, and thereby on communicative action, grows even more marked in the later works. It is precisely in communication that he hopes to find a foundation for his critical social theory.

> Habermas's entire project, from the critique of contemporary scientism to the reconstruction of historical materialism, rests on the possibility of providing an account of communication that is both theoretical and normative, that goes beyond a pure hermeneutics without being reducible to a strictly empirical-analytic science. (McCarthy 1984, p. 272)

It is in this vein that we find Habermas elucidating the notion of 'systematically distorted communication', expounding a 'theory of communicative competence', and setting forth the conditions for the 'ideal speech situation' (1970a, 1970b). The ideal speech situation is one that is free from systematic distortion, allows unimpaired self-presentation by participants, and is characterised by mutuality of expectations rather than one-sided norms. In such a situation, discourse is 'unrestrained and universal' and enables an 'unconstrained consensus' to emerge whereby the idea of truth can be analysed (Habermas 1970b, pp. 370–2). For Habermas, as Anthony Giddens observes:

> The ideal-speech situation, held to be immanent in all language use, provides an energising vision of emancipation. The more social circumstances approximate to an ideal-speech situation, the more a social order based on the autonomous action of free and equal individuals will emerge. (1991, p. 213)

Habermas goes on to set forth a theory of discourse and a consensus theory of truth (1973). Discourse is distinguished from communicative action. The latter is the interaction that takes place in everyday life and in it claims to validity are more or less naively accepted. Discourse, on the other hand, constitutes an unusual form of communication in which the participants subject themselves to the force of the better argument, with the view of coming to an agreement about the validity or invalidity of problematic claims. In discourse the beliefs, norms and values that are taken for granted in everyday interaction are expressly thematised and subjected to critique. And, according to Habermas, discourses become institutionalised for certain domains, one such domain being that of practical questions and political decisions. 'It should be obvious that it is the institutionalization of this last type of discourse (practico-political) that is the guiding light of Habermas's critical social theory' (McCarthy 1984, p. 293).

In 1976 Habermas published *Communication and the Evolution of Society*, which contains his essay 'What is universal pragmatics?'. Here his thought has moved to a broader understanding of communicative action and focuses more sharply on moral reasoning. He is arguing the case for a cognitive—indeed, a communicative—ethics as the normative basis of critical theory. Where there is consensus about norms that is free from constraint and representative of the common good, Habermas is ready to accord it universality. Moreover, this normative principle of universalisation is, for him, the stepping stone to social critique, which is always his ultimate goal. He accepts the need to ground this principle and finds a basis for it in the general presuppositions of communication. He argues that competent speakers raise invariable and universal validity claims. As Habermas puts it, 'the general and unavoidable—in this sense transcendental—conditions of possible understanding have a normative content' (1979, p. 2). The project of discovering and articulating these general presuppositions of possible understanding is what Habermas refers to as 'universal pragmatics'.

> Habermas's work on universal pragmatics . . . represents a much stronger attempt to provide a normative foundation for social theory through an examination of communicative competence, understood in terms of the ability of a speaker to master the rules for embedding utterances in speech

acts. Such an examination, in the form of a universal pragmatics, attempts to uncover the general and unavoidable presuppositions of communication by identifying and reconstructing the universal conditions of possible understanding. Habermas attempts to synthesise the work of Chomsky, Hymes, Austin and Searle in the framework of a general theory of social action. (Roderick 1986, p. 97)

As the title of his 1976 work attests, Habermas is addressing not only communication (in his universal pragmatics) but also social evolution. He sees the evolution of society proceeding by way of processes of learning that go on within it and adaptations that occur at every level of learning to accommodate the learning processes. Most importantly, there are always contingent forces at work to induce new learning levels. Habermas makes much of the systems problems that occur in any given society. These create crises and demand a response. The systems problems, along with the learning processes that emerge in response to them, provide the dynamism for social development.

There are two dimensions to these processes of learning: they involve moral–practical knowledge (developments in the relations of production) and empirical–analytic knowledge (development in the forces of knowledge). This sounds Marxist enough and, in fact, Habermas sees his theory of social evolution as a reconstruction of historical materialism. 'The analysis of developmental dynamics', he writes (1979, p. 123), 'is "materialist" in so far as it makes reference to crisis-producing systems problems in the domain of production and reproduction; and the analysis remains "historically oriented" in so far as it has to seek the causes of evolutionary changes in the whole range of . . . contingent circumstances'.

In 1981 Habermas once more returned to Frankfurt. He had left Frankfurt for Starnberg ten years earlier to become director of the Max Planck Institute for Research on Living Conditions in the Scientific and Technical World. His return to Frankfurt coincided with the publication of his two-volume *The Theory of Communicative Action*, which encapsulates the program for an interdisciplinary social theory he had developed over the decade spent at Starnberg.

It was intended to provide the normative basis and the fundamental conceptual framework for the programme, sketched out at the close of the two volumes, for an updated critical theory of society: a programme of interdisciplinary research into the selective patterns of capitalist modernization that had led to the collision between the imperatives of the economic and political system, on the one hand, and the original communicative structures of the life-world, on the other. (Wiggershaus 1994, p. 658)

What Habermas begins in *The Theory of Communicative Action* he continues in *The Philosophical Discourse of Modernity*, originally published in Frankfurt in 1985. The focus remains on what Wiggershaus has termed a collision between economic and political imperatives and the communicative structures of the lifeworld. Against a backdrop of political and ethical concerns, which he elaborates more expressly in still later writings, Habermas analyses two ways of considering reason. First, there is the understanding of reason that comes to us in modernity. Here the question of reason is framed, as Rasmussen (1990, p. 4) points out, 'within the philosophy of consciousness with its concern for the development of a subject'. What modernity seeks is a justification of subject-centred reason. Over against that project, however, another endeavour has emerged. The contemporary philosophy of language repudiates the subject so central to the project of modernity, 'finding whatever reason there is within the confines of linguistic usage' (1990, p. 4). These are two quite different agendas. From them arises the question whether the dilemmas of modernity can be reformulated under the rubrics of a philosophy of language centred on a theory of communication. This, in fact, was 'the question which is at the core of the post–1981 Habermasian reflection' (1990, p. 4).

The critical theory of the Frankfurt School, as Horkheimer's distinction between traditional theory and critical theory shows, sought from the start emancipation from the tyranny of instrumental reason. This was carried out in terms of a philosophy of consciousness and Habermas himself engaged in this enterprise in his earlier work. Now, by situating the issue within a philosophy of language instead, he looks to achieve what he sees earlier critical theory failing to achieve. He also looks to achieve what he sees postmodernism failing to achieve. Thus, *The Philosophical Discourse of Modernity* critiques Nietzsche and especially Heidegger, as a lead-in to a critique of Foucault and Derrida. For Habermas, postmodernism, 'having placed itself under the Heideggerian banner, represents a certain moral vacuity, an absence of the proper place for the normative question' (Rasmussen 1990, p. 109).

What, then, is Habermas's answer to the question that has just been posed? Can the dilemmas of modernity be reframed in terms of a philosophy of language and a theory of communication? Clearly, Habermas's answer is in the affirmative. For him, communicative reason is not the same as subject-centred, instrumental reason. The very structure of communicative discourse is emancipatory because 'embedded within the linguistic paradigm, under the rubric of communication, one finds the fundamental assertions of the project of modernity in their reconstructed

form, as essentially scientific claims' (Rasmussen 1990, p. 6). Undoubtedly, 'the project of modernity can be redeemed' (1990, p. 5).

*Reason. Language. Communication. A normative foundation for social
critique.* These have been constants throughout most of Habermas's
intellectual history. Not that it is easy to track the course that these
elements of his thought have taken. Habermas's thought never stands
still. Yet pursuing such a quarry is well and truly worth the effort. Highly
theoretical as his thought may be, it needs to be remembered that theory
for Habermas 'is a product of and serves the purpose of human action'
and 'is essentially a means to greater human freedom' (Craib 1984,
p. 206). Writing of the historical and theoretical work done in the cause
of radical theory, Roderick (1986, p. 173) points up the eminently
practical and essentially democratic purposes Habermas has in mind.
'Habermas's own work, read as a supplement to Marx and not as
a replacement, also contributes to this continuation of radical theory
by forging a link between Marxism and a radical democracy in which
all political decisions are subjected to the discussion of a reasoning
public.'

PAULO FREIRE'S PEDAGOGY OF THE OPPRESSED

Research in the vein of critical inquiry cannot escape the influence of
Paulo Freire (1921–97), whose best known work is *Pedagogy of the
Oppressed* (1972a).

Freire was a Brazilian educationalist who launched literacy programs
among the peasant peoples of north-east Brazil in and around Recife in
the early 1960s. He was a member of the Movement of Popular Culture
in Recife and spent a lot of time in the slums, engaged in dialogue with
the poor. So, while he received his doctorate from the University of
Recife in 1959 and became its professor of the history and philosophy
of education, he was no armchair academic but spelled out in his own
life and practice what he was later to articulate in his writings: that
reflection without action is empty 'verbalism'.

Freire's very effective approach to teaching literacy became so well
known that in 1963 Brazil's Ministry of Education agreed to a large-scale
literacy campaign employing his approach. Training courses for coordi-
nators started up throughout the country and it was estimated that
within a year there would be 20 000 groups in operation. This would
enable some two million people at a time to pursue the three-months
course that was envisaged. Clearly, within a few years such a campaign
would make significant inroads into Brazil's illiteracy problem.

The campaign, however, was not to last for a few years. In April 1964 the Brazilian government was toppled by a military coup. Freire was jailed for 75 days and declared expelled from the University of Recife. He was released but forced into exile. He went first to Chile, where he set up his literacy program once again. However, with the assassination of Allende and the inauguration of Pinochet's repressive regime in that country, Freire found himself once more in exile. Out of the country at the time of the assassination, he was declared *persona non grata*. He began teaching at Harvard University, later becoming a special consultant to the Office of Education of the World Council of Churches in Geneva.

What is it about Freire's way of teaching people to read and write that proves such a threat to the powers-that-be? In seeking an answer to this question, we might take note of his starting point. Freire does not begin by teaching his peasant groups the alphabet or showing them how to spell words chosen for them to learn. Instead, he spends time with the communities, learning himself the words that are meaningful to the people, words that evoke responses in them. These he calls 'generative words' and it is these words that he portrays in visual form and invites the people to discuss as a community. He suggests that they dissect these words and put them together in different forms. He wants them to feel that they have power over their words and can exercise power over them. This is no mere pedagogical technique. It intimately reflects Freire's philosophy of existence, as we shall see.

Freire's method proved highly successful not only in developing literacy skills but in arousing critical awareness among the peasants and workers. Understandably, it met with constant criticism and attack from the upper and middle classes in Brazil. These enjoyed a monopoly of power and privilege, both because illiterate people were not eligible to vote and because lack of social and political awareness made it easy to manipulate those of the lower classes who did vote. These beneficiaries of the *status quo* were the people who supported the 1964 military coup and it is not surprising that they found Freire-style literacy programs threatening.

The word most associated with Freire is 'conscientisation'. According to Freire, the word first came to be used at the Institute of Brazilian Studies in the late 1950s. While Freire did not originate the word, it was he who popularised it and bestowed upon it the rich content it possesses today. Etymologically, the word is straightforward enough. To conscientise is to render conscious. Conscientisation is an awakening of, or increase in, consciousness. When describing the process of conscientisation, Freire also uses terms like 'critical consciousness', 'critical perception', or 'critical thinking'. In one key passage (Freire 1972a, pp. 65–5) he defines critical thinking as 'thinking which discerns an indivisible solidarity between the world and men'. Critical thinking, he adds, 'perceives reality as process and transformation, rather than as a static entity'. It is 'thinking which does not separate itself from action' (pp. 64–5).

In these words we discern the philosophical underpinnings of Freire's pedagogy. Freire is known primarily as a Marxist. He certainly draws upon Marxist thought, and, of course, upon the revolutionary and liberationist literature of Latin America. Yet he can also be said to stand in the tradition of existential phenomenology and we find him citing such thinkers as Husserl, Buber, Ortega y Gasset, Marcel and Sartre. In the words just cited, Freire links conscientisation to the relationship between humans and their world, to the essentially historical character of human being, and to 'praxis' as a form of reflection that stems from, and remains indissolubly wedded to, active human intervention in reality. In short, he brings together his notion of conscientisation and his understanding of what it means to be human.

FREIRE AND HUMAN BEING

As Freire has said, there is indivisible solidarity between humans and their world. No dichotomy can be made between the two. 'Authentic reflection considers neither abstract man nor the world without men, but men in their relations with the world' (Freire 1972a, p. 54). A favourite phrase of Freire's puts it this way: we are not only 'in' the world, but also 'with' the world, that is, essentially related to it (1972b, p. 51).

In this view of things the world is *our* world in a very radical sense. We are rooted in this world, and in us humans the world has come to consciousness. Because of this, the world is now subject not merely to natural evolution but to an historical evolution in which human beings have a guiding hand. Our task is to exercise in the world the creative responsibility that is our characteristic as persons.

As conscious beings, humans are endowed with creative imagination. This means that they find themselves confronted not by brute factuality, sheer material circumstance, but by what can only be described as a *human* situation. This is a situation that holds creative possibilities, for humans are able to see it not only in terms of what it is but also in terms of what it can be. They can do something about their situation and, precisely as human beings, they are called to do something about it. This, and only this, is the kind of freedom human beings enjoy. It is a situated freedom, an embodied freedom—not the freedom to realise absolute, abstract ideals as such, but the freedom to address themselves to their situation, seize upon its growing points, and out of the worse to create the better.

The 'point of departure of the movement', Freire tells us, lies in human beings themselves. Since humans do not exist apart from the world, the movement must begin with the relationship they have with their world. This means the 'here and now'—the situation within which they are submerged. They must emerge from that situation, reflect upon it, and intervene in it. They are able to do this only if they perceive their state not as the outcome of inexorable fate, not as something unalterable, but merely as limiting and therefore challenging (Freire 1972a, p. 57).

This is a never-ending enterprise. As we continue to modify our environment through our human activity, that is, as we continue to fashion 'culture', ever new challenges and ever new tasks arise for us. It is the story of this ongoing interplay between us and our world that constitutes human history and characterises us as essentially historical beings. Animals have no 'historical sense' and merely adapt to the world, but human beings have 'an historical and a value dimension' and a 'sense of "project"' (Freire 1972b, p. 21).

Although there is 'indivisible solidarity' between human beings and their world, they are not in the world as one object alongside other objects. As a thinking and free being (or, to use Freire's frequent expression, as a 'Subject'), the human being is in the world in a unique way. Because of this unique human presence, it is, in fact, never a merely material universe but always a human world (Freire 1972a, p. 55) and what humans do in it never has physical consequences only. In constantly transforming their environment, women and men are shaping the very conditions for their existence and their life. They are changing themselves, therefore. The call of human beings to creative initiative extends to their own being, so that human freedom comes ultimately to mean a self-creating.

This self-creating too is a never-ending historical project. 'Historical', yes. As the famous phrase of Ortega y Gasset puts it, human beings have no nature; what they have is history (1964, p. 41). Freire expresses the same thought. Human beings must be seen 'as beings in the process of becoming—as unfinished, uncompleted beings in and with a likewise unfinished reality' (Freire 1972a, pp. 56–7). They are beings who move forward and look ahead. For such beings immobility represents a fatal threat. There is 'no history *for* men; there is only history *of* men, made by men and (as Marx pointed out) in turn making them' (1972a, p. 101).

Accordingly, to ask who human beings are or what it means to be human is to ask what human beings have made of themselves.

PRAXIS AND DIALOGUE

The solidarity between human beings and their world bridges the classical objective/subjective dichotomy. Freire's epistemology rejects both 'mechanistic objectivism' (wherein consciousness is considered to be merely a copy of objective reality) and 'solipsism' (which reduces the world to a capricious creation of consciousness) (Freire 1972b, p. 53). On the contrary, we must recognise the unity between subjectivity and objectivity in the act of knowing. Reality is never simply the 'objective datum' but is also people's perception of it (1972b, p. 31).

Sadler expresses this same viewpoint:

> The classical distinction between subject and object, between consciousness and thing, between interpretation of the mind and objective facts has broken down . . . Experience is completely a mixture of subjective and objective, of fact and interpretation, of consciousness and thing. (1969, pp. 14–16)

To denote the fact that the dynamic structure of consciousness is inseparable from the objects that inform it, in other words, that 'authentic thought-language' is generated in and out of a dialectical relationship between human beings and their concrete historical and cultural reality (Freire 1972b, p. 13), Freire uses the word employed by Brentano, Husserl and the phenomenologists generally—intentionality. The intentionality of consciousness means that consciousness is never a mere reflection of material reality but is a reflection *upon* material reality (1972b, p. 53). Consciousness is already an active intervention into reality. Critical reflection is already action (Freire 1972a, p. 99).

Authentic action and reflection are indissolubly united, therefore. This is Freire's understanding of *praxis*. It is 'reflection and action upon the world in order to transform it' (Freire 1972a, p. 28). True praxis can never be merely cerebral. It must involve action. Nor can it be limited to mere activism. It must include serious reflection (1972a, pp. 40–1). Freire regards reflection without action as sheer verbalism, 'armchair revolution', whereas action without reflection is 'pure activism', that is, action for action's sake (1972a, p. 41).

Action and reflection must go together even in the temporal sense. Freire insists (1972a, p. 99) that praxis cannot be divided into a prior stage of reflection and a subsequent stage of action. Action and reflection take place at the same time. When they do—when action and reflection are united—they become creative. They 'constantly and mutually illuminate each other' (Freire 1976, p. 149).

It is praxis that leads to conscientisation. 'Conscientisation', writes Freire (1976, p. 146), 'cannot be arrived at by a psychological, idealist subjectivist road, nor through objectivism'. Praxis is the only route (Freire 1972b, p. 78).

The action referred to is what Freire refers to as critical self-insertion into the reality of one's own situation. As he never tires of pointing out, human beings are called to be re-creators, not mere spectators, of the world (1972a, p. 49). They are meant to be Subjects and not merely objects of their history. For them, the world is to be seen not as some kind of static reality but as a reality in process. They are called to transform it—and thereby to transform themselves. Hence we find Freire speaking of 'the unfinished character of men and the transformational character of reality' (1972a, pp. 56–7).

It is this kind of action—human beings engaged in intervention in the world as transformers of that world—that results in the development of critical consciousness (Freire 1972a, p. 47). This critical conscious-ness, in its turn, leads to further action (1972a, p. 81). In and through such action, people cease to see their situation 'as a dense, enveloping reality or a tormenting blind alley'. Instead, it emerges as 'an historical reality susceptible of transformation'. (1972a, p. 58).

Yet, if humans are to take charge as Subjects and not mere objects of their own history, what direction are they to give to that history? If they must intervene in the reality of their own situation, seeing that situation as capable of transformation, to what end are they to intervene? What kind of transformation are they to effect? Freire's answer is summed up in the word 'humanisation'. When people confront their situation, they discover in it the obstacles to their humanisation and a call to struggle against them (Freire 1972a, p. 90).

The historic task of human beings, and their central problem as well, is to become more fully human. No one escapes this 'ontological and historical vocation' of becoming more fully human (Freire 1972a, p. 58). Freire sees dehumanisation as both a possibility and an historical reality. Unlike other animals, which cannot be de-animalised, humans can be dehumanised. They can fail to become fully human. They can become less human (Freire 1972b, p. 55). Such dehumanisation is the charac-teristic of exploitation, oppression and all other forms of injustice, marking both those whose humanity is stolen and those who have stolen it. It is the result of an unjust order that engenders in the oppressors a violence that in turn dehumanises the oppressed. So emerges 'the great humanistic and historical task of the oppressed', namely, to liberate themselves and their oppressors as well (1972a, pp. 20–1).

In confronting us with this task of conscientisation—of moving towards humanisation through praxis—Freire is not addressing us as individuals. Conscientisation does not take place in abstract beings but in real people and in actual social structures. For Freire, this is proof enough that it cannot remain on the level of the individual (1976, pp. 146–7). The pursuit of full humanity, he tells us (1972a, p. 58), cannot be carried out in isolation or individualism. It can only take place in fellowship and solidarity.

Action/reflection in fellowship and solidarity is precisely what Freire means by dialogue. Without dialogue, there can be no conscientisation. Conscientisation is a 'joint project'. It takes place in human beings among other human beings. These are human beings united by their action and their reflection upon that action and upon the world (Freire 1972b, p. 75).

Nor, without dialogue, can there be liberation. As Freire puts it (1972a, p. 103), 'we can legitimately say that in the process of oppression someone oppresses someone else; we cannot say that in the process of revolution someone liberates someone else, nor yet that someone liberates himself, but rather that men in communion liberate each other'.

For its part, true dialogue cannot exist without critical thinking. This is a two-way street, however, for only dialogue is capable of generating critical thinking (Freire 1972a, pp. 64–5). For this reason, Freire's adult literacy programs are, as he believes all education ought to be, programs of vital dialogue from start to finish—'dialogical *par excellence*' (1972a, p. 81). In dialogical education, learners and educators are regarded 'as equally knowing subjects' (Freire 1972b, p. 31). The educator is the students' partner as they engage together in critical thinking and a quest for mutual humanisation (Freire 1972a, p. 49).

Over against this kind of education stands what Freire calls the 'banking' concept of education. In banking education the teacher resembles someone putting money into a bank, the students being regarded as empty receptacles into which the teacher deposits knowledge. The method is monological, not dialogical. This, of course, has been a common approach to education and it serves the interests of the *status quo* and those who are its beneficiaries, for it results in acceptance and adaptation rather than any move towards change (Freire 1972a, p. 47).

Freire contrasts this with a pedagogy of the oppressed in which the teacher/students dichotomy vanishes. The teacher is no longer merely the one who teaches, for the teacher is also taught in dialogue with the students. And the students, while being taught, also teach. In this way, teacher and students become jointly responsible for a process in which all of them grow (Freire 1972a, p. 53).

While banking education is a mechanistic theory that reduces the practice of education to a complex of techniques, Freire's pedagogy of the oppressed—dialogical education—is radically different. He describes it as 'cultural action for freedom' (1972b, p. 13). If this sounds revolutionary, it is because it *is* revolutionary. Freire sees cultural action for freedom and cultural revolution as but two moments in the one revolutionary process. The difference is simply that, while cultural action for freedom takes place in opposition to the dominating power, cultural revolution takes place in harmony with the revolutionary regime. Authentic revolution, that is, political change that is no mere *coup d'état* or the development of 'sclerotic bureaucracy' (Freire 1972b, p. 82), can be effected only through conscientisation. Consequently, it can be effected only through dialogue, the *sine qua non* of conscientisation.

And this dialogue out of which revolution is born must persist. It must become 'a permanent process of self-scrutiny' (Freire 1972b, p. 83).

THE CULTURE OF SILENCE

In all this Freire is led by a concern for 'the oppressed'. These are the masses upon whom, within culturally alienated societies, a regime of oppression is imposed by the power elites. Freire speaks 'as a man of the Third World' (1972b, pp. 16–17). Yet, when he left Latin America and went to the United States in 1967, he discovered that the 'Third World' is not a geographical concept but essentially socio-political in character. The blacks and other minorities in the USA, he learned, constitute the Third World within North American society, just as the elites in Latin America play the role of the First World *vis-à-vis* the workers and the peasant communities. So it is for oppressed peoples everywhere that Freire seeks conscientisation and liberation.

Conscientisation does not come easy, however. For the oppressed to become critically aware of their true situation, intervene in its reality and thus take charge of their destiny, is peculiarly difficult because they belong to 'the culture of silence'. Freire uses this term because, in their condition of oppression, the masses are 'mute'. They have no voice. They are excluded from any active role in the transformation of their society and are therefore 'prohibited from being' (Freire 1972b, p. 30). Not only do they not have a voice, but, worse still, they are unaware that they do not have a voice—in other words, that they cannot exercise their right to participate consciously in the socio-historical transformation of their society (Freire 1972b, p. 30).

In the culture of silence, the dominated have introjected the cultural myths of the dominators. The oppressed internalise the image of the oppressor and adopt the oppressor's guidelines. As Freire points out many times, the oppressor comes to be 'housed' within the oppressed and they seek to be like the oppressor. Freire points to oppressed people who want agrarian reform, not to become free, but to become 'bosses over other workers' (Freire 1972a, p. 23). Among the myths that they internalise is the myth of their own natural inferiority (1972b, p. 30). They come to see themselves as the oppressor sees them, and needs to see them, and needs to have them see themselves—as incompetent, lazy, prodigal, and so on.

In this way, the very situation of exploitation and oppression begets lack of awareness, apathy, fatalism, absence of self-respect—even a fear of freedom. 'Functionally, oppression is domesticating.' This is the culture of silence. The oppressed are submerged in their situation and, as long as they remain so submerged, they cannot be active Subjects intervening in reality; they cannot become engaged in the struggle for their own liberation (Freire 1972a, pp. 27–8). They need help to emerge and engage in that struggle.

How to help in this process of emergence? Unsurprisingly, Freire totally rejects the donor–recipient approach that finds solutions *for* the people instead of *with* the people and imposes these solutions upon them. This approach will not do. It must be remembered at all times that the oppressed 'are fighting not merely for freedom from hunger, but, to quote Fromm's *The Heart of Man*, for ". . . freedom to create and to construct, to wonder and to venture. Such freedom requires that the individual be active and responsible, not a slave or a well-fed cog in the machine"' (Freire 1972a, p. 43).

The only valid approach, Freire believes, is the way of dialogue. Whether we are speaking of education as cultural action for freedom or of the further phase of cultural revolution, the oppressed cannot be liberated without their reflective participation in the act of liberation (Freire 1972a, p. 41). This must be 'not pseudo-participation, but committed involvement' (1972a, p. 44).

To foster participation of this kind, there must be trust in the oppressed and their ability to reason (Freire 1972a, p. 41). True enough, in a situation of alienation people may be impaired in their use of that power. Those promoting dialogue among them may therefore need to be critical. Their faith in the people will not be naïve. Nevertheless, a basic belief in the oppressed's power 'to make and remake, to create and re-create' remains indispensable. Without such faith, 'dialogue is a farce which inevitably degenerates into paternalistic manipulation' (Freire 1972a, pp. 63–4).

Given this faith in human beings, Freire looks to a methodology that is 'dialogical, problem-posing and conscientising' (1976, p. 157). In 'problem-posing' we strike another key word in Freire's thought. He wants to place the oppressed in a consciously critical confrontation with their problems (1976, p. 16). This is Freire's 'problematisation', a peda-gogical process that presents the concrete, existential situation of those involved in the dialogue as a set of problems. The problems are consid-ered challenges to intervene in the reality of their situation and transform it. This problem-posing approach requires them to emerge from their situation and reflect upon it. They have a 'focalised' view of their own reality that the culture of silence has imposed upon them and they must move from this to a view that sees their reality as a totality—with all its causes and consequences. This is critical thinking.

Critical thinking sounds the death knell to the popular myths that have hitherto shackled the people's consciousness. Problematisation is at the same time a 'demythicisation'. Hence we find Freire pointing up 'the oft-emphasised necessity of posing as problems the myths fed to the people by the oppressors' (1972a, p. 132).

With this demythicisation comes a new view of reality and a founded hope for freedom. It makes possible a conscientised people. These are people who encounter one another in the common search to be more human. They are people emerging from their situation to reflect upon it and cast aside the culture of silence that has held their consciousness submerged. They are people whose critical awareness melds reflection and action and enables them to transform their lives in a new-found spirit of hope and courage.

DRAWING ON FREIRE

A number of questions remain.

In Freire, for instance, we find little of, say, Alinsky's preoccupation with community organisation (Alinsky 1972). Yet, when people become critically aware and take action to humanise their situation, their social and political organisation and the creation of necessary institutions assume central importance. Freire is very aware of this, at least by the time he comes to write *Pedagogy of the Oppressed*, but seems to offer little help in this connection beyond demanding that social and political organisation be dialogical and not authoritarian, so as to preserve authentic freedom at all times.

Another question touches the relevance of Freire's thought to our kind of society. Applying Freire's approach to a society like ours requires that we first identify the forms—often very subtle forms—that oppression takes in a society like ours. Freire's later works, especially *Pedagogy of the City* (1993), are of more help in addressing such questions.

In these later works as in the earliest, Paulo Freire speaks with authority and passion. As we ponder the spirit of critical inquiry brought by researchers to methodologies such as action research and critical ethnography, his is not an easy voice to ignore.

CRITICAL INQUIRY TODAY

Critical forms of research call current ideology into question, and initiate action, in the cause of social justice. In the type of inquiry spawned by the critical spirit, researchers find themselves interrogating commonly held values and assumptions, challenging conventional social structures, and engaging in social action.

Fuelling this enterprise is an abiding concern with issues of power and oppression. Critical inquiry keeps the spotlight on power relationships within society so as to expose the forces of hegemony and injustice. It is at all times alive to the contribution that false consciousness makes to oppression and manipulation and invites researchers and participants (ideally one and the same) to discard false consciousness, open themselves to new ways of understanding, and take effective action for change.

Critical inquiry cannot be viewed as a discrete piece of action that achieves its objectives and comes to a close. With every action taken, the context changes and we must critique our assumptions again. Viewed in this way, critical inquiry emerges as an ongoing project. It is a cyclical process (better seen, perhaps, as a *spiralling* process for there is movement forward and upward) of reflection and action.

The goals of critical inquiry—the just society, freedom, equity—may appear utopian. Nevertheless, while critical inquirers admit the impossibility of effecting consummate social justice, they believe their struggle to be worthwhile. It can lead at least to a more just and freer society than we have at the moment.

Kincheloe and McLaren (1994, pp. 139–40) offer us a picture of 'criticalist' researchers and theorists. They believe that criticalists, people who use their work as a form of social or cultural criticism, accept these basic assumptions:

- that all thought is fundamentally mediated by power relations that are social in nature and historically constituted;
- that facts can never be isolated from the domain of values or removed from ideological inscription;
- that the relationship between concept and object, and between signifier and signified, is never stable and is often mediated by the social relations of capitalist production and consumption;

- that language is central to the formation of subjectivity, that is, both conscious and unconscious awareness;
- that certain groups in any society are privileged over others, constituting an oppression that is most forceful when subordinates accept their social status as natural, necessary or inevitable;
- that oppression has many faces, and concern for only one form of oppression at the expense of others can be counterproductive because of the connections between them;
- that mainstream research practices are generally implicated, albeit often unwittingly, in the reproduction of systems of class, race and gender oppression.

Of obvious and, indeed, primary concern to critical theorists are dominative relationships. Critical inquiry illuminates the relationship between power and culture and, in this picture of things, culture comes to be looked upon with a good measure of suspicion. For most of our civilised past it has not been seen in this light. In fact, culture has tended to be canonised. Marcuse (1968) points out how, from Plato on, culture is seen as a realm apart from the nitty gritty of social life and material necessity. The ancients were honest enough about this. They accepted ('with good conscience', Marcuse says) that most people had to spend their lives providing for material necessities while a smaller number could devote themselves to enjoyment and truth. In this view, culture was at least able to act as the critic of society, society coming to be seen as an imperfect and inferior mode of existence with 'culture' upholding the ideal.

This 'good conscience', according to Marcuse, disappears with the emergence of capitalism. Bourgeois society transforms culture into a matter of the 'soul', the inner self, setting up a dichotomy between 'the real and the ideal, the transitory and the permanent, the material and the meaningful, the outer world of ugly fact and an inner world of harmony called the soul' (Brenkman 1987, p. 6). Strangely, the one now becomes the justification for the other. Instead of challenging and condemning the visible world of society, culture becomes a justification of it and an apologia for it. It becomes, in Marcuse's term, 'affirmative'. We can now play down the fact that so many people are excluded from the earth's material riches because, it is claimed, they all have equal access to the richness of culture. This, Marcuse tells us, is 'the thesis of the universality and the universal validity of "culture"' (Marcuse 1968, p. 93). Meaning, value, truth—they are there, without discrimination, for all who want them. In this fashion, affirmative culture 'exonerated external conditions from responsibility for the "vocation of man", thus stabilizing their injustice' (1968, p. 120).

In contradistinction to this view of culture as affirmative is the recognition by critical inquirers that culture is not a realm apart from the give-and-take of everyday society but mirrors its contradictions and oppressions. More than once we have recalled Marx's tenet: social being determines consciousness, not the other way round. Consequently, the 'violence that founded and continues through our social history is also a violence against consciousness' (Brenkman 1987, p. 4).

This is why criticalists cannot share the unalloyed confidence interpretivists tend to place in accounts of experience turned up by their research. Where most interpretivists today embrace such accounts as descriptions of authentic 'lived experience', critical researchers hear in them the voice of an inherited tradition and a prevailing culture. John Dewey (1929, p. 34) alerted us to that voice many decades ago. Our experience 'seems to be fresh, naïve empirical material'. Yet, Dewey warns us, it is 'filled with interpretations, classifications, due to sophisticated thought'. It 'is already overlaid and saturated with the products of the reflection of past generations and by-gone ages'. According to Dewey, these 'incorporated results of past reflection' are likely to 'obfuscate and distort' unless they are detected. Criticalists make a sustained effort to detect them. In addition, they emphasise, as Dewey did not, that the tradition echoing though personal accounts of experience is a tradition founded on exploitation and resounds with overtones of domination and unfreedom. Where most intepretivists are content to adopt a professedly uncritical stance *vis-à-vis* the culture they are exploring— indeed, may demand such a stance—criticalists insist that the culture and the accounts it informs be radically called into question.

Critical inquiry may be as radical as Adorno's negative dialectics or Freire's movement towards conscientisation—or it may not. The spirit of social critique, as we have seen, expresses itself in many ways. Through all this diversity, however, critical inquiry remains a form of praxis—a search for knowledge, to be sure, but always emancipatory knowledge, knowledge in the context of action and the search for freedom.

It is in this mood of critical reflection on social reality in readiness to take action for change that critical researchers come to the tasks of human inquiry.

8

FEMINISM: RE-VISIONING THE MAN-MADE WORLD

... and these are the forces they had ranged against us
and these are the forces we had ranged within us,
within us and against us, against us and within us.

Adrienne Rich, 'Poem XVII'

How do feminists envisage the human world they inhabit? And what, in consequence, are the assumptions that feminist researchers bring to their various forms of human inquiry?

These questions, formulated here to target feminism and feminist research, are questions we have already addressed to positivism, interpretivism and critical inquiry. In doing so, we have in each case been forced to take account of the pluralism that obtains. For a start, as we saw, there are many positivisms. The same must be said of interpretivism. Not only has interpretivism emerged historically in the threefold guise of hermeneutics, phenomenology and symbolic interactionism, but each of these assumes a range of distinct forms that are not easily reconciled and are sometimes irreconcilable. Critical inquiry too has a long history. The divergences found to arise within just one 'school' in this tradition are warning enough that we cannot facilely lump together theoretical stances whose differences are as striking as their commonalities. Nor can we ignore the differences in social research posture and procedure that these stances call for.

It would be unrealistic to expect feminism to be different. Here too we come up against a wide-ranging pluralism. People may speak and write of 'feminism' in the singular, just as they speak and write of 'positivism', 'interpretivism' and 'critical theory' in the singular, but there are, of course, many feminisms. Feminists make sense of the world in a myriad of ways and bring differing, even conflicting, assumptions to their research. Feminism speaks with one voice in characterising the world it experiences as a patriarchal world and the culture it inherits as a masculinist culture, but this unity is short-lived. What do patriarchy and masculinism mean? How do patriarchy and masculinism arise? What, in sociological terms, is the paramount *locus* wherein patriarchy and masculinism are encountered and identified? From where do patriarchy and masculinism draw their essential support? And are these, in fact, the questions it is most relevant to ask? Merely to raise issues like these is to point up the heterogeneity of feminist thought.

Here once more, then, there is place for some 'sorting out'.

For a male to presume to do such sorting out, even when relying overall on women's texts, calls for a good measure of courage or foolhardiness. Probably both. There are those who would assert without qualification that a man can have nothing valid or useful to say about feminism or feminist research. While the literature carries references enough to male feminists and feminist males, to a large number of feminist writers these terms are oxymorons.

> We reject the idea that men can be feminists because we argue that what is essential to 'being feminist' is the possession of 'feminist consciousness'. And we see feminist consciousness as rooted in the concrete, practical and everyday experiences of being, and being treated as, *a woman*. (Stanley and Wise 1983, p. 18)

Given Stanley and Wise's definition of 'being feminist', theirs is impeccable logic. The definition is not unchallengeable, of course, and it surely has anomalous implications. On these grounds, a woman emerges as a genuine feminist if, espousing a weak form of liberal feminism, she is content to see meagre gains for women in workplace opportunities which leave all systems and structures in place and essentially intact, male-derived though they are. Not so a far more radically minded male who insists that sexism permeates the very fabric of society and the culture that sustains it and warns that women will never experience justice or achieve any measure of equality without fundamental changes to cultural thought patterns and societal structures. The mantle of feminism is denied to the latter because he is male and therefore unable to share feminine consciousness.

The same logic would deny to whites the possibility of their being in any formal sense members of the black movement for civil rights. However anti-racist their sentiments and whatever they might do for the cause, they are unable to share the consciousness and experience of people of colour. Yet the important role whites have played in movements for emancipation and racial justice cannot be denied. Feminist writer Alison Assiter writes of how African people have revealed the Eurocentrism of modern science. Those who have played this role are 'African people who spoke from a commitment to the emancipation of Africans from white domination'. She adds, however: 'One does not have to be African to hold these values; potentially, anyone would be able to join the relevant community' (1996, p. 87).

Echoing around us, at the same time, is Freire's clear assertion, referred to in the previous chapter, that no one can liberate somebody else. As Freire sees it, no one can even liberate herself or himself. Instead, people together—yes, people in fellowship—liberate one another. That being so, there is no escaping the need for the women of this world, in solidarity with one another, to engage in a movement for deliverance from oppression and the attainment of equality. No one can do it for them. It can only be their movement. Women must lead it and constitute its core.

Nevertheless, a 'movement'—a much looser concept than, say, 'institution' or 'organisation'—allows for a broad range of affiliations and diverse modes of participation and action. Just as whites have joined blacks in their struggle, to the advantage of the movement as a whole, men can surely join women in theirs—peripherally, to be sure, but not the less wholeheartedly for that. Nor is such involvement to be seen as some kind of exercise in altruism. Men's own interests are utterly at stake. They are, after all, victims as well as perpetrators of patriarchy and sexism. At one point it became something of a truism in feminist literature but it bears repeating: patriarchy and sexism are not fetters worn by females only; they severely limit human possibility for males as well.

THE MANY FEMINISMS

How does one go about sorting out feminist issues? Perhaps one should start by listing and describing the various forms that feminism takes? While it appears logical enough to begin in that fashion, offering a typology of feminisms turns out to be a tricky thing to do. It is not just that a movement of such intricate diversity resists categorisation but that the very act of categorising has implications of its own. Not the least of these implications is the 'maleness' of the act of categorising, which a number of feminist thinkers are swift to allege. Among them are Stanley and Wise (1983, p. 40), who judge 'one-dimensional forms of classification' to be 'dichotomous ways of construing reality'. It matters not whether these are established ways of construing reality or new ways of construing reality. In either case, categorisations of this kind 'are concerned with pin-pointing differences', 'portray political ideologies as clearly demarcated, fixed and unchanging', and privilege one side of the dichotomy over the other. This, Stanley and Wise conclude, is 'an essentially masculinist way of interpreting'.

Such misgivings about classification on the part of feminists have not proved totally inhibiting. Rosemarie Tong (1995), for example, offers us no fewer than seven forms of feminism to consider. In her much-cited typology, she suggests that feminism may be 'liberal, Marxist, radical, psychoanalytic, socialist, existentialist, or postmodern'. As the title of her Introduction proclaims, these are 'The Varieties of Feminist Thinking'. She refers to them variously as 'categories', 'labels', 'strands', 'perspectives' and 'views' (1995, pp. 1–9).

Liberal feminism is grounded in the humanism of liberal political thought. Such humanism privileges the autonomy of the person and views the just society as a system of individual rights that safeguard personal autonomy and allow self-fulfilment. There are liberals and liberals, all the same. Classical, or libertarian, liberalism wants the state to protect rights and provide equal opportunity, but to interfere as little as possible. Welfare, or egalitarian, liberalism has an eye for social justice rather than civil liberties and calls for forthright state intervention in the cause of equity. Tong believes that, in contrast to many nineteenth-century liberal feminists, who appear as classical (libertarian) liberals, most twentieth-century liberal feminists present as welfare (egalitarian) liberals.

Tong herself leans towards the egalitarian form of liberalism. 'An egalitarianism that worries about all women's basic needs is probably more feminist than a libertarianism that is concerned only about a few women's rights.' For this reason, she chooses for consideration liberal feminists in whom 'the drift of their thought is away from some of the less feminist assumptions of classical liberalism and toward some of the more feminist assumptions of welfare liberalism' (1995, p. 13). These are earlier feminists (Mary Wollstonecraft, John Stuart Mill, Harriet Taylor) and, in our own day, Betty Friedan (the Betty Friedan of *The Second Stage* rather than the Betty Friedan of *The Feminine Mystique*).

Such egalitarianism takes feminists beyond liberal feminism's traditional invitation to individual women merely to cast off their conditioning and reject traditional sex roles. 'Sexual equality', Tong observes (1995, p. 38), 'cannot be achieved through women's willpower alone'. Even modest goals relating to equal opportunity tend to demand a significant measure of economic reorganisation and resource redistribution and rather profound changes in consciousness.

Unlike liberal feminism, *Marxist feminism* is revolutionary, not merely reformist. Liberal feminism may be led to address issues of structure but this is less a matter of principle than a means to an end. It is not the same with Marxist feminism. For the latter, as we would expect from our considerations of Marxism to this point, structural change is the major goal. The structure that it targets is, of course, the class structure. From this perspective, without radical change to the class society, the equal opportunity sought by liberal feminists is a chimaera. Women's oppression began with the introduction of private property and is now to be seen as 'the product of the political, social and economic structures associated with capitalism' (Tong 1995, p. 39). It is capitalism that has shaped the institution of the family as we know it. It is capitalism that leads women's domestic work to be dismissed as not real work. It is capitalism that ensures that women are generally given the most monotonous jobs and the smallest remuneration. How can women liberate themselves from oppression as long as the structures of capitalism remain in place?

Marxist feminists, understandably, concentrate on issues relating to women's work—both their paid employment and their unpaid work in the home. They expect that radical changes in the one will induce changes in the other. Margaret Benston (1969) insists that, as long as domestic work remains a matter of private production and the responsibility of women, equal access to jobs will not provide equality but will simply force women into carrying a double workload. What Benston wants to see is a socialisation of domestic work. This, she believes, will bring home to everyone how socially necessary domestic work is. Mariarosa Dalla Costa and Selma James (1972) go further, arguing that domestic work is not merely useful but productive, even in the Marxist sense of creating surplus value. By their work in the home, women are already in the productive workforce. This should be acknowledged and women should be receiving a wage for their domestic labour. While socialisation of domestic work and the provision of a wage for domestic work may not seem revolutionary targets, Marxist feminists are in a position to develop the revolutionary consciousness of working women and lead them into revolutionary action (Tong 1995, p. 69).

For *radical feminism*, the oppression of women is the oldest, most profound and most widespread oppression of all. It is the view of some radical feminists that the oppression of women causes more suffering than any other form of oppression. Some propose the oppression of women as the model for understanding any other form of oppression.

This awareness of the depth and extent of women's oppression has led some radical feminists into separatism. Despairing of ever forging a community with males in which there would be equality, freedom and respect, they have directed their efforts instead to developing an exclusively female culture. 'Womanculture' is likely to comprise a specifically female aesthetic (art, literature, music, dance), specifically female science, and specifically female religion. It may also include a specifically female sexuality wherein lesbianism, autoeroticism or celibacy replace heterosexual relations.

While not all radical feminists choose the separatist path, all are preoccupied in one way or another with women's sexual and reproductive issues. Tong (1995, p. 51) lists these as 'contraception, sterilization, and abortion; pornography, prostitution, sexual harassment, rape, and woman battering'. Addressing such issues starkly reveals just how radically disordered the patriarchal society is and how radically it must therefore be transformed. It will not be enough to make human society more libertarian or more egalitarian, as liberal feminism is suggesting. That might even make matters worse. As Farganis states in expounding the views of Erikson:

> Women becoming equal to men, in the sense of their becoming like men, allow men to impose their notions, misguided and incorrect though these may be, of what is humanly desirable and humanly possible on women. This imposition enslaves women, continues to entrap men, and precludes any genuine dialectic of an ideal of being human. (1986, p. 117)

Nor will it be enough to rid human society of its capitalistic structures, as Marxist feminism calls upon us to do. The patriarchal system as such, with all its social and cultural institutions, has to be eliminated. Radical feminists may be far from unanimous as to how that might be achieved, but there is impressive uniformity in the strength of their conviction and the passion of their commitment.

Psychoanalytic feminism grounds women's oppression in the depths of the female psyche. In this form of feminism, arising as it does out of Freudian theory, sexuality is at centre stage. Freud, of course, is seen by many as an implacable foe of all feminism. His talk of penis envy and his alleged biological determinism have drawn incisive critiques on the part of writers such as Betty Friedan (1974), Kate Millett (1970) and, with more qualification, Shulamith Firestone (1970). However, there are a number of feminists who identify in Freud—in Freud himself, that is, in contradistinction to many of his latter-day followers—insights that prove liberating rather than domesticating. This, to be sure, necessitates a break with the biological determinism so routinely ascribed to Freudian theory. It also occasions a spirited challenge to the Freudian notion that men's sense of justice and morality is more highly developed than women's. With that break made and that challenge mounted, a number of feminists have found it useful to remain within a Freudian framework. Some of them work towards a non-patriarchal understanding of the Oedipus complex, while others prefer to concentrate on the pre-Oedipal stage in which the relationship between mother and infant is at its peak. The influence of Jacques Lacan has led a number of these psychoanalytically oriented feminists into a post-structuralist reading of feminism.

In Tong's listing of feminisms, *socialist feminism* is deliberately placed after psychoanalytic feminism rather than after Marxist feminism. She believes that socialist feminism represents 'the confluence of Marxist, radical and, more arguably, psychoanalytic streams of feminist thought' (1995, p. 173). Socialist feminists find that Marxism, taken alone, is inadequate for the analysis of women's oppression. Hartmann claims (1981, pp. 10–11) that '*Marxist categories, like capital itself, are sex-blind*'. Radical feminism, on the other hand, while it offers a more comprehensive gender analysis, presents such a univocal picture of patriarchy that it blurs important distinctions that need to be made. As a number of writers have pointed out, purdah, suttee, foot binding and clitoridectomy may all come to be dismissed as abominations perpetrated by a patriarchal system, without due regard being paid to the significance each of these possesses in its respective culture. Psychoanalytic feminism is similarly limiting. It too is guilty of blanket statements about patriarchy and generally bases its analysis on psychic structures alone.

Socialist feminists attempt to overcome these limitations by bringing these strands together and drawing on the strengths of each of them. In doing so, some thinkers focus particularly on patriarchy and capitalism, believing that these go hand in hand. Others insist that patriarchy and capitalism are quite distinct and need to be treated differently. Either way, there is widespread concern among socialist feminists to unify feminists under one banner and have them speak, as far as possible, with one voice.

Existentialist feminism locates its source in the pre-eminent figure of Simone de Beauvoir and her major text, *The Second Sex* (1953). Her partner was Jean-Paul Sartre, who, along with Maurice Merleau-Ponty, spearheaded the advance of existential phenomenology. This was in the wake of Heidegger's *Being and Time* (1962), which, in developing its radical ontology, invoked a number of traditional existentialist themes. Numerous commentators have regarded Sartre's *Being and Nothingness* (1956) as, in large measure, a commentary on *Being and Time*.

Unlike the ancient Greeks and the medieval Christians who found comfort and security in the notion of a stable, orderly cosmos operating according to immutable laws, existentialists find the world contingent, indifferent, even absurd. In this view of things, as conscious and self-conscious human beings, we are thrown back upon our freedom and called to respond to our human situation.

In expounding his version of existentialism, Sartre makes a cardinal distinction between *en-soi* (the 'in itself') and *pour-soi* (the 'for itself'). These are modes of being. The *pour-soi* is conscious being; the *en-soi* is being-as-object. Flowing out of this distinction is Sartre's further distinction between 'Self' and 'Other'. By Other he means another personal being. Even though the Other is itself a *pour-soi*, we dissociate ourselves from it as from an *en-soi*. This is a mutual dissociation: we each constitute the Other as an object and perceive it as a threat.

Simone de Beauvoir takes this Sartrean distinction between Self and Other (perhaps it was hers in the first place?) and uses it to illuminate the relationship between man and woman. She construes man as Self and woman as Other. The Other being a threat to Self, woman must be seen as a threat to man and he needs to make her subordinate. Hence the oppression of women that we find throughout history. Relegated to the status of Otherness, women find themselves in a condition of subjection and dependency. This has led males in the course of time to construct a series of myths about woman so as to control her better. As de Beauvoir sees it, such myths express an ideal image of woman that offers men all that they as men lack. To fulfil this purpose, the image must be chameleon-like: it must be able and ready to change at will. Woman can be a reminder of life or of death. She can be angel or devil. These myths beget the social roles to which women are assigned and which play a pivotal role in holding them subject. Breaking such fetters is no easy task for women but, de Beauvoir believes, joining the work-force, entering the ranks of the intellectuals, and taking part in the socialist transformation of society are all steps in the right direction.

Postmodern feminism is Tong's final category. The feminist thinkers she has in view are Hélène Cixous (1937–), Luce Irigaray (1932–) and Julia Kristeva (1941–). Until recently, Tong observes, what she is calling postmodern feminism has been referred to as 'French feminism'. This, along with a linking of postmodern feminists to Derrida and Lacan, is indication enough that Tong sees no need to distinguish between post-structuralism (an eminently French phenomenon stemming from the equally French phenomenon of structuralism) and postmodernism (a phenomenon much broader both geographically and in terms of the issues it raises and addresses). While Tong is by no means alone in doing this, it will be suggested in Chapter 9 that the distinction between postmodernism and post-structuralism remains a useful distinction to make. In the light of that distinction, it can be argued that the three feminists referred to are post-structuralist rather than postmodernist. Certainly, Kristeva, for one, has expressly declined to be described as postmodernist.

Whatever of the nomenclature, Tong links postmodern feminism very closely to deconstruction, characterising this as a process that is universally and radically critical, anti-essentialist, and fiercely committed to breaking down traditional antinomies such as reason/emotion, beautiful/ugly, self/other, and the conventional boundaries between established disciplines. Deconstruction makes a major theme of 'the positive side of Otherness—of being excluded, shunned, "frozen out", disadvantaged, unprivileged, rejected, unwanted, abandoned, dislocated, marginalized' (Tong 1995, p. 219).

While mention of deconstruction summons up for us the personage of Jacques Derrida (1930–), postmodern feminists have drawn as well on the thought of another Jacques—Jacques Lacan (1901–81). Lacan's structuralism will be discussed in Chapter 9 but here we may focus on his use of Freudian theory.

The relationship between infants and their parents has a pre-Oedipal phase and an Oedipal phase. Pre-Oedipally (or in what Lacan terms the 'Imaginary') infants are at the start so much at one with the mother that they do not know where their body ends and the mother's body begins. Then, in a 'mirror' phase, they move to an awareness of their self. While this weakens their earlier, undiscriminating unity with the mother, they remain firmly attached to her. The Oedipal phase follows. During this stage the child must internalise the Symbolic Order, that is, the linguistic rules of society that need to be inscribed in the unconscious. Here the father comes very much into the picture. The child separates to some extent from the mother and gains a kind of rebirth—a birth into the symbolic world of language. Language provides a medium for a continued link to the mother but it is, of course, not the same. Because of their anatomy, girls cannot make this shift as well as boys do. Fear of symbolic castration is the prime motive but that can hardly move girls to the same extent. They fail to emerge fully from the Imaginary and remain trapped within it. For this reason, girls are seen to be left at the very margins of the Symbolic Order or at best are repressed within it.

Cixous, Irigaray and Kristeva have all been influenced by Lacan's ideas but, far from following him slavishly, have each drawn on his thought in their own way for their own purposes. Lacan holds that the phallus will always dominate and women will always be at the margins of the

Symbolic Order. Since they cannot fully internalise that order ('the law of the fathers'), it will be imposed upon them via the masculine language with which they are endowed. Cixous, for one, refuses to share this pessimism. Women can break free of this circumscribing order, which expresses itself above all in the binary oppositions we inherit—activity/passivity, sun/moon, culture/nature, day/night, speaking/writing, high/low, and so on (Cixous and Clement 1986, pp. 63–5). Exploration of the body, finding strength in 'oral drive', 'anal drive', 'vocal drive', 'gestation drive', a 'desire to live self from within', and a 'desire for the swollen body, for language, for blood', will enable women to escape the dichotomies of the conceptual order in which they find themselves (Cixous 1981, p. 261).

Lacan views women's entrapment in the Imaginary in a quite negative light, but Irigaray declines to follow suit. She wants to find possibilities for women within the Imaginary. All that women hear about womanhood and female sexuality has come from a male point of view. Irigaray looks for a non-phallic feminine, a feminine feminine, one not articulated by men, and for a way to selfhood and language that is not mediated by men. 'Thus', writes Clough (1994, p. 50), 'Irigaray gives voice to the preoedipal daughter, a voice already full of confusion, anger, and desperation'.

In a move that parallels the modernist attack on 'identity logic' launched by thinkers such as Adorno, Irigaray unleashes a fierce onslaught on 'Sameness'. She finds Sameness to be endemic within a history of ideas stretching back to the ancient Greek philosophers. It is Sameness that leads people to understand woman in the light of what they hold about man—for instance, to interpret woman, in Freudian mode, as a little man deprived of a penis. To combat Sameness, it is important, first of all, to address the nature of language. However, for all the sexism everyday language displays, it is not Irigaray's aim to render it gender-neutral. Her tactic, instead, is to insist on the use of the first person and the active voice, which at once puts her practice at variance with the language of science. In this way, science, philosophy and psychoanalysis are forced to assume responsibility for what they say. They can no longer indulge in the false security provided by the anonymous third person and the passive voice that distances subject from object.

To combat Sameness, it is also important not to describe female sexuality in terms provided by male sexuality. The female sex organs are not just the absence of the male organ but are in themselves a most meaningful multiplicity. Nor will the understanding begotten by a direct addressing of that multiplicity be limited to sexuality. It will reach out to all forms of human expression. It can even transform social structures.

Finally, to combat Sameness, Irigaray provocatively suggests that women mime the very miming to which they have been subjected. 'If women exist only in men's eyes, as images, women should take those images and reflect them back to men in magnified proportions' (Tong 1995, p. 228). By its very exaggeration, such mimesis will strip phallocentric discourse of its power to oppress.

Kristeva, for her part, is not comfortable talking about women in general or woman in the abstract. To talk of woman as such or the feminine as such is to embrace an essentialism that Kristeva rejects wholeheartedly. Politically, one may talk in such terms but philosophically she finds it untenable. People may say, 'We are women', as they struggle for freedom to use contraception and abortion, the availability of day-care centres, or equal opportunities in the workplace. Yet, at a deeper level, 'We are women' is an unwelcome phrase for Kristeva. She does not even want to hear women saying, 'We are', for she believes a woman cannot 'be' but must always be 'becoming'. If this sounds a matter of words, we need to be mindful of Kristeva's focus on language. For her, the pre-Oedipal is the 'semiotic' rather than Lacan's 'Imaginary'. She contrasts the semiotic with the symbolic stage that follows, conceptualising the two stages as engaged in continual interplay, a back-and-forth movement between disorder and order.

The symbolic stage, as we have seen, occurs as a post-Oedipal development. It is this post-Oedipal development that induces disgust, the characterisation of something as 'abject' (Kristeva 1982). Identifying the oppression of Jews, ethnic minorities, homosexuals and so on, along with the oppression of women, as the outcome of this very process, Kristeva calls for the marginalised discourses of such groups to be unleashed upon language to transform it. Social revolution, for her, is always poetic revolution (Kristeva 1984).

Feminist 'epistemology'

Tong's categories have led us on a long journey. While this has been a speedy journey and we are left rather breathless, our fleeting glimpses of feminist landscapes along the way bring home to us the richness and diversity of feminist thought. We may well feel moved to retrace our steps and study these vistas at our leisure.

For the moment, however, we need to consider something that caught our attention at the start. Notwithstanding our gratitude to Tong's categories, we recall the reservations many feminists evince about any categorisation of feminist thought—or, for that matter, about the categorisation of any thought whatsoever. Tong herself warns that her categories can prove limiting and distorting. What she has in mind in saying this is that some of the theorists she presents are difficult to fit under one label and may need to be dealt with under several. This notwithstanding, she believes her categories serve a useful analytic purpose. In her own case, they have helped her to locate herself on the spectrum of feminist thought and serve to reveal inconsistencies, or points of growth, or both, in her own understanding of feminism (Tong 1995, p. 8).

Others are much more sceptical about the development of typologies. As we have already seen, Stanley and Wise consider it a quintessentially male thing to do. This is not their only concern. In the typologies they study, they find the types presented in very clear-cut terms with each so definitely separated from the others that there is no overlapping. Moreover, the various positions come to be laid out one after the other, stretching from the 'most correct' to the 'least correct'. Stanley and Wise, quite rightly, take issue with these forms of typologising. Tong, however, would have to be acquitted of both charges. On the one hand, she explicitly recognises overlaps, acknowledging 'just how artificial are the boundaries between the various feminist perspectives'. On the other hand, she expresses respect and gratitude for all the perspectives, emphasising that each 'has made a rich and lasting contribution to feminist thought' (1995, pp. 7–8).

What, then, about the further charge that making clear-cut classifications of this kind is a very masculine thing to do? That this form of categorising is carried out overwhelmingly by males goes without saying. It reaches its peak in empirical science as we know it, itself a very male affair, and it embodies the desire to have control of things and to know what is likely to happen. It issues in the kind of binary opposites we have found feminists, especially postmodernist feminists, decrying so vigorously—antinomies such as thought/language, nature/culture, reason/emotion, theory/practice, white/black, and especially men/women. Not that all males do such categorising or create these hierarchical oppositions without question. As we have already seen in Chapter 6 and will see again in Chapter 9, there are male thinkers aplenty who have argued, for quite some time and in quite radical fashion, against categorisation of this kind. Theodor Adorno, for one, never failed to assail the view of the 'concept' that lies at the root of all such categorisation.

Feminists arguing against this categorising and these oppositions do so from a special standpoint, however. Where, for others engaging in this debate, the male/female antinomy is one binary opposite among many, for feminists it tends to be *the* binary opposite, serving as a synecdoche for all the others. Thus, in a paper delivered at the University of Leicester in 1978 and cited by Stanley and Wise (1983, p. 29), Dale Spender asserts that 'few, it appears, have questioned our polarisation of reason/emotion, objectivity/subjectivity, reality/phantasy, hard data/soft data *and examined them for links with our polarisation of male/female*'. The emphasis in this citation is ours, not Spender's. It is added because it is the linking of the issue to the feminist question and feminist critique that distinguishes the questioning of binary oppositions by feminists from the questioning that has taken place in modernist and postmodernist thought more generally.

Needing to be viewed in much the same light is Chester's claim that radical feminism offers 'a much more optimistic and humane vision of change than the male-defined notion of the building towards a revolution at some point in the distant future, once all the preparations have been made' (1979, p. 15). Chester believes that one of the most important attitudes she has learned from radical feminism has been to 'bring revolutionary change within the realm of the possible'. The notion of building towards a future revolution is indeed found in male thinkers and may well be seen as male-defined. Once again, however, it has to be said that not all males have thought in this fashion. Paulo Freire's pedagogy of the oppressed, considered in the last chapter, is a praxis requiring the oppressed to reflect and act *now* and he denies that it 'could be divided into a prior stage of reflection and a subsequent stage of action' (1972a, p. 99). Freire is forever underlining that revolution is possible. In his 'problem-posing' pedagogy, as we have noted, the oppressed come to understand their situation, not as 'a dense, enveloping reality or a tormenting blind alley' (Freire 1972a, p. 81), not as 'fetters or . . . insurmountable barriers' (1972a, p. 72), but as a challenge that can and must be met.

It may therefore be important to qualify claims like Chester's about specifically feminist insights. Perhaps there is place for a *caveat* like that entered by Seigfried when writing of the feminine traits she finds within pragmatism. Seigfried is careful to note that these 'can be understood as the expression of a feminine style without implying that all women think this way or that no men do' (1991, p. 11). Similarly, we find Assiter expressing scepticism about the role assigned to 'feminine desire' by Irigaray, that is, its capacity to reveal as illusory 'the hypothesis that the symbolic realm gives us access to knowledge and certainty'. We do not need female desire to reveal the impossibility of acquiring certain knowledge, Assiter insists (1996, p. 47). 'This claim has been questioned by "phallocentric" male philosophers as diverse as Hegel, Wittgenstein and Feyerabend (and this is to exclude Derrida and Lacan).'

Qualifying such feminist claims—or, better, making clear what is distinct about them—has importance. If feminist insights are seen as hinging on their being in themselves uniquely feminine insights, the claims themselves may be facilely dismissed and the value of the insights unappreciated if it can be shown that few women share them or that a number of men do. The real point is, not that feminists gain insights never glimpsed by others, especially not by males, but that, as feminist insights, they are grounded in, and stem from, a specifically feminist standpoint. Adorno may rail against classification but he does so on different grounds. His is a different critique from that of Spender, therefore. Chester's awareness of the need to see change as possible and to take action now is different from Freire's awareness of this need. Hers has been taught to her, as she states, by radical feminism. It stems from a specifically feminist standpoint, is set against a feminist backdrop, and for that reason is to be seen as a critique distinct from that of Freire.

A specifically feminist standpoint? That is surely more correct than any talk of *the* specifically feminist standpoint. Assiter concurs with Jane Flax in arguing that, because there cannot be just one way in which patriarchy permeates thinking, there cannot be just one women's standpoint. Where Assiter locates feminist unity is not in a single standpoint, for 'it is certainly the case that there is a multiplicity of standpoints, values, outlooks amongst feminists', but in 'collective commitment to the undermining of oppressive gender-based power relations'. This commitment constitutes 'a shared set of values that makes feminists feminist' (Assiter 1996, p. 88).

Here Assiter is casting doubt on 'the idea of a specifically *women's* epistemological standpoint' (1996, p. 88). She does not hold that women 'know' in a different way from men so that a group of women would, together, inevitably have a specifically women's form of knowledge. 'Rather than suggesting that an epistemological stance follows from the identity of the group holding it', writes Assiter (1996, p. 89), 'my own position allows for a multiplicity of individuals to come together, in an epistemic community, so long as the members of that community share certain values in common'.

In adopting this position, Assiter is setting herself against what has been a very strong current in feminist thought. Alcoff and Potter write of 'feminist epistemology' and of how feminist theorists 'have used the term variously 'to refer to women's "ways of knowing", "women's experience", or simply "women's knowledge"' (1993, p. 1).

The use of the word 'epistemology' in this context is problematic. Alcoff and Potter recognise that the usage is 'alien to professional philosophers and to epistemology "proper"' (1993, p. 1). If talk of women having their own epistemology is taken to mean that the fundamental act of knowing is different for women, this has enormous, and unwelcome, consequences. *How does one know what one knows? What is the relationship between the knower and the known? What status is to be ascribed to knowledge? In other words, what truth claims can be made on its behalf?* These are epistemological questions and, if one must answer them in a radically different way when referring to women, women emerge as alien beings indeed and one wonders how there could ever be dialogue of any kind between them and males.

'Feminine epistemology' can, however, be understood in another sense—one that suggests, not that women *know* in a way fundamentally different from that of men, but that they *theorise the act of knowing* in a way different from that of men. In 'doing' epistemology, they express concerns, raise issues and gain insights that are not generally expressed, raised or gained by male epistemologists. Few would want to quarrel with that.

Still, many feminists would not be content with that version of 'feminine epistemology'. They insist that women's knowing is, in important respects, different from that of men. Some might accept that they are talking about women's psychology, or their philosophical anthropology perhaps, rather than women's epistemology. Their sociology, even? Fonow and Cook, after all, take epistemology to mean 'the study of assumptions about how to know the social and apprehend its meaning' (1991, p. 1). Yet it would be impoverishing to let semantics impede our engagement with this important stream of feminist thought.

Gilligan (1982) has been very influential in suggesting that women speak 'in a different voice'. She believes women and men have different ways of perceiving the world and relating to it. Their concept of the self is different. In particular, their mode of addressing moral issues is different. For this reason, she takes issue with Kohlberg's stages of moral development and proceeds to rewrite them so that they take account of the way in which women approach the task of moral reasoning. In all of this, men are seen to set a premium on autonomy, generality, abstract impartiality. Women, on the other hand, prize caring, nurturing, bonding and the formation of interpersonal community. Harding too (1983) is found 'suggesting (in a way quite similar to that of Gilligan) that the rational is gendered, that is, that it varies according to sex' (Farganis 1986, p. 181).

Characteristics of the kind postulated by Gilligan and Harding have been used to set women's forms of research over against male forms of research. Some have gone as far as identifying quantitative research as male and qualitative research as female. In introducing their symposium of writings on 'feminist scholarship as lived research', Fonow and Cook (1991, p. 8) reject this point of view. They agree 'that carefully designed research grounded in feminist theory and ethics is more useful to understanding women's experiences than an allegiance to any one particular method as more "feminist" than another'. 'A well crafted quantitative study', they add, 'may be more useful to policy makers and cause less harm to women than a poorly crafted qualitative one'.

What Fonow and Cook do see as a 'major feature of feminist epistemology' is attention to the affective components of the research act. They refer to 'women's greater familiarity with the world of emotions and their meaning' and the 'notion that "women care" at both a practical and an interpersonal level'. Then, drawing on the outcomes of Gilligan's research, they point to the emphasis on caring that emerges in different ways in the essays they have edited. What all this suggests to Fonow and Cook is 'an attempt among feminist scholars to restore the emotional dimension to the current concepts of rationality'. While recognising similar endeavours within the critical theorists of the Frankfurt School, Fonow and Cook see this attention to emotions as part of the critical reflexivity that 'characterizes feminist approaches to knowledge' (1991, pp. 9–11).

In this linking of emotion and knowledge, Fonow and Cook look to Alison Jaggar. Jaggar identifies 'a continuous feedback loop between our emotional constitution and our theorizing such that each continually modifies the other and is in principle inseparable from it'. To recognise this is to embrace an 'alternative epistemological model', one that 'shows how our emotional responses to the world change as we conceptualize it differently, and how our changing emotional responses then stimulate us to new insights'. In this model an important role is ascribed to what Jaggar calls 'outlaw' emotions. These are conventionally unacceptable emotional responses, as when people of colour respond to a racist joke with anger rather than amusement, or when women experience discomfort and even fear, instead of flattery, in the face of male sexual banter. Outlaw emotions can inspire new investigations, Jaggar feels, and may lead to different perceptions of the world (1989, pp. 144–8).

As a feminist, Jaggar has particular interest in the outlaw emotions of women. This is not because she accepts 'the stereotypes of cool men and emotional women'. There is in her essay no parallel to Fonow and Cook's talk of women's greater familiarity with emotions and their meaning. To the contrary, as she sees it, 'there is no reason to suppose that the thoughts and actions of women are any more influenced by emotion than the thoughts and actions of men'. The stereotypes continue to flourish, however, and they lead to the myth of 'the dispassionate investigator'. This is a very powerful myth. It is classist, racist and especially masculinist.

> It functions, obviously, to bolster the epistemic authority of the currently dominant groups, composed largely of white men, and to discredit the observations and claims of the currently subordinate groups, including, of course, the observations and claims of many people of color and women. The more forcefully and vehemently the latter groups express their observations and claims, the more emotional they appear and so the more easily they are discredited. (Jaggar 1989, p. 142)

It is above all to counter this myth and its consequences that Jaggar proposes her 'alternative epistemological model' with the key role it assigns to emotions in general and outlaw emotions in particular. As she points out, 'some, though certainly not all, of these outlaw emotions are potentially or actually feminist emotions'. How do emotions become feminist emotions? Jaggar's answer is unequivocal. 'Emotions become feminist when they incorporate feminist perceptions and values' (Jaggar 1989, p. 144). In this way, Jaggar comes close to what we have already found Assiter asserting, that is, that a group's 'epistemological stance' does not stem from the identity of the group members (the sheer fact, in this case, that they happen to be women) but arises from their sharing certain values in common (in this case, their collective commitment to undermining oppressive gender-based power relations). As Stanley and Wise point out (1990, p. 27), a feminist standpoint is 'a practical achievement, not an abstract "stance"'. It demands, Harding tells us (1987, p. 185), an 'intellectual and political struggle'. Farganis agrees (1986, p. 196): 'Feminism is a movement to change the way one looks at the world and feminist theory is part of that struggle'.

FEMININE THOUGHT OR FEMINIST VALUES?

There would appear, then, to be two rather disparate strands within feminist theory, both invoking the concept of 'feminist epistemology' and its associated themes, and both of compelling interest from the viewpoint of research methodology. The two are by no means mutually exclusive and in the end, paradoxically, they come together.

In the one case, feminist researchers bring a feminist standpoint to their research. Because of their commitment to feminist values and the feminist cause, and given the feminist purposes they bring with them, they do research in a different way from others, especially men. Whether this means that there are distinctive feminist methodologies, that is, methodologies unique to feminist researchers, is the subject of much discussion. For many, it is more a question of feminist perspectives entering into existing methodologies. The debate may be chiefly a matter of semantics. A methodology that embodies a feminist orientation is essentially very different from a methodology that does not, even if the methods it selects and shapes look to be the same. Just as a critical ethnography is vastly different from an ethnography informed by anthropological theory or symbolic interactionism even though all rely on participant observation, so a feminist ethnography will be different again.

In the other case, the claim to distinctive patterns of research rests upon a prior claim to a different pattern of knowing. Women are said to have different ways of knowing and will therefore do research in different ways to men. Some would want to say that what this postulates is feminine forms of research rather than feminist forms of research. Mies (1991, p. 60) invokes this distinction when she asks, 'Women's research or feminist research?' and demands involvement in the women's movement for research to qualify as the latter. Furthermore, a similar debate to the one just mentioned can be detected here too. Are there distinctive feminine methodologies, that is, methodologies unique to female researchers? Or does a feminine style come to inform existing methodologies? However one responds to them, these questions imply that there *is* a feminine style in research which reflects feminine traits and makes a significant difference to the research that is carried out. On this basis, claims are made that, because the researcher is a woman, the approach taken is likely to be, say, qualitative rather than quantitative . . . constructivist rather than objectivist . . . experiential rather than cerebral . . . interactive rather than non-involved . . . caring rather than dispassionate . . . a seeking of shared understanding rather than an attempt to prove a point . . . action-oriented rather than theoretical . . . collaborative and participatory rather than otherwise . . . And so on.

Some difficulties with this point of view have been considered already. Women form a far from homogeneous grouping, and selecting certain features as categorically feminine and shaping women's research in definite ways will always prove contentious. It is also difficult (impossible, perhaps?) to pinpoint feminine characteristics that are not shared by a significant number of men. Even when it is a question of undoubtedly feminist and not merely feminine insights, many of these, as we have seen, appear to be attainable by routes other than feminism. We may point to the Spenders and Chesters of this world but the Adornos and Freires of this world persist in putting their hand up too. Alcoff and Potter might set out to put together a symposium on 'feminist epistemologies' but in the end they find themselves having to answer the question, 'Why, then, retain the adjective "feminist"?' (1993, p. 4).

For all that, as we have also seen, feminist commitment and feminist orientation are able to transfigure the insights in question and make them well and truly distinctive. It is not so easy to say the same of insights that are attributed, not to feminist perspective and participation in the feminist struggle, but to feminine style. When all that can be said of their genesis is that in these cases they come from women, are we talking about feminist insights, or even specifically feminine insights? Or are we talking merely about insights found among men and women alike?

True enough, we may be talking about features—ways of thinking, feeling, behaving—that are found among women much more than among men. They may divide quite strongly along sex lines. Not only are they far more characteristic of women than men but they may be said to come together in a complexus that constitutes feminine style and is unique to women. From this perspective, there are numerous feminists for whom features characteristic of women and therefore constituting the feminine are central to their feminism, and they roundly celebrate the 'difference'.

At this point it becomes important to ask about the origin of such feminine traits. Are they innate and inherent? Are they social products? Or is there some kind of middle position here?

Whether, or to what extent and in what way, innate or inherent features of femininity exist remains very much a matter of dispute. 'It may well be', writes Sondra Farganis (1986, p. 1), 'that there are no traits particular to a single sex'. On the other hand, as 'sceptical feminist' Janet Radcliffe Richards sees it (1982, p. 155), 'there is no reason to presume that there cannot be *any* inherent feminine and masculine characteristics' and 'it is overwhelmingly likely that there are some'. In her view, the actual attributes of men and women spring from a combination of specifically sexual characteristics with others that may be equally distributed between the sexes. It is hardly surprising if this process issues in some non-sexual traits that are more commonly found in one sex than the other.

Despite the apparent difference of opinion, neither of these writers considers the existence of specifically feminine traits to be central to her concerns. For Farganis, the existence or otherwise of such traits is not what is 'at issue' in her work (1986, p. 1). Instead, she is concerned with how women are *perceived* and, in this more limiting sense, how gendered characteristics are understood. While Richards may be more inclined to accept the existence of inherent, or innate, feminine characteristics, she too does not consider them 'at issue in the great debate about women and femininity'. The question of 'how many there are, what they are, or what effect they have' is not at the centre of that debate as she understands it. Women may have inherent or innate attributes but these are not the ones that are a matter of concern. Instead, 'the fuss about femininity' is 'about what it is thought that the sexes *ought* be like, and about what measures need to be taken to achieve whatever that is'. Accordingly, she believes, most feminists have no worries about inherent tendencies to differences between the sexes. They are, however, justifiably indignant about what these differences are often alleged to be and are deeply concerned about the discrimination that these perceived differences supposedly legitimate. 'The feminist concern about femininity is not about such inherent characteristics. It is rather the fact that *men and women are under different social pressures*, encouraged to do different kinds of work, behave differently, and *develop* different characteristics, which is important' (Richards 1982, p. 155–7).

Once again, then, we find ourselves with the feminist agenda rather than with allegedly inherent features of femininity. The pivotal problem that emerges has to do with inherited and prevailing perceptions of what it means to be a woman and how women ought to live and act. Not that these perceptions can be kept apart from the feminine characteristics we have been discussing. Earlier in this book, when dealing with social constructionism, we considered the notion of reification. It is a process whereby something that is not a 'thing' is posited as a 'thing'. By just such a process of objectification, socially derived expectations of women become putatively 'inherent' features of femininity.

Thus, what are said to be characteristically feminine traits and behaviour turn out to be historical and cultural constructions. Unless we postulate some sort of essential feminine nature and are willing to wear the charge of being essentialist and ahistorical, we need to see it in this light. This is not to deny a role to biology. Nature has a hand in it, to be sure. Female anatomy and physiology play their part. Yet the feminine qualities and actions we encounter in social life do not equate to the mere functioning of genes and hormones. Lying between the basic ground plans for our life that our genes lay down and the precise behaviour that we in fact execute is 'a complex set of significant symbols under whose direction we transform the first into the second, the ground plans into the activity' (Geertz 1973, p. 50).

> Chartres is made of stone and glass. But it is not just stone and glass; it is a cathedral, and not only a cathedral, but a particular cathedral built at a particular time by certain members of a particular society. To understand what it means, to perceive it for what it is, you need to know rather more than the generic properties of stone and glass and rather more than what is

common to all cathedrals. You need to understand also—and, in my opinion, most critically—the specific concepts of the relations between God, man, and architecture that, having governed its creation, it consequently embodies. It is no different with men: they, too, every last one of them, are cultural artifacts. (Geertz 1973, pp. 50–1)

Geertz's use of the generic masculine stands out in the clearest relief in the context of the present chapter. 'It is no different with men.' While this was originally written well over 30 years ago and we may be tempted to feel indulgent about the author's language in this respect, we may also feel the temptation to shout back, 'It is no different with women!'. And this, as it happens, is the precise point we are concerned with at the moment. Women, along with men—yes, 'every last one of them'—are cultural artifacts. Simone de Beauvoir tells us (1953, p. 273), 'One is not born, but rather becomes a woman'. Farganis agrees. Proposing that 'theories of the feminine cannot be divorced from the social conditions of their formulation', Farganis draws on and expands the thought of English sociologist Viola Klein.

The feminine, according to Klein, is a constellation of cultural roles, attitudes and abilities related to, but not necessarily growing out of, the biological traits held to constitute being a woman, that is, grounded in chromosomes, anatomy and hormones. 'Feminine' includes cultural influences in a way that 'female' does not . . . In allowing for the importance of human intervention, action, and transcendence in becoming a person, one counters the determinism of simple biological or cultural explanations. The biological within a cultural context rooted in time is at the core of the social and the sociological, and it moves beyond the simplistic as well as specious dichotimization of nature/nurture, biology/culture, genes/environment. (Farganis 1986, p. 4)

There are those who would privilege the nature–biology–genes side of the divide to which Farganis refers us. The movement in this direction reached its zenith in the sociobiology that waxed strong in the 1970s and sought, as in the writings of E.O. Wilson, to explain animal behaviour, including human behaviour, through genes and gene selection. One of the sociobiological strategies is to draw parallels between humans and other species—especially our ape cousins, most of whose genetic material matches our own. Here sociobiologists pay a great deal of attention to sex roles, sexual displays and sexual practices, so that their work is certainly of interest to people involved with feminism. Sociobiology has had a bad press in feminist quarters, not least because it suggests a determinism that would leave women at the mercy of their genetic inheritance and biological functions. Still, there are feminist writers who do not hesitate to appeal to instinctual female drives, for example, to motherhood in particular or to nurturing in more general terms.

There are others who would privilege the nurture–culture–environment side of the divide mentioned by Farganis. Cultural, or social, anthropology certainly emphasises the role of the symbol system that serves to direct what we as humans do. On the basis of citations we have already considered, Geertz emerges as an anthropologist who offers that emphasis without losing sight of the biological basis. He calls for 'analyses of physical evolution, of the functioning of the nervous system, of psychological process, of cultural patterning, and so on—and, most especially, in terms of the interplay among them' (1973, p. 53). His talk of 'interplay' resonates with Farganis's appeal for a 'dialectical method' in the analysis of feminist issues. For the most part, feminists are certainly on the side of the culturalists rather than the sociobiologists. Nevertheless, Farganis echoes the finding of Smith that there is an essentialism to be found not only in sociobiology but in certain strands of feminist theory as well. 'A dialectical method', Farganis believes (1986, p. 118), 'often absent from feminist theory and never found in sociobiology, would be the corrective to or antithesis of each of these paradigms and would counter a universalism that is historically untenable'.

There is a point to be carefully noted here and it holds regardless of whether we want to downplay the role of culture (as in sociobiology) or maximise the role of culture (as in certain versions of anthropology). If, in any way and to any extent, we consider the inherited and prevailing understandings of womanhood to be a social construction, we need to be suspicious of them. These understandings have been forged in and out of the give-and-take of society. They are a cultural product. Since that society is a patriarchal society and that culture a masculinist culture, one can only conclude that the picture of femininity we have inherited has been developed by males to serve male purposes. In consequence, the first task of feminists may well be that of opening themselves in phenomenological fashion to the immediate experience of being a woman, thereby calling into question the meanings inevitably imposed upon them in hegemonic fashion by their culture.

It is in this very spirit that Adrienne Rich (1990) directs women to the literature they have inherited, as we noted when discussing hermeneutics. In pointing up the kind of oppression that women suffer under patriarchy, Rich writes of 'the visible effects on women's lives of seeing, hearing our wordless or negated experience affirmed and pursued further in language' (1990, p. 483). Language has trapped women as well as liberated them. The very act of naming has been until now the prerogative of males. Rich does not call for a boycott of this masculinist literature. What she calls for instead is 're-vision'—a radical feminist critique of literature that will use literature as a clue to how women have been living and a pointer to how women can begin to see things differently, name things authentically for themselves, and so bring themselves to a new way of being and living. 'We need', says Rich, in a statement that we have already considered but which bears repetition, 'to know the writing of the past, and know it differently than we have ever known it; not to pass on a tradition but to break its hold on us' (1990, p. 484).

Rich's call should not be limited to literature. All human life and every human situation can be seen as text. As they address that life and those situations, women need to lay aside the cultural understandings imposed upon them, inevitably sexist as those understandings are, and interpret life and situation anew—yes, reading them as they have never been read before.

Research as re-vision, then? That may not be a bad way to describe feminist research in a nutshell. When feminists come to research, they bring with them an abiding sense of oppression in a man-made world. For some, this may be little more than an awareness that the playing field they are on is far from level and they need to even things up. For others, the injustice is more profound and severe. They perceive the need for very radical change in culture and society—for a revolution, no less. Feminist research is always a struggle, then, at least to reduce, if not to eliminate, the injustices and unfreedom that women experience, however this injustice and unfreedom are perceived and whatever intensity and extent are ascribed to them.

This striving for equity and liberation marks feminist research indelibly. To all outward appearances, feminist researchers may share methodologies and methods with researchers of other stripes; yet feminist vision, feminist values and feminist spirit transform these common methodologies and methods and set them apart. Far more than ways of gathering and analysing 'data', methodologies and methods become channels and instruments of women's historical mission to free themselves from bondage, from the limiting of human possibility through culturally imposed stereotypes, lifestyles, roles and relationships.

Like Rich's reading of literature, feminist research addresses the world to 'know it differently than we have ever known it'—yes, and to fashion it anew.

9

POSTMODERNISM: CRISIS OF CONFIDENCE OR MOMENT OF TRUTH?

Toute pensée émit un coup de dés.
All thought brings forth a throw of the dice.

Stéphane Mallarmé, 'Un Coup de dés'

Postmodernism is the most slippery of terms. It encompasses a broad variety of developments, not only (and certainly not first) in philosophy and social science, but also in architecture, the arts, literature, fashion, and many other spheres of human endeavour. The term is used, and defined, in a multitude of ways. So too is the 'modernism' to which it is related by virtue of the preposition 'post', which in its turn is understood in almost equally inconsistent fashion.

Given that state of affairs, the explanation of postmodernism that follows in this chapter cannot purport to be the only way in which the sense and implications of the term might be unfolded. Instead, in keeping with the purposes stated at the outset of this book, what is contained in this chapter is offered as 'scaffolding' only and not as anything in the way of a finished edifice. It is simply one way—hopefully a useful way—of 'sorting things out'.[15]

'POST' WHAT?

The Latin word *post* means 'after'. In terms such as postmodernism, it does not mean this in a chronological sense—or at least it does not necessarily mean this in a chronological sense. One might talk here of logical succession rather than a succession in time. 'Postmodernism' certainly does not imply that once there was a modernism and now this has been replaced by postmodernism. We will recall from earlier discussions that the emergence of post-positivism has not meant the demise of positivism. Nor has it meant that in post-positivism something utterly different has come to be. Post-positivism, we know, remains in the broad tradition of positivism and retains a number of its features. Similarly, we should expect that postmodernism remains in broad continuity with modernism and embodies many of its concerns.

Do we find this to be the case as we peruse the literature? Yes. And no. It depends on what we are reading. In some accounts, postmodernism is seen to emerge out of, and in reaction to, modernism, with the continuity between the one and the other strongly maintained. Milner writes, for example, of the postmodernist style's 'deeply derivative relationship to high modernism' (1991, p. 108). In other accounts, postmodernism is presented as a definite rupture with modernism; it calls into question—indeed, stands in total opposition to—virtually all that modernism asserts and holds dear.

Why this disparity? It is, of course, because modernism means different things to different people.

Modernism is not a word found too often in sociology or the social sciences generally. There is far more talk of 'modernity' and 'modernisation'. If the word 'modernism' is used, it tends to be a synonym for one or both of these. In the textbooks, we find modernity accepted as 'the key concept in the study of social change' and defined as 'patterns of social life linked to industrialization' (Macionis 1991, p. 617). Consequently, modernisation becomes 'the process of social change initiated by industrialization' (1991, pp. 617, 619). As the textbooks see it, the industrial revolution ushered in a new form of human society. To be sure, across different societies, there are 'infinite gradations of modernity', one form of society displaying 'a relatively low level of modernization' and another 'a relatively high level of modernization' (Waters 1989, p. 403). Such gradations notwithstanding, we live now in a modern world and it is qualitatively different from the world that preceded it.

What is this modern world like? More than any other feature that might be cited, modernity is typically described in the textbooks as 'rational'. Especially following Weber, the modern world is viewed as a world in which instrumental reason holds full sway. The rationality of modern society is embodied especially in the certainty and precision of its science and the astounding control and manipulation of nature that its science makes possible. In pointing this up, modernity is claiming its birthright as the child of the Enlightenment. With that intellectual movement of the seventeenth–eighteenth centuries, the world is seen to have been changed forever. The Enlightenment meant a radical and permanent break with the alleged irrationality and superstition of preceding ages.

Modernism, then, in the sense of modernity and modernisation, evinces great faith in the ability of reason to discover absolute forms of knowledge. Science and the scientific method are paraded as the paramount way in which this self-professedly universal and valid hold on reality is achieved. Modernism, taken in this sense, is proclaimed the path to emancipation, for it delivers us from the fetters of ignorance in which we were once held fast. According to Horkheimer and Adorno (1972, p. 3), the program of the Enlightenment 'was the disenchantment of the world, the dissolution of myths and the substitution of knowledge for fancy'. In this way, modernisation is seen as synonymous with progress.

As Horkheimer and Adorno point out (1972, p. 3), the Enlightenment 'has always aimed at liberating men from fear and establishing their sovereignty'. Establishing their sovereignty indeed. In bringing clarity and certitude and banishing ambiguity, modernism, as modernity, posits an autonomous individual self that is self-reliant and very much in control.

> Autonomy and instrumentality are the correlative qualities constituting modern subjectivity in a liberal, democratic social order. The modern subject is the product of the Enlightenment program. (Posnock 1991, p. 56)

If this is modernism, postmodernism is a thoroughgoing rejection of what modernism stands for and an overturning of the foundations on which it rests. Postmodernism refuses all semblance of the totalising and essentialist orientations of modernist systems of thought. Where modernism purports to base itself on generalised, indubitable truths about the way things really are, postmodernism abandons the entire epistemological basis for any such claims to truth. Instead of espousing clarity, certitude, wholeness and continuity, postmodernism commits itself to ambiguity, relativity, fragmentation, particularity and discontinuity. In the place of what may be seen as the arrogance and pomposity of Enlightenment modes of thought, postmodernism delights in play, irony, pastiche, excess—even 'mess'. In the course of all this, postmodernism typically engages in a radical decentring of the subject, privileging 'nonidentity (or the dispersal of identity) over any stable self-conception' (Dallmayr 1997, p. 41).

This, it has to be said, is a clear-cut way of dealing with postmodernism and modernism. One is quite simply the antithesis of the other. It is problematic, all the same. The problem lies in the fact that the characteristics attributed here to postmodernist thought are not specific to postmodernism. While postmodernism (though not the postmodern) is commonly taken to have emerged since the 1960s, the things it is saying of modernity have been said long before that. In some cases they were said even before the turn of the twentieth century.

Already in this book we have considered the way in which constructionism has long rejected the objectivism inherent in the Enlightenment theory of knowledge. We have seen Adorno fighting against the tyranny of the concept and have heard his invitation to remedy the inadequacy of thought and thing 'in the thing' by looking to the important remainder that slips through the conventional conceptual net. 'It is striking', writes Dews (1987, p. 233), 'that, in many contemporary accounts of "postmodern" culture, central emphases of Adorno's work of forty years ago are reproduced'. Even Henry James (1843–1916), writing before and around the turn of the century, is a 'hero of ambiguity' and 'practices a politics of nonidentity', 'refusing to resolve paradoxes or dissolve differences into identity' (Posnock 1991, pp. 16, 66, 74).

Yet constructionists are not *per se* postmodernist. Adorno, let alone Henry James, cannot be seen as postmodernist. Nor, on the other hand, can they be classified as modernist on this understanding of modernism. There are glaring anomalies to be faced if we simply set postmodernism over against modernism understood as modernity/modernisation.

As it happens, this is not the only way in which we might conceptualise the matter. Modernism may not be a word commonly found in social science writing but it is certainly common enough in other spheres of thought and action. It looms very large in the vocabulary of art and literature where it is by no means identified with modernisation and modernity. Instead, it represents a *response* to modernisation and modernity that emerged originally towards the close of the 1800s and has continued in various forms throughout the present century. 'Modernism', writes Sarup, 'concerns a particular set of cultural or aesthetic styles associated with the artistic movement which originated around the turn of the century'. Modernism, as Sarup describes it (1993, p. 131), emphasises 'experimentation', explores 'the paradoxical, ambiguous and uncertain, open-ended nature of reality', and manifests a 'rejection of the notion of an integrated personality'.

Sarup uses the word 'ambiguous'. The modernist response was, and is, thoroughly ambiguous. The Enlightenment brought a modern world into being, but modernism is neither an enthusiastic embracing of the Enlightenment project nor an outright rejection of the Enlightenment world. In those closing decades of the nineteenth century, there were plenty who did reject modernity and engaged in nostalgic longings for a return to the (putatively) idyllic days of a more bucolic past. Echoes of such a response can be seen in Tönnies's antinomy between the *Gemeinschaft* ('community') of the past and the *Gesellschaft* ('association') of the present and in vitalist philosophies like those of Dilthey and Bergson. But this is antimodernism, not modernism. Modernism does not reject modernity. It accepts modernity—but its acceptance is made in full awareness of the many anomalies it holds. Lewis says of Weber that he 'did not contemplate his age of reason with equanimity or with the cheerful complacency of so many subsequent British and American sociologists and economists, but with a sardonic acceptance of the inevitable' (1975, p. 85). Weber's is a modernist attitude.

In certain respects, Weber can, in fact, be seen as leading the way down the modernist path. In a phrase he has borrowed from the poet Schiller, he defines modernity as the 'disenchantment of the world'. For him, the world has been robbed of its enchanting quality. It has lost its magic. The robber, above all other contenders for the title, is bureaucratisation. 'Precision, speed, unambiguity', along with 'unity, strict subordination, reduction of friction', are what bureaucracy most values (Weber 1970, p. 214). In such a world, Weber points out, 'there are no mysterious incalculable forces that come into play'. Instead, 'one can, in principle, master all things by calculation'. In consequence, 'the world is disenchanted' (Weber 1968, p. 298). With the magic gone, we are left with the world of reason, 'a world in which men lose their manifold natures in the specialised division of labour, devoting themselves in unambiguously defined tasks' (MacRae 1974, p. 87). Weber's life, MacRae adds, is a struggle against such a destiny.

Struggle he might, but Weber's struggle is within, and not apart from, the world of modernity. The same has to be said of Benjamin and Adorno, authentic modernists both of them. While 'neither Benjamin nor Adorno is entirely immune to the lure of nostalgia', Posnock points out, 'this moment of regression is far outweighed by their commitment to anatomizing modernity on its own terms rather than lamenting the allegedly unalienated past' (Posnock 1991, p. 99).

Weber, Benjamin and Adorno typify the struggle of modernism generally. Modernism is far from retreating from the bourgeois world it finds itself inhabiting. Instead, it mounts a challenge to bourgeois beliefs and values from within, drawing not on relics of the past nostalgically preserved but on what the modern itself has to offer. Within the context of the modern and in essential relationship to the modern, modernist art and literature replace bourgeois realism with something quite different. The capitalist world, heir as it is to the Enlightenment and the progress of science, presents its forms of understanding as precisely 'the way things are'. In doing that, it needs the support of a bourgeois art that, as a genre, conforms to such a project. For this reason, we find social realism pervading the arts and literature of the bourgeois world. Modernism, however, inaugurates a departure from bourgeois realism. 'Modernism', writes Lash (1991, p. xiii), 'challenged previously existing aesthetic realism's assumptions that aesthetic value came from some sort of correspondence between artistic representation on the one hand, and reality on the other'.

Picasso, for example, became modernist as he moved from the orthodox realism of his 1901 portrait of Señora Canals 'to 1906, when he began to experiment with distortions and generalizations of the human image based on primitive Iberian and African art, to 1911, when, in paintings like *Ma Jolie*, the human image has disappeared entirely' (Hardison 1989, p. 2). Hence the jolt Picasso's work tends to cause in a society whose very mindset upholds the paramountcy of the autonomous human subject.

In architecture, nothing has provided a greater jolt to these same sensibilities than the building of the Eiffel Tower. Gustave Eiffel was a bridge builder. What he created to commemorate the centennial of the French Revolution was 'a bridge rotated from horizontal to vertical and, at the same time, a fully realized abstract sculpture' (Hardison 1989, p. 90). As Hardison goes on to describe, the leaders of the French establishment (Alexandre Dumas and Guy de Maupassant included) protested mightily 'in the name of art and French history'. What they wanted, of course, was a realist monument that affirmed the social and political order obtaining at that time. Architecture that expressly reflects the liberating event of the Revolution and symbolises the order of things the Revolution has ushered in would fit the bill very nicely. The Tower fulfils neither of these functions.

> Being abstract—devoid of historical allusions to the French Revolution—it can be read as a symbol of almost anything: a prophecy of flight, an expression of man's aspiration for the infinite, a phallic symbol, an enlarged toy. It is none of these. It forces the viewer to look beyond historical myths to the revolution that surrounds him. (Hardison 1989, p. 93)

In literature, likewise, the modernism that emerged in the late nineteenth century was, in large measure, an eschewing of bourgeois realism. Henry James is an outstanding example of this. Often described as the first modern American novelist, he portrays 'movements beyond the conventional codes that impose intelligibility upon individual behavior' (Posnock 1991, p. 3). In 1904 James returned to the United States after many years of living abroad. In *The American Scene* he presents what he describes in the Preface as his 'gathered impressions'. He deliberately refrains from offering 'information'. In fact, he states that he is 'incapable of information'. A year before *The American Scene* was published, H.G. Wells had produced a book that reported on his travels in the United States. Wells's book, titled *The Future in America*, is informative. It is essentially what James declares he does not want his book to be. Posnock describes *The Future in America* as the work of 'a scientific socialist' and a 'hymn to "material progress"'. Henry James's work is very different. It dissociates itself from 'the authority of utilitarian, abstract reason (embodied in the journalist's gathering of information) in a world dedicated to the Enlightenment ideal of progress' (Posnock 1991, p. 148). Instead, James gives free rein to his 'restless curiosity' as he wanders New York's Lower East Side, or Charles Street in Boston, or the many other places to which his aimless meanderings (his *flânerie*, to use a term invoked by many others as well, Baudelaire, Simmel and Walter Benjamin among them) had brought him.

James is led on by what his autobiographical writings describe as 'the play of strong imaginative passion'. 'Fed by every contact and every apprehension', this passion 'constitutes in itself an endless crisis' (James 1956, pp. 454–5). In James's view, writers who share such passion, that is, writers possessed of the 'largest responding imagination before the human scene', are found 'washing us successively with the warm wave of the near and familiar and the tonic shock, as may be, of the far and strange' (1962, p. 31).

The far and strange. Here we are coming close to the basic purposes of the modernist endeavour. Modernity holds us firmly under the sway of what it presents as the sure and the true, but modernism shares the phenomenological purpose of calling such received notions into question. Posnock writes of 'the ferment of experimental literary, artistic and intellectual activity that occurred roughly from 1875 to 1925'. Much of this experimental activity, he tells us, 'erupted in protest against the bureaucratic dominance of abstraction, rational cognition, and instrumentality that had disambiguated modern life in obedience to the Enlightenment (or Baconian) imperative of efficiency'.

> Thus modernism insists on an obdurate difficulty expressed in formal innovation that refuses the familiar comforts of realist presentation. Instead, defamiliarisation—a making new by estranging the familiar—characterizes modernism's project to reunify human sensibility, dissociated by the hegemony of positivist science. Paradoxically, the healing of the breach between thought and feeling is achieved through deliberate shock tactics of dissonance. (Posnock 1991, p. 56)

This is highly reminiscent of the Russian formalist school of literary criticism, which came to see art as having the purpose of defamiliarisation. 'In order to recover the sensation of life', writes Merquior (1986, p. 22), describing the views of Viktor Shklovsky, 'art had to *defamiliarize*, to make objects unfamiliar by making forms difficult, shattering the layer of custom on our humdrum perceptions'. Poetry in particular is considered a genre that does violence to language, thereby bringing about *ostranenie*, the process of defamiliarisation. *Ostranenie* is 'the making strange of reality in order to create it anew' (Bogdan 1990, p. 116). It is an attempt, Hawkes tells us, to 'counteract the process of habituation encouraged by routine everyday modes of perception'. It is a modernist purpose through and through.

> We very readily cease to 'see' the world we live in, and become very anaesthetized to its distinctive features. The aim of poetry is to reverse that process, to *defamiliarize* that with which we are overly familiar, to 'creatively deform' the usual, the normal, and so to inculcate a new, childlike, non-jaded vision in us. The poet thus aims to disrupt 'stock responses' and to generate a heightened awareness: to restructure our ordinary perception of 'reality'. (Hawkes 1977, p. 62)

The anti-bourgeois orientation emphasised in this account of modernism is not its only characteristic. Nor has modernism succeeded in displaying anti-bourgeois sentiment with total consistency. Still, its status as a spirited, if ambiguous, response to modernity, rather than a movement identified with modernity itself, is difficult to challenge.

What, then, on this accounting, is postmodernism?

Any answer to this question should be prefaced with a careful distinction between postmodernism and postmodernity. In discussing modernism, we have distinguished between modernism and modernity and we need to make a comparable distinction here as well. Postmodernity, like modernity, is a distinctive historical stage in societal development. Postmodernism, like modernism, is a response to a qualitatively new society, 'a profound mutation in recent thought and practice' (Sarup 1993, p. xi). On the one hand, as Crook puts it, postmodernity has to do with a 'structural transformation of advanced industrial societies'. On the other hand, postmodernism 'implies the exhaustion of the dynamic principles of modern art, music and literature and heralds major transformations in the very idea of "art" and in its relation to other social practices' (Crook 1991, p. 4).

As these words of Crook suggest, besides being a response to the postmodern world, postmodernism arises out of, and in reaction, to modernism. Milner underlines both aspects. Postmodernism denotes 'a whole set of contemporary literary and cultural movements (for example, in painting or architecture) which self-consciously define themselves in opposition to earlier, equally self-consciously modernist cultural movements' (Milner 1991, p. 104). At the same time, in at least some of its dimensions, it 'alerts us to the possibility that postmodernist culture might have deep structural roots in some distinctively postmodern socio-political reality' (1991, p. 108). Postmodernity, then, is postmodernism looked at as a moment in time, as an historical epoch in which world and society are seen to have been transformed. Postmodernism-as-postmodernity stands over against postmodernism-as-cultural response. With the emergence of this radically new socio-political reality, a new kind of cultural logic is required to understand it. Moreover, to convey the understanding that arises, there must be new forms of representation and communication. Such essentially different ways of thinking, representing and communicating constitute postmodernism as a cultural response to postmodernity.

Milner makes yet another distinction we may find helpful. This distinction—between 'postmodernism' and the 'postmodern debate'—is a distinction between a complex of human behaviours and the attempt to conceptualise these behaviours theoretically. Milner has defined postmodernism as primarily a set of literary and cultural movements. It is, he observes, 'only secondarily a set of efforts from within cultural theory to define the specific nature of these movements'. For this secondary meaning of postmodernism, that is, its sense as postmodernist theory, he suggests the term 'postmodernist debate' (1991, p. 104).

In short, the form of society in which we live has radically changed. Our world is now a world of *postmodernity*. Throughout many spheres of human activity—art, literature, philosophy and social science among them—experience of such a world elicits *postmodernism-as-cultural-response*. Furthermore, analysts and interpreters of this complex scene offer us a *mélange* of *postmodernism-as-theory*.

With these distinctions in mind, we return to our question: If modernism is taken to be Posnock's 'ferment' of experimental activity erupting within modernity but in reaction against its abstraction, rationalisation and instrumentality, what is postmodernism? Obviously, postmodernism has emerged out of this modernism, and in reaction to this modernism, but what is left to it that is not found in modernism itself? This is an important question because, as we have already seen, much of what is attributed to postmodernism today, even paraded as its very hallmark, is already found well entrenched in the modernist tradition. After listing the 'basic features of modernism', Sarup (1993, p. 131) writes: 'One of the problems with trying to understand modernism is that many of these features appear in definitions of postmodernism as well'. Similarly, Richard Wolin reminds us that 'in many respects postmodernism has merely carried out the legacy of modernism qua "adversary culture"' (1992, p. 8). Jonathan Rée goes so far as to claim that 'the fact that modernism is itself acutely critical of modernity threatens the coherence of the whole project of philosophical postmodernism' (1991, p. 256).

Take Loyal Rue's presentation of postmodernism as an example. Rue describes postmodernism as 'a philosophical orientation that rejects the dominant foundational program of the Western tradition'.

> There are no absolute truths and no objective values. There may be local truths and values around, but none of them has the endorsement of things as they really are . . . As for reality itself, it does not speak to us, does not tell us what is true or good or beautiful. The universe is not itself any of these things, it does not interpret. Only we do, variously. (Rue 1994, pp. 272–3)

'I find the postmodernist perspective theoretically agreeable', Rue concludes (1994, p. 274). But is he embracing postmodernism or modernism? Everything he asserts here of postmodernism can already be found loud and clear in the modernist tradition. If Rue's position is postmodernist, it is not merely because it embraces constructionism and anti-foundationalism. Our question remains to be answered, therefore. What would make Rue's position postmodernist? What sufficiently characterises postmodernism as to enable us to talk logically of both modernism and postmodernism rather than just one or the other?

Milner answers our question by pinpointing an aspect of postmodernism not found in modernism, or at least not found so prominently in modernism. It is the 'progressive deconstruction and dissolution of distinctions' lying at the very heart of postmodernism (Milner 1991, p. 106). Ihab Hassan had this in mind when, as Wolin points out (1992, p. 206), he 'aptly characterized postmodernism as a movement of "unmaking"'.

> It is an antinomian moment that assumes a vast unmaking in the Western mind—what Michel Foucault might call a post-modern epistēmē. I say 'unmaking' though other terms are now de rigueur: for instance, deconstruction, decentering, disappearance, dissemination, demystification, discontinuity, différance, dispersion, etc. Such terms express an ontological rejection of the traditional full subject, the cogito of Western philosophy. They express, too, an epistemological obsession with fragments or fractures, and a corresponding ideological commitment to minorities in politics, sex and language. To think well, to feel well, to act well, to read well, according

to the *epistēmē* of unmaking, is to refuse the tyranny of wholes; totalization in any human endeavor is potentially totalitarian. (Hassan, in Wolin 1992, p. 206)

What this progressive eradication of distinctions means for Milner in the first instance is a collapse of the antithesis found in the context of modernism 'between high and low, elite and popular'. In pointing to this antithesis, Milner is placing the spotlight on the mass culture that developed contemporaneously with modernism. Modernism may have brought new aesthetic self-consciousness, daring experimentalism and formalist innovations, but alongside all this there grew 'a whole range of technically novel cultural forms each of which is in principle near universally available (yellow journalism, penny dreadful and later paperback fiction, radio, cinema, and so on)' (Milner 1991, pp. 105–6). Contemporaries though they are, high modernism and mass culture have never been allies. 'Modernist art', Milner insists, 'emerges as an autonomous social institution, the preserve and prerogative of an increasingly autonomous intellectual class and thereby necessarily counterposed to other non-autonomous arts' (1991, p. 106). Kipnis too writes of the 'antinomies with the popular that constituted aesthetic modernism from its inception' (1989, p. 154).

With postmodernism, this adversarial relationship between modernist and mass culture is considered to have come to an end. In the context of a new world variously characterised by, or as, radical internationalism and transnationalism, post-industrialisation (even post-capitalism), mass communications and telecommunications, universal consumerism, hyperreality, and (as Milner, for one, insists) hypermilitarisation, modernism has been unable to retain its elitist character. Postmodernism is characterised, instead, by 'the deletion of the boundary between art and everyday life; the collapse of the hierarchical distinction between élite and popular culture; a stylistic eclecticism and the mixing of codes' (Sarup 1993, p. 132). It is not that mass culture has broken down the barriers and forced a merger. Instead, it has been 'an endogenous transformation, internal to elite culture itself' and stemming from an inner 'crisis of faith' on the part of modernism (Milner 1991, p. 107).

All along, modernism's challenge to modernity has been fuelled by its firm conviction that, operating within and as part of modernity, it can be at once subversive and redemptive. The emergence of postmodernity means for modernism a 'collective crisis of faith in its own previously proclaimed adversarial and redemptive functions' (Milner 1991, p. 107). All kinds of divisions and distinctions are evaporating within the world in the face of mass media, mass marketing, mass capitalisation, mass commodification, mass entertainment, rapid transport systems, and the rest, to the extent of calling into question even the distinction between the virtual and the real. How, then, can modernism, embodied in a distinct group of aesthetes and thinkers, retain faith in its ability to contribute effectively to the solution of the world's problems?

And, with the dissolution of differences and distinctions, the process moves inexorably on. Fragmentation takes the place of totality and completeness. Ambiguity reigns where once there was clarity. The old certainties vanish, leaving us with the tentative, the provisional, the temporary, the contingent. Even our cherished antinomies are denied to us, those hierarchical oppositions between thought and language, nature and culture, reason and emotion, theory and practice, white and black, men and women. In the place of clear-cut distinctions and earnest logic, there is widespread irony, parody, pastiche, playfulness.

True enough, much of this denial is already there in the modernist movement. Now, however, set in the historical and socio-political context of postmodernity, it emerges as something different. The very setting prevents us from launching ourselves into challenging, subversive innovations with anything like a messianic vision for the future or any hope of redeeming the situation. As we have seen, owing to the extent and degree of the massification that has occurred, society is experiencing a state of implosion in which distinctions are obliterated and a postmodern condition of radical ambiguity, hyperreality, and simulation prevails. In such a society, the battle cry 'This way lies salvation!' is well and truly muted. Modernism, Huyssen reminds us, 'always upheld a vision of a redemption of modern life through culture'. In other words, it always offered an alternative. Postmodernism upholds no such vision and offers no such alternative. 'That such visions are no longer possible to sustain may be at the heart of the postmodern condition' (Huyssen 1988, p. 210).

Accordingly, with the evaporation of differences and the rejection of the goal of wholeness, the modernist emphasis on the redemptive role of aesthetic and intellectual work goes by the board. What, then, of positions that claim to be postmodernist but continue to hold out hope of redemption? Some feminist theory would seem to fall into this category. Milner distinguishes within second-wave feminism between 'a largely American, politically interventionist, and often pseudo-popular, feminist cultural practice which is indeed often subversively postmodernist' and 'a largely French, theoretical, feminist post-structuralism, which is in fact almost classically modernist in character'. 'Kristeva, Irigaray and Cixous', writes Milner (1991, p. 113), 'do remain committed to the archetypically modernist notion that modern life can indeed be redeemed through culture, through writing in fact'. Waugh would seem to endorse this view. As she sees it, 'feminism cannot sustain itself as an emancipatory movement unless it acknowledges its foundation in the discourses of modernity' (1992, p. 190).

In argument of this kind, you will notice, postmodernism and post-structuralism are well and truly distinguished from each other. Yet, in social science literature they are usually found closely allied. Sometimes the terms are used interchangeably. Here, too, some 'sorting out' would seem to be in order.

(POST-) STRUCTURALISM

There seems to be no limit to the number of ways in which the relationship between postmodernism and post-structuralism is portrayed in the literature.

For a start, there are those who want to identify them out of hand. Rée suggests, for example, that in the 1970s postmodernism 'was adopted within philosophy as a rough synonym for deconstruction and poststructuralism' (1991, p. 256). 'There are', Sarup tells us (1993, p. 144), 'so many similarities between post-structuralist theories and postmodernist practices that it is difficult to make a clear distinction between them'.

Others, however, are anxious to distinguish the two. Thus, Fink-Eitel (1992, p. 5) goes to some pains to introduce Foucault 'not as a post-modernist, but rather as a poststructuralist'. Conceiving Foucault as a postmodernist, he claims, 'would be too much of a generalization and consequently would not do justice to the complexity of his work'. It would seem that, for Fink-Eitel, post-structuralism is subsumed under postmodernism as a more specific form of thought under the more general. If this is so, Fink-Eitel certainly does not stand alone. According to Blackburn (1994, p. 295), postmodernism has 'post-structuralist aspects'; indeed, post-structuralism is a 'variety of postmodernism defined by its reaction against structuralism in France'. As it happens, a number of authors consider that post-structuralism, developed in France in reaction to structuralism, has provided orientations and ideas that postmodernism, a much broader movement geographically and conceptually, has made its own, enlarged, and applied to an extended range of subject areas. Nor has this happened only at the start. As Marcus (1994, p. 564) sees it, postmodernism, in the United States at least, 'has been given theoretical substance by the works of the French post-structuralists (who themselves had little use for the term, save, momentarily, Lyotard), which only became available through frequent translation in the early 1980s'.

Wolin strikes a different chord in discussing the work of Lyotard. From Lyotard's point of view, he tells us, postmodernism is a 'non-sentimental adieu—a farewell without tears—to the traditional metaphysical longing for totality, holism, and presence', with post-structuralism becoming 'the epistemological—or better: anti-epistemological—corollary of this epochal cultural transvaluation' (Wolin 1992, p. 9). Then there is Patti Lather (1991, p. 4), who uses '*postmodern* to mean the larger cultural shifts of a post-industrial, post-colonial era and *poststructural* to mean the working out of those shifts within the arenas of academic theory' (blithely adding that she also uses the terms interchangeably!).

Post-structuralism a corollary of postmodernism? A theorising of postmodernism? A strain within postmodernism? A synonym for postmodernism? Well, certainly not the last. Milner is surely right in asserting that 'the two are by no means synonymous' (1991, p. 110). As for post-structuralism being a corollary of postmodernism, it may well be the case that some post-structuralisms have developed in direct relation to the postmodern condition and are themselves instances of postmodernism-as-cultural-response. Whether they relate in any close way to postmodernism-as-theory, that is, to the 'postmodern debate', is another matter. 'The major post-structuralist thinkers', says Milner (1991, p. 111) 'have been almost entirely absent from the debate'.

The absence of major post-structuralist thinkers in the postmodern debate does not mean that their thought has not been influential. Postmodernists have certainly drawn on their thought, as we have seen Marcus indicating in the case of the United States. Waugh (1992, p. 189) writes of 'a Postmodernism that has absorbed the lessons of post-structuralism'. It is therefore possible to envisage postmodernism and post-structuralism informing one another, each promoting the development of the other, without their becoming in any true sense identified. There are post-structuralisms that are not at all postmodernist. And there are forms of postmodernism that are neither structuralist nor post-structuralist (see Figure 6).

Those who see structuralism and post-structuralism as very much a French matter are surely correct. Émile Durkheim (1858–1917), the 'first French academic sociologist' (Coser 1971, p. 143), is widely acknowledged as at least the precursor of structuralism. While Milner sees Durkheim as 'protostructuralist' (1991, p. 62), others are ready to attribute a more developed structuralism to his social theory. Lash, for example, describes him as 'the structuralist among sociology's classics' (1991, p. x). Durkheim, in fact, invokes many systems to indicate how there is 'a whole world of sentiments, ideas and images which, once born, obey laws all of their own' (1976, p. 424). Language, whose 'laws

Figure 6

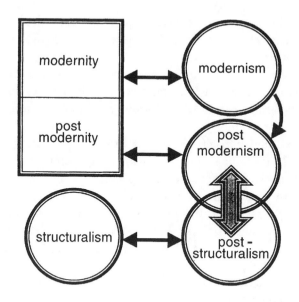

are not those of thought' and which expresses 'the manner in which society as a whole represents the facts of experience' (Durkheim 1976, pp. 75, 434), is one of them.

Durkheim's contemporary, Ferdinand de Saussure (1857–1913) also understands systems as the decisive factor in human affairs. However, he replaces Durkheim's emphasis on consciousness with an emphasis on language. For him, language is not only in itself *a* system, one of many (as with Durkheim), but *the* system, that is, the ultimately determining system.

The centrality accorded to language in Saussure's thought has remained uncontested in the structuralism that forms his legacy. Language is a system of signs and later structuralists owe to him the notion of a 'science that studies the life of signs within society' (de Saussure 1974, p. 16). His theory of the sign expounds it as a union of *signifier* (a form, or symbol) with *signified* (an idea). This is an entirely arbitrary union. True, it stems from the web of relationships found within language as a whole but in that web the signified is not a thing but a concept. The units of language, as the discrete system that it is, 'can be identified only in terms of their relationships to each other, and not by reference to any other linguistic or extra-linguistic system' (Milner 1991, p. 63). It is a self-enclosed system. That is why, according to Saussure (1974, p. 67), '*the linguistic sign is arbitrary*'. This arbitrary sign becomes the focus of his efforts. In dealing with it, Saussure makes his well-known distinction between *langue* (language), a system shared by all speakers of a certain language, and *parole* (word), the individual speech-act in which language-as-system is expressed and embodied. Language is an institution; word is an event.

The structuralist movement emanating from Saussure received immense impetus from the use made of his thought by anthropologist Claude Lévi-Strauss (1908–). In studying symbolic relationships—kinship systems, for example—in the lives of Indian communities in Brazil, Lévi-Strauss found himself dissatisfied with the prevailing anthropological method of empirical observation. The technical elements in Saussure's structuralist approach to linguistics and its purported scientific character had special appeal and Lévi-Strauss conceived a role for a Saussurean approach within anthropology. This means an intersection of the linguistic and the social. Lévi-Strauss now looks to essentially linguistic structures as the source of social meaning 'on the assumption that however much one language may vary from another there is a fundamental structure common to them all, an essence without which no language could be a language' (Sturrock 1993, p. 43).

Lévi-Strauss's work in the late 1950s encouraged other anthropologists, as well as researchers in other disciplines, to adopt more robustly structuralist and more specifically linguistic forms of analysis. In the decade that followed, the 'linguistic turn' came very much to the fore. By this time there was plenty of material for structuralist-minded researchers to draw upon. Plenty of French material, at any rate. There was the work of Roland Barthes (1915–80), Louis Althusser (1918–90), and Michel Foucault (1926–84). Such thinkers led the movement into its moment of high structuralism and later, at least in the case of Barthes and Foucault, on into post-structuralism. Along the way they influenced, and were influenced by, a large contingent of other thinkers.

Structuralism? High structuralism? Post-structuralism? We are obviously at a point where some more 'sorting out' is in order. We may read 'high structuralism' as shorthand for the moment when an elite group of structuralists came to prominence and gave structuralism an edge. But what is structuralism? Not everyone is brave enough to venture a definition. Milner courageously offers us this:

> . . . for our purposes, and very broadly, structuralism might well be defined as an approach to the study of human culture, centred on the search for constraining patterns, or structures, which claims that individual phenomena have meaning only by virtue of their relation to other phenomena as elements within a systematic structure. (1991, p. 61)

Milner goes on to narrow this definition. More specifically, structuralism is the claim 'that the methods of structural linguistics can be successfully generalised so as to apply to all aspects of human culture' (Milner 1991, p. 62).

The formal structure found in language thus becomes the source of meaning for the structuralist. Since this structure is considered a self-regulating entity, such that linguistic signs are independent of non-verbal reality, structuralism cuts human understanding adrift from its moorings in mundane reality and espouses, epistemologically, a thoroughgoing subjectivism. This subjectivism is inherent in Saussure's emphasis on the arbitrariness of linguistic signs. What the signifier signifies is not a reality in the world but a concept. Rather than taking account of reality in any true sense, we conform to a system of social meaning embedded in language.

Milner (1991, pp. 65–6) points to five characteristics of structuralism:

- *positivism* ('it can be described . . . pejoratively as scientistic');
- *anti-historicism* ('structuralisms typically inhabit a never ending theoretical present');
- *a possible, though non-mandatory, commitment to the demystification of experiential reality* ('a peculiarly enfeebled, and essentially academic, version of intellectual radicalism, in which the world is not so much changed, as contemplated differently');
- *theoreticism* (a 'science of stasis, marked from birth by an inveterate anti-empiricism, becomes almost unavoidably preoccupied with highly abstract theoretical, or formal, models');
- *anti-humanism* ('if neither change nor process nor even the empirical instance are matters of real concern, then the intentions or actions of human subjects, whether individual or collective, can easily be disposed of as irrelevant to the structural properties of systems').

Milner proceeds to identify these characteristics in the work of the early Barthes, the early Foucault, and Althusser. He could have started with earlier structuralists, had he so chosen. Geertz has said of Lévi-Strauss's structuralism, for example, that it 'annuls history, reduces sentiment to a shadow of the intellect, and replaces the particular minds of particular savages in particular jungles with the Savage Mind immanent in us all' (1973, p. 355).

Barthes's early interests had to do with the images and messages (he calls them 'myths') to be found in popular culture (Barthes 1972). Here he cuts a wide swathe, looking at advertising, consumer goods, wrestling, striptease, the Negro soldier saluting the French flag, and other intriguing phenomena. His interests then extend to the general rules and constraints of the narrative and to the nature of literariness. In a well-known text (1977, pp. 142–8), he comes to declare 'the death of the author'. When dealing earlier with the question of hermeneutics, we considered historical trends in literary criticism and reading comprehension theory, noting particular periods that privilege, respectively, the author, the text or the reader. In his essay on the death of the author, Barthes stands with those who, in their search for the source of meaning, look to the text rather than to authorial intent or the activity or abilities of any reader. Yet, even here, Barthes's concern is 'not with the intrinsic properties of the text, but with the conventions that render it intelligible to the reader' (Milner 1991, p. 69). His structuralism represents a shift of interest from meaning to the conditions for meaning.

Foucault denies that he was ever a structuralist but there certainly seem to be structuralist elements in his early work. As Milner observes, in *Madness and Civilization* and *The Birth of the Clinic*, both published in the early 1960s, Foucault is concerned with the systematic nature of the understandings of madness and illness that were dominant in the seventeenth and early eighteenth centuries. He wants to contrast these with the equally systematic understandings that emerged later in the eighteenth century. In each case and on their own terms, Foucault views these understandings as possessing validity. Later in the 1960s, in works such as *The Order of Things* and *The Archaeology of Knowledge*, Foucault becomes preoccupied with the notion of discourse. His focus is on discursive formations or *epistemes*. Milner explains *epistemes* as 'systematic conceptual frameworks which define their own truth criteria, according to which particular knowledge problems are to be resolved, and which are embedded in and imply particular institutional arrangements' (1991, p. 70). This too is structuralist enough.

Althusser, as we noted in Chapter 6, is a Marxist. He came to prominence in the 1960s at a time when a number of European Marxist intellectuals, disillusioned with Stalinism, were interested in forging new links to philosophical currents. There were efforts, for example, to link Marxism to a revitalised Hegelianism and to inject into Marxism elements of contemporary philosophical stances such as existential phenomenology. Some found the bridge they needed in the works of the early (and allegedly more humanistic) Marx. Set against the background of this intellectual thrust, Althusser's attempt to defend Marxist orthodoxy while threading a pathway between Stalinism, on the one hand, and a humanist version of Marxism, on the other, takes a novel form.

Althusser sets the early Marx against the later Marx. The former is an ideologue, the latter a scientist. This fits with Althusser's belief that 'the theoretical practice of a science is always completely distinct from the ideological practice of its prehistory' (1977, pp. 167–8). The science that the later Marx brought forth was dialectical materialism, as a theory of social formations and the manner in which they are structurally determined.

Here Althusser is introducing his own way of defending orthodox Marxism. He incorporates certain key concepts of structuralism into his explication of Marxism. As Milner tells us (1991, p. 70), Althusser proceeds to 'reread Marx's marxism as if it too were a structuralism'. Economics, politics, and ideology itself, as instances of society, are all presented as structures existing within an overarching structure of structures.

> The complex and uneven relationship of the instances to each other was called by Althusser a 'conjuncture'. Every conjuncture was said to be 'overdetermined' in that each of the levels contributed to determining the structure as well as being determined by it: determination was always complex. (McLellan 1995a, pp. 22–3)

It is not difficult to find a basis in the thought of each of these three philosophers for the five characteristics of structuralism that Milner has identified for us. We will not attempt here to substantiate this claim in terms of all five for all three. Suffice it to say, for a start, that their positivism has been widely acknowledged. Thus, Mészáros (1989, p. 182) writes of 'the positivist Althusserian interpretation' of Marxism and 'the positivistic misconceptions of science ascribed to Marx by the Althusserian school'. 'Foucault's earlier writings are also deeply positivist in inspiration', says Milner (1991, p. 70).

It may appear contradictory to describe structuralism as positivist. After all, we have already judged it to be, in epistemological terms, quite subjectivist. Have we not said, right back at the start, that positivism embodies an objectivist epistemology? How can we say that structuralism sees meaning as inherent in the object (objectivism) and, at the same time, that it imposes meaning on the object from elsewhere (subjectivism)? We can do so because we are talking about two different objects. In relation to one, structuralism is subjectivist; in relation to the other, it is objectivist. If what we have in mind as object are realities in the world to which meaning is ascribed, we are right to characterise structuralism as subjectivist, since the formal structure from which meaning is said to derive functions independently of those worldly realities. It is a self-enclosed, self-regulating system. But what if we take the formal structure itself as object? Now we are faced with an object that, according to structuralists, is in itself well and truly meaningful. Meaning resides in it independently of any individual consciousness and it can be studied scientifically. In this respect, structuralism proves to be objectivist and arguably a form of positivism.

Another apparent contradiction arises when Foucault is accused of being ahistorical.[16] After all, historical accounts loom large in what he writes, even early in his career. Nevertheless, as Milner insists (1991, p. 70), the thought of the early Foucault is not essentially historical and remains 'unable to judge between *epistemes* or to explain the shift from one to another'.

As for the invitation to demystification found in structuralism, we should note Barthes' attempts at structuralist demystification in his wide-ranging analysis of 'myths'. Foucault does the same in his analysis of modern psychiatry and modern medicine. And the theoreticism of all three is clear enough from even a cursory study of their writings.

Nor can one doubt the anti-humanism they evince. Barthes is clearly anxious to remove the reader from centre stage in his study of the act of reading. By this move he impugns the more humanist under-standing of the reading of literature. This is no isolated instance but typifies what is for Barthes a general anti-humanistic stance. Of Foucault's anti-humanism there is evidence aplenty. That 'philosophy is still—and again—in the process of coming to an end' and that 'the question of language is being posed' are two facts, he declares, that 'prove no doubt that *man is in the process of disappearing*' (1970, p. 385).

> As the archaeology of our thought easily shows, man is an invention of recent date. And one perhaps nearing its end. If those arrangements were to disappear as they appeared . . . then one can certainly wager that man would be *erased like a face drawn in the sand at the edge of the sea.* (Foucault 1970, p. 387)

In a 1971 interview (1977, pp. 221–2), Foucault describes humanism as 'everything in Western civilization that restricts the *desire for power*'. Indeed, 'it prohibits the desire for power and excludes the possibility of power being seized'. He is not saying this in any laudatory sense: he goes on to advocate 'desubjectification' through political struggle and 'the destruction of the subject as a pseudosovereign' through an attack on culture. The latter would include:

> . . . the suppression of taboos and the limitations and divisions imposed upon the sexes, the setting up of communes, the loosening of inhibitions with regard to drugs; the breaking of all the prohibitions which form and guide the development of a normal individual. I am referring to all those experiences which have been rejected by our civilization or which it only accepts in literature. (Foucault 1977, p. 222)

Althusser is no humanist either. In the complex 'overdetermination' postulated for every conjuncture of society, the 'structured causality resulted in a reading of history as process without a subject—as opposed to the tendency of, for example, Sartre or the early Marx to see human beings as the active subjects of the historical process' (McLellan 1995a, p. 23). In this respect, if we think back to what we discussed in Chapter 7, a striking contrast emerges between the anti-humanist Althusser and the humanist Freire, Marxists though they both claim to be.

Althusser never transcends his structuralism. At most, he may be seen as an intermediary figure between structuralism and post-structuralism. 'Althusser', says Crook (1991, p. 149), 'attempts to hold the line between modernist radicalism and its "post-structuralist" critique; his is a liminal modernist radicalism'. Liminal or not, he remains structuralist and modernist to the end. It is not the same with Barthes and Foucault. They move on to become pivotal figures in the development of post-structuralism, joined by such eminent names as the deconstructionist Jacques Derrida, psychoanalyst Jacques Lacan, and feminists Luce Irigaray and Julia Kristeva.

Another eminent name warrants mention here, the name of a philosopher long dead. To date, you and I have not had occasion to talk about Friedrich Nietzsche (1844–1900) other than in passing. He deserves far better. We have noted Nietzsche's impact on Weber but, in fact, few thinkers since his time have escaped his influence. Harrison (1991, p. 175) describes this influence as 'subterranean'. There have been political reasons for the long repression of Nietzsche's thought. As Harrison points out, those political reasons no longer obtain and we have witnessed 'Nietzsche's return', 'a more direct appropriation of Nietzsche's thought'. Where? 'The two most important receptions of Nietzsche's work in recent times have both occurred in the context of what is conventionally called French poststructuralist thought.' What Harrison instances are Foucault's 'genealogy' and Derrida's 'deconstruction', both of them pivotal concepts within post-structuralism. Accordingly, as we move on to consider post-structuralism, including the thought of Foucault and Derrida, the figure of Nietzsche will loom large, even if we lack the space to spell out its impact in detail.

THE CHARACTER OF POST-STRUCTURALISM

Post-structuralism retains structuralism's commitment to de Saussure's view that the meaning of words derives from their relationship to one another and not from any postulated relationship to non-linguistic reality. However, it places a much more intense focus on the origins of language. As one would expect, there is no unified voice to be heard here. We find language being situated within societal relationships of power (Foucault) and within the unconscious (Lacan), to give just two examples. In such exercises, the difference between post-structuralism and structuralism stands forth in clear relief. Structuralism looks for decisive shaping factors in structural forms discoverable within society or the unconscious, or both. Not so post-structuralism. Structures no longer offer the life line they were once seen to be throwing to the shipwrecked. There is no life line to offer. Post-structuralism has abandoned positivism. It remains ahistorical and theoretical. It still offers its mild invitation to demystify the experience of reality. Above all, it is as anti-humanist as ever. But claims to being 'scientific' have well and truly gone.

> Indeed, for all the *éclat* with which the transition from structuralism to post-structuralism has invariably been announced, the latter clearly exhibits a remarkable fidelity to all but one of the five major structuralist *motifs* we identified above: positivism seems the sole casualty of this bloodless revolution in thought. (Milner 1991, p. 76)

In the move to post-structuralism, Barthes takes his 'death of the author' a step forward. He writes of the distinction between 'readerly' (*lisible*) and 'writerly' (*scriptible*) texts, that is, between texts that envisage a merely passive, receptive reader and those that call upon the reader to be an active creator of meaning. This is an important ingredient in his post-structuralism. The readerly text is bourgeois text. It is realist or classical in form and confirms readers in the subject position assigned to them by culture. Writerly texts, on the contrary, are texts that explode convention and shatter the reader's wholeness. In similar vein, Barthes contrasts 'the text of pleasure' with 'the text of bliss'. The former is comfortable, the latter unsettling and crisis-provoking. Writerly texts, or texts of bliss, are destabilising for both society and the individual ego (Barthes 1975).

Foucault's move from the structuralist orientation he displayed in the 1960s to his 1970s post-structuralism can be detected in his treatment of power.

> His work in the 1960s focused on language and the constitution of the subject in discourse. The individual subject was an empty entity, an intersection of discourses. In his later work Foucault shifted from linguistic determination to the view that individuals are constituted by power relations, power being the ultimate principle of social reality. (Sarup 1993, p. 73)

In Foucault's later work on power, we detect no positivist searching for meaning in linguistic structures or social institutions. Power as he envisages it is not a reality lying there for its meaning to be discovered. It is itself a generator of reality and meaning. Power 'reaches into the very grain of individuals, touches their bodies and inserts itself into their actions and attitudes, their discourses, learning processes and everyday lives' (Foucault 1980, p. 39). 'For Foucault', states Sarup (1993, p. 74), 'conceiving of power as repression, constraint or prohibition is inade-quate: power "produces reality"; it "produces domains of objects and rituals of truth"'. There is no standing back from this power and the discourses it effects. All that one can do is to engage with the dominant discourse from within (shades of Adorno's 'immanent critique'?), attempting to disrupt and demystify it by revealing its indeterminacy and, paradoxically, the possibilities it thereby has to offer.

In this respect at least, as Milner makes clear (1991, p. 75), Foucault manifests an affinity with Derrida 'despite their apparent mutual ani-mosity'. Like Camus and Althusser, Jacques Derrida is Algerian-born. Unlike Barthes and Foucault, he is not a convert from structuralism. In fact, since bursting onto the French academic scene in the late 1960s, he has been a stern critic of structuralism. One of his prime targets has been the positivism it displays. Derrida does not accept the possibility of general laws governing the nature of reality. Nor does he accept the split between subject and object that is required if one is to attempt an 'objective' description of things. For him, as for anti-positivists generally, there can be no description of reality into which the standpoint and interests of the observer have not entered.

One form that Derrida's anti-structuralism takes is a fierce opposition to the fixed relationship that structuralism posits between signifier and signified. In describing the sign, he breaks apart what for Saussure is an essential unity of word and concept. For Saussure word and concept are like sides of a lens that is at once concave and convex. For Derrida, however, word and concept never come together definitively in this fashion. 'He sees the sign', Sarup observes (1993, p. 33), 'as a structure of difference: half of it is always "not there" and the other half is always "not that"'. And signifiers and signifieds refuse to stand still. Signifiers constantly turn into signifieds, which keep turning into signifiers. As we search for meaning, we find ourselves led along a whole concatenation of signifiers/signifieds—an infinite regress of signification.

So words need to be put *sous rature*, Derrida maintains. Literally translated, this means 'under erasure'. Drawing on a device used earlier by Heidegger, Derrida crosses words out but leaves the crossed-out words in the text. It is a move reminiscent of Adorno's negative dialectics. By it Derrida is indicating that, while the word is inadequate, it is still necessary. One must be ready to hold word and concept in precarious tension. What this means, above all else, is that in every sign there remains the trace of 'the other' that eludes our grasp. Something is always absent. Philosophy, of course, has characteristically predicated itself not on absence but on presence. Derrida reverses this. He rejects 'the metaphysics of presence' and directs our attention to absence. 'Our attention is therefore to be constantly displaced', writes Yates (1990, p. 224). 'Every boundary to context, like that of structure and its centre, is no more than a mark within a chain of signifiers in which there are no a priori fixed points, places of certainty or security.'

Suppose we were to read a text with all this in mind. Instead of assuming a definite sense in what is written, we remain aware of the infinite regress of meaning just referred to. We find ourselves engaged in 'a remorseless worrying away at the other possible meanings of words' (Milner 1991, p. 74). We read the text 'so closely that the author's conceptual distinctions on which the text relies are shown to fail on account of the inconsistent and paradoxical use made of these very concepts within the text as a whole'; the very 'standards or definitions which the text sets up' are 'used to unsettle and shatter the original distinctions' (Sarup 1993, pp. 34–5). In such an ironic exercise, we are following in Derrida's footsteps and carrying out what has come to be known as 'deconstruction'.

Sounds like fun, doesn't it? There is, indeed, a playful (or 'ludic') dimension to what Derrida is doing. Yet Derrida is dealing with matters of great moment. The ambiguity associated with the sign mirrors a much deeper ambiguity within human existence itself. As Derrida insists, deconstruction is not neutral but 'intervenes' (1981, p. 93). Reflecting on this, Wolin underscores the need to discover how deconstruction intervenes and on what basis it can claim any privilege or priority as a mode not only of interpreting texts but also of influencing daily social life. As Wolin sees it (1992, p. 199), whether deconstruction 'possesses sufficient conceptual resources for the tasks of contemporary cultural criticism' is a question that must be asked. Derrida, it seems, would agree. Certain of his statements constitute a forthright invitation, issued to all deconstructionists, to engage in self-criticism. 'It is', says Wolin (1992, p. 217), 'an initiative that should be seized'.

Any such self-criticism would need to examine the deconstructionist attitude towards metaphysics. From Derrida's standpoint, metaphysics anal-yses the world in terms of polarities. Derrida lists some of the polarities for us: 'normal/abnormal, standard/parasite, fulfilled/void, serious/non-serious, literal/non-literal, briefly positive/negative and ideal/ non-ideal'. These are 'value oppositions clustered around an ideal and unfindable limit'. One member of each opposition is always subordinated to the other. In this way metaphysics becomes the 'enterprise of returning "strategically", ideally, to an origin or to a "priority" held to be simple, intact, normal, pure, standard, self-identical, in order *then* to think in terms of derivation, complication, deterioration, accident, etc.' (Derrida 1977, p. 236). Derrida's strategy is to address these binary oppositions so beloved of the metaphysicians and to subvert them from within. 'What Derrida does', writes Yates (1990, p. 208), 'is to locate the lacunae and blind-spots within this system, and to attempt to use their unforeseen and unperceived problems and contradictions to invert the terms, overturn the hierarchy and work differently within the field they demarcate'.

In all this, let us note, Derrida focuses on the written rather than the spoken word. It was not that way with Saussure. Speech came first for Saussure, as it has done for Western philosophy generally. As Derrida sees it, Saussure's emphasis on the unity of the sign in speech causes him to collapse voice into thought. The signifier fades from the picture and the concept is allowed to occupy pride of place. 'The exteriority of the signifier seems reduced', complains Derrida (1981, p. 22). Why is this unfortunate? Because it admits 'the possibility of thinking *a concept signified in and of itself*, a concept simply present for thought, independent of a relationship to language, that is of a relationship to a system of signifiers' (Derrida, 1981, p. 19). Derrida rejects such 'phonocentrism', the privileging of the spoken word, and makes writing, rather than speech, his starting point. He goes so far as to say (1976, p. 158), '*There is nothing outside of the text*'. Speech has been traditionally privileged because it appears closer to the presence of meaning. Writing is discounted because it appears a step further away. This is a 'logocentric' way of viewing things. It assumes a 'transcendental signified' (a *logos*), that is, an essence or form of truth in which beliefs can be grounded. It assumes a presence of meaning one might be close to or far removed from. Derrida has no time for a philosophy of presence of this kind. Logocentric as it is, it represents an unwarranted concession to metaphysics.

We have noted above that, for Derrida, the sign is a structure of 'difference'. It is founded as much on the absence of what it is not as on the presence of what it is. Derrida writes of the 'play of differences'. No element of discourse is simply 'present in and of itself'; instead, it bears 'the trace within it of other elements in the chain', so that everywhere there are 'differences of differences and traces of traces' (Derrida 1981, p. 26). In our search for meaning, therefore, we are sent to difference, and meaning is deferred. To capture this twin significance of difference and deferral, Derrida invents a word of his own—*différance*. One is reminded of Heidegger's 'dif-ference' (*Aus-trag*), a movement in which 'Being and beings are borne or carried outside of one another yet at the same time borne toward one another' (Caputo 1982, p. 148).

Already, in this necessarily brief account of Jacques Derrida, we have encountered much that is prominent in post-structuralist literature. 'It would be of little value to produce a list of post-structuralist "concepts"', says Yates (1990, p. 206), 'but many of those we might wish to include stem from Derrida's work'.

Another noted thinker in this tradition is Jacques Lacan. With Lacan, psychoanalysis strides onto the structuralist/post-structuralist stage. Taking the unconscious to be structured like language, Lacan has translated Freud's categories into linguistic forms. As Merquior puts it (1986, p. 149), 'Lacan "Saussureanized" psychoanalysis'. He has been helped in this task by the work of Russian formalist Roman Jakobson (1896–1982), who brought together the literary dichotomy of metaphor/metonymy and Saussure's analysis of language. Lacan seizes upon this same dichotomy to cast light on the workings of the unconscious. He believes, for instance, that one can give Freud's concepts of condensation and displacement greater precision by recasting them as metaphoric and metonymic processes, respectively.[17] 'He sees censorship and repression, the classical Freudian mechanisms, as symbol mills, ever churning out metaphors and metonymies' (Merquior 1986, p. 153).

Taking the unconscious to be structured like language has the further outcome that language and sexuality arrive together. We might revisit what we have already considered about this aspect of Lacan's thought.

> For Lacan, the child originally inhabits a pre-Oedipal 'imaginary' characterised by speechless identity between child, mother and world. Entry into the symbolic order of language, and the acquisition of subjectivity, are achieved only at the price of a loss of this imaginary identity with the mother. The symbolic order is thus masculine, it is, in short, the law of the father. (Milner 1991, p. 95)

Lacan has had significant influence on French feminism. This is evident in the work of Luce Irigaray and Julia Kristeva, whose contributions we considered in the previous chapter. We noted there that, while both are indebted to Lacan, neither has proved to be an orthodox disciple. Irigaray was expelled from Lacan's school at Vincennes because of her divergent views on female sexuality. Kristeva, for her part, significantly reworks Lacan's analysis of the pre-Oedipal situation. Where Lacan posits 'the imaginary', Kristeva talks of 'the semiotic' and, while accepting that the semiotic is repressed, she insists, contrary to Lacan, that it is not superseded. The semiotic—'the "raw material" of significantation, the corporeal libidinal matter that must be harnessed and appropriately channelled'—is a 'movement of "cutting through", breaking down unities' (Sarup 1993, pp. 124, 126).

This cutting through and breaking down entails, among other things, an intertextuality that brings the 'plurality of the text' to the fore. Intertextuality brings all texts together as a matrix within which one text is transported into another. Kristeva expounds intertextuality with impressive insight and considerable originality. Owing particularly to her influence, intertextuality has become a stock theme within post-structuralist discourse. We should not underestimate its impact. It has played a key role, Bannet reminds us, in 'bringing the human sciences together' and enabling post-structuralists 'to give their marginalised disciplines a new centrality and importance'.

> . . . it made it possible for Lacan, Barthes, Foucault and Derrida to roam at will among different types of discourse and among different types of text, pulling things together and making what sense of them they would, without conforming to the traditional limitations and prescriptions of any one discipline or any one text. (Bannet 1989, p. 244)

This constant intertwining and blending of elements once seen as distinct, and the consequent need to disentangle them and redefine them as best we can, is not just true of texts and the disciplines that study them. Everywhere we look, if we are looking through post-structuralist eyes, the once clear-cut lines of demarcation appear blurred. Hierarchical oppositions seem to meld even as they stand apart. The traditional antinomies, so dear to our heart—where have they gone? The focus is now on cutting through and breaking down. It is a process of disentanglement that brings us back to what we have already found to be postmodernism's pivotal theme.

This confluence does not justify an identification of post-structuralism with postmodernism. For the most part, post-structuralism has not come to its standpoint in and out of an encounter with the postmodern world precisely as postmodern world. Claims made on its behalf that it is itself a postmodernism hardly stand up to close scrutiny. 'In general', states Milner (1991, p. 111), 'French post-structuralism has been far too preoccupied with the high modernist canon to accord any serious attention to a contemporary culture that has acquired an increasingly postmodernist complexion'. In regard to Derrida in particular, Wolin makes the comment that he 'has intentionally avoided associating deconstruction with the postmodern turn in criticism and the arts' (1992, p. 206), even if more recently 'he has taken an increasing interest in postmodern architectural theory and practice' (1992, p. 249). For all that, as we return from our excursion into post-structuralism to a consideration of more strictly postmodernist thought, we find ourselves better able, as a result of the former, to appreciate and evaluate the latter.

Back to the postmodern

We may feel safe enough in classifying Jean-François Lyotard (1924–) as postmodernist, if only because he makes an express claim to being just that. Not that this deters commentators from referring to him instead, or in addition, as post-structuralist. It depends, of course, on how one conceptualises the two terms. Wolin, as we have seen, looks to Lyotard's own understanding of the matter, suggesting that, from this perspective, post-structuralism emerges as the epistemological corollary of postmodernism. This allows Wolin (1992, p. 16) to locate Lyotard among post-structuralist thinkers while still emphasising the way in which he engages with the postmodern.

Lyotard does engage with the postmodern and he does so in his own fashion. For him the postmodern is found within the modern, not in any sense apart from it.

> The postmodern would be that which, in the modern, puts forward the unpresentable in presentation itself; that which denies itself the solace of good forms, the consensus of a taste which would make it possible to share collectively the nostalgia for the unattainable; that which searches for new presentations, not in order to enjoy them but in order to impart a stronger sense of the unpresentable. (Lyotard 1984, p. 81)

This takes us to the heart of the postmodernist stance. It is not just a jettisoning of Enlightenment claims to reproduce reality faithfully. Such claims have been well and truly thrown out in the course of the modernist revolt. We noted in Chapter 6 how Adorno uses 'mimesis' and Benjamin's 'constellation' to characterise human thought—not as something 'true' that captures reality conceptually and represents reality-as-it-is, but as a mere mimicking of reality in full recognition that reality is too rich for reason.

Lyotard is not just repeating these modernist strictures against Enlightenment epistemology. He goes much further.

In rejecting objectivist epistemology and the bourgeois realism that feeds on it, modernist forms of cultural criticism offer themselves as alternatives. From the modernist standpoint, we may no longer have clarity and certitude but at least we have a creative and liberating embrace of ambiguity. If we must lose the firm grip we have on reality, we can remind ourselves of the price we pay for having that firm grip in the first place—the repression of so much of reality's richness. We can tell ourselves, in fact, that relaxing the grip will mean a rewarding return of the repressed. Benjamin's and Adorno's constellation resembles the technique that modernist poetry is said to have drawn from painting—'a juxtaposition of details to make a field of force, not an argument' (Donoghue 1994, p. 25). In other words, while a constellation lacks the force of argument, it has a force all its own. There is no doubt about it. Modernist criticism presents itself to us overwhelmingly in redemptive pose.

Lyotard, on the other hand, offers no such redemption. Unlike the modernists, Lyotard does not substitute mimesis or representation for what Enlightenment thinking offers as a grasp of the real. Even such mimetic representation is denied to us, for it is in itself one of the grand narratives (*grands récits*) of modernity that, on Lyotard's accounting, are no longer credible. No matter that the modernist narrative speaks of emancipation rather than speculation. The grand narratives of speculation and emancipation are in the same boat. 'The grand narrative has lost its credibility, regardless of what mode of unification it uses, regardless of whether it is a speculative narrative or a narrative of emancipation.' Both have witnessed 'the decline of the unifying and legitimating power' (Lyotard 1984, pp. 37–8). Included in this decline is each and every 'metadiscourse of this kind making an explicit appeal to some grand narrative, such as the dialectics of Spirit, the hermeneutics of meaning, the emancipation of the rational or working subject, or the creation of wealth' (1984, p. xxviii). What we are left with is not a modernist form of presentation but a 'sense of the unpresentable'—at best, the possibility of a 'stronger' sense of the unpresentable. 'Finally', writes Lyotard, 'it must be clear that it is our business not to supply reality but to invent allusions to the conceivable which cannot be presented' (1984, p. 81).

This is not entirely new. Some phenomenologists certainly glimpsed this radical unpresentability of reality. Gabriel Marcel (1889–1973), for one, loves to tell us that experience is mystery. It is an error 'to take experience for granted and to ignore its mystery' (Marcel 1965, p. 128). How, then, are we to explore the mystery of experience? Not by reasoning discursively and logically about it, as Enlightenment thought would have us do. Marcel is quick to point up the contrast between his 'phenomenological description' and any kind of 'logical schema' (1964, p. 176). Far from reasoning about experience, we listen to it. As musicians might listen to voices joined with them in producing a

THE FOUNDATIONS OF SOCIAL RESEARCH

symphony, we listen to what is for us a grand symphony of being (Marcel 1963, pp. 82–3). Yet, for all our investigation of it, Marcel reminds us, the mystery of being remains mystery and cannot be converted into the content of thought. We cannot describe such mystery. We can only allude to it as poets and musicians do (Marcel 1952, p. 299).

Yet Marcel is no Lyotard. Postmodernism not only brings this acknowledgment of reality's unpresentability to centre stage but links it forcefully to the postmodern condition in which we find ourselves. The postmodern world is at once, and paradoxically, a world of massification and a world of fragmentation. The mass society obliterates time-honoured distinctions and without those distinctions we have no sense of how the whole might fit together. As Lyotard insists, there is no metanarrative that can bring things together for us. There is no meta-language and our language games are thoroughly fragmented.

> In the name of *Lyotard* postmodernism says we're now living with/in the 'postmodern condition', where something funny is happening to the 'metanarratives' we live by—those big stories (of science, progress, Marxism, humanism . . .) that cultures tell themselves in order to understand and legitimate their practices. These narratives are fragmenting into a disorderly array of little, local stories and struggles, with their own, irreconcilable truths. (MacLure 1995, p. 106)

Earlier in this chapter this postmodern condition was described as an implosion and a blurring even of the distinction between the virtual and the real. This fits well enough with what Lyotard is saying to us. However, the word 'implosion' is associated more expressly with the name of Jean Baudrillard (1929–) and it is Baudrillard who, more than any other, focuses on the character of hyperreality and its displacement of what we once considered 'the real'. Baudrillard leaves us with 'simulation' and 'simulacra' in an obliteration of all distinction between the imaginary and the real.

There are other postmodernist theorists, to be sure. Mention might be made of Fredric Jameson, who sees postmodernism as the cultural logic of late capitalism, and Richard Rorty, who has developed a postmodernist version of American pragmatism. There is not space here to give these (or the many others) the attention they deserve. Hopefully, enough has been said to provide something of the flavour of postmodernism.

What the postmodernist spirit has brought into play is primarily an overpowering loss of totalising distinctions and a consequent sense of fragmentation. The boundary between elite and popular culture, between art and life, is no more. Along with that boundary has gone the messianic sense of mission that modernists have allowed themselves.

Under the influence of post-structuralism, even the clear distinction between different texts has gone, with intertextuality inviting us to move at random between them and to read one into the other.

What were formerly regarded as clear-cut differences in style appear to have vanished too. Where, in the past, artists and writers were seen to create particular styles, which could then be parodied, this is no longer the case. All art is repetition. Parody continues, but it is a specifically postmodernist form of parody. It is parody without fun—'pastiche', to use the word that Jameson has popularised in this connection. Pastiche is a mimicking of various styles. These may well be what Sarup (1993, p. 146) dubs 'dead' styles. Dead styles are found, for example, in the nostalgia film. In these films and other media dealing sentimentally with the past, styles long gone from the human scene are revived, thrust together and set before us. This, Dickens tells us (1994, p. 90), is 'a generalization of pastiche onto the collective level'.

Yet, if parody has lost its funniness, there is still a playfulness and carnival spirit in postmodernist work—the ludic element. Irony is forever to the fore, along with allegory, artifice, asymmetry, anarchy.

With all this in mind, we have a number of questions to face. What happens when the postmodernist turns to research? What kind of envisaged world forms the backdrop for postmodernist research? What assumptions does the postmodernist bring to it? What form is the postmodernist's analysis of the human scene likely to take? Given what we have discussed in this chapter, we know there are no tidy answers to any of these questions. They are questions we cannot sidestep, all the same.

10

Conclusion

It is with literature as with law or empire—an established name
is an estate in tenure, or a throne in possession.

Edgar Allan Poe, 'Preface, Letter to Mr B . . .'

It has been a long journey. What are we to do now?

If we are about to engage in a piece of research, should we link our
proposed methodology and methods to one or other of the lines of
thought we have been considering here? More specifically, should we be
saying, 'This research is Heideggerian in orientation', 'My research
follows Gadamer's form of hermeneutics', 'This is critical inquiry of the
type spelled out by Habermas'? Is this the sort of claim we should be
making?

Perhaps. 'Eponymous' research of this kind is found often enough in
the literature.

Invoking the name of one or other icon to characterise one's approach
does raise some interesting and important questions, however. Why one
wants to do that is one of them. What it *means* to do that is another.
And implicit in the latter question is yet another: How faithful does one
need to be to the thought and procedures of the scholar concerned? How
true, for example, does one need to be to Heidegger to justify calling
one's process Heideggerian?

A purist stance would insist that, if we claim to be Heideggerian, or
Gadamerian, or Foucauldian, we must apply to our area of research
precisely and exclusively the approach that Heidegger, Gadamer or
Foucault has enunciated. We will be asking, in effect, 'How would

214

Heidegger, or Gadamer or Foucault have gone about this piece of research?'. This may serve some valid purposes. Of course, following such a path would require a thorough understanding of the mindset and practices of the thinker in question.

We need not be so purist. It is possible to be more or less Heideggerian, more or less Gadamerian, more or less Foucauldian. There may well be aspects of the thinker's thought that we want to dismiss, while other aspects come together to form a useful avenue to what we want to study. In her *Disciplining Foucault*, Jana Sawicki uses Foucault very effectively in this fashion to ground her feminist analysis. On the face of it, this is an improbable enterprise, given the charge of misogyny so often levelled against Foucault. Unsurprisingly, *not* identifying with certain aspects of his discourse proves to be a necessary feature of the task. On the other hand, Sawicki attempts at certain points to flesh out Foucauldian concepts that she finds less than fully developed in Foucault himself. She is thinking feminism *through* Foucault but does not hesitate to think *beyond* Foucault to develop a 'viable Foucauldian feminism' (Sawicki 1991, p. 15).

Picking and choosing of this kind is legitimate enough. Here too, however, we need to have a comprehensive grasp of what Foucault is about. Otherwise, we are in no position to indicate, as Sawicki does, what is authentically Foucauldian and what is not. We would not know whether we were pulling up short of Foucault or moving beyond him. And, of course, in picking and choosing, in pulling up short or going beyond, there easily comes a point where we diverge so far from Foucault that it is no longer legitimate to invoke his name at all. When, for example, the name of Foucault (or Heidegger) is invoked to characterise an analysis that is utterly humanistic from start to finish, surely that point has well and truly been passed.

This is not to preclude a transactional reading of Foucault—or of Heidegger, Gadamer, Habermas or anyone else. Under the rubric of hermeneutics we have discussed a way of reading that makes no attempt to capture what the author meant but engages with the text in very creative mode to develop new meaning. This is not meaning that the author has put into the text; it is not meaning considered to reside in the text; nor is it meaning brought to the text by the reader. It is meaning that comes into being in and out of the reading and only in and out of the reading. Transactional reading is highly commendable. Yet, when such reading is done, the outcomes cannot be laid at the feet of the author. When our engagement with Heidegger's texts brings us to new insights, we cannot in all integrity say, 'This is the thought of Heidegger', 'This is Heideggerian'. We will acknowledge our debt to his texts as our partner in the generation of new meaning, but that is as far as we can go.

Nor should we feel under any compulsion to wrap our research process in the mantle of an eminent scholar in the first place. To take that tack, we need to believe that Heidegger's approach to things, or Gadamer's, or whoever's, will *as such* usefully illuminate the area of human affairs we are researching. That is not always the case. In fact, it is very often not the case.   f

Why, then, have we spent so much time delving into the ideas and modes of analysis of so many thinkers? Certainly not in order to pluck a research paradigm off the shelf. As we noted at the outset, the purpose of our survey is essentially formative. As researchers, we have to devise for ourselves a research process that serves our purposes best, one that helps us more than any other to answer our research question. Having perused and mused over the opinions and procedures of this array of scholars and practitioners, we are in a much better position to do that. We engage in a running conversation with these thinkers. We knock our ideas against theirs. We glean from them an understanding of what is possible in research. We learn how to evaluate strengths and weaknesses in research. Importantly, we become better able to set forth the research process in ways that render it transparent and accountable. All this is educative, not prescriptive.

For all that, it may suit our purposes at times to link methodology—in an explicit fashion and in all its dimensions—to one or more established line of thought. We have dealt in this book with many recognised approaches to research. Invoking one or several of them may help us to set forth the process we plan to follow and, even more importantly, to expound the process we have in fact followed. Could we then be accused of doing what we agreed we should not do? Are we guilty of merely plucking a research approach off the shelf? No, we are not. Rather than selecting established paradigms to follow, we are using established paradigms to delineate and illustrate our own.

What, then, in the end, has this journey meant for us—these ponderings of ours on the foundations of social research? It should mean at least that we can look to the research task with greater clarity and a better sense of direction than we would otherwise have done. Today, Denzin and Lincoln tell us (1994, p. 15), is a 'messy' moment for social research. The study you and I have made has not removed the mess. It has not even reduced it significantly. But it should help us to make our way through it. And that, we may feel, is reward enough.

NOTES

1 *Constructivism* is also used, often interchangeably with constructionism. In Chapter 3 we consider a useful distinction that can be made between the two.

2 Some are ready to level accusations of Cartesian dualism at the very sight of the words 'subject' and 'object'. Nevertheless, every one of us, including every philosopher and social scientist, invokes the concepts of subject and object, if only by talking about them or employing the words 'I' and 'it'. Thereby we posit a *conceptual* distinction between them. Descartes's error was to posit a *real* or *substantial* distinction between, in the first instance, mind (or soul) and body, thus making them distinct things in the world, that is, a *res cogitans* (a 'thinking thing') over against a *res extensa* (an 'extended thing'). This real distinction between mind and body entails a real distinction between mind and everything else in the material universe. This suggests that we can engage in a scientific study of that universe utterly divorced from any considerations of mind (or subject). This is the famous Cartesian split and it has had enormous consequences. Avoiding it, however, does not require us to collapse subject into object (as some forms of realism do) or object into subject (as some forms of idealism do).

3 This understanding of *post-positivism* is not the only way in which the word is used in the literature. For some, post-positivism means 'non-positivism'. Lather, for instance, includes under its umbrella 'phenomenological, hermeneutic, naturalistic, critical, feminist, neo-Marxist, constructivist' forms of social inquiry (1991, p. 7).

4 To *reify*, or engage in *reification*, is to take as a thing (in Latin, *res*) what is not a thing.

5 *Foundationalism*: the epistemological view that knowledge has secure and certain foundations.

6 *Askesis* (in English more commonly *ascesis*, from which 'ascetic' derives) means self-denial. This is self-denial in the sense of denying oneself the use of things. It represents abstemiousness, an extreme frugality.

7 Given the understandings of objectivism, constructionism and subjectivism set out in the Introduction, it is arguable that by and large our meanings are epistemologically subjectivist. For all our talk of constructionism, we do import meanings to the objects, after all. We import them from our culture. From the constructionist viewpoint, however, while this is true of us as individuals, it is not true of us as participants in a given culture. Historically, the culturally inherited meanings did arise out of interaction between humans and the realities in their world. In structuralist, post-structuralist and some postmodernist approaches, this relationship to the world ('intentionality') is not taken account of. Here human understanding sheds its links to mundane reality, sets itself firmly in a self-regulating structural system, and comes to be framed within a quite subjectivist orientation.

8 In 1996, Alan D. Sokal, Professor of Physics at New York University, published an article titled 'Transgressing the boundaries: Towards a transformative hermeneutics of quantum gravity' in the Spring/Summer issue of *Social Text*. Simultaneously, he published an article in another journal revealing that 'Transgressing the boundaries' was a hoax. It was intended to be a parody of epistemological and other theoretical understandings fervently espoused today in social and cultural studies. He made much of the fact that his article, while 'liberally salted with nonsense', was still accepted for publication in what purported to be a respectable journal. The Sokal Affair sparked off an intense, if brief, debate among many scholars, Stanley Fish included.

9 Why only 'in the normal course of events'? For a start, there are occasions when our customary ways of making sense of things just fail to work and we must address them and make sense of them anew. These are normally moments of great trauma. Kurt Wolff (1984, pp. 194–5) talks of the 'extreme situation' when there is 'deep confusion, the unshakeable grip by something new, the feeling that everything is a riddle, that there is no sense to the world'. On such occasions, he reminds us, 'our traditional, habitual, customary methods fail'. Again, it is readily acknowledged that poets and other aesthetes have an ability to read realities in new, unconventional ways at variance with the received notions about them. Then there is phenomenology. Phenomenologists, for their part, make a spirited and methodical attempt to break with conventional understandings and see things afresh. As Spiegelberg describes it (1982, p. 680), phenomenology is 'a determined effort to undo the effect of habitual patterns of thought and to return to the pristine innocence of first seeing'.

10 *Weltanschauung* means 'worldview'; that is, the way one understands the world to be. For the most part, this is an implicit understanding and, as Peirce is suggesting, not a critical process.

11 Side by side with this transformation of phenomenology into what can justly be termed a variant of ethnography, another form of phenomenology emerged in North America. This is ethnomethodology. Launched by Harold Garfinkel, who

published his *Studies in Ethnomethodology* in 1967, it has assumed several contrasting forms. Garfinkel's ethnomethodology focuses on an everyday world
characterised by consistency, coherence, planfulness, method and reproducibility.
The 'members' of that everyday world have to work hard to make it appear
organised and accountable in this way. They have their own ways of identifying
properties of this kind and making them accountable to themselves. Accounts
of such 'methods', revealed in members' behaviour (*ethno*-methods, therefore,
since they belong to the 'people' or the 'folk'), form the focal point of
ethnomethodological investigation. Ethnomethodologists invoke their own form
of the phenomenological reduction, putting in brackets all beliefs and understandings about the everyday world except the practices that members use to
produce and maintain the setting as something understandable, consistent and
accountable.

12 *Historicism* is a much abused term. For some it means an acknowledgment of
historically situated social evolution. Understood in this way, historicism means
that there are laws of historical development at work. 'Historicism', writes Blaikie
(1993, p. 22), expounding the term as Popper understands it, 'aims at developing
laws of historical development, laws that link up the successive historical periods,
laws of process and change rather than uniformities'. In this same vein, Sarup
(1993, p. 2) points to the structuralist and post-structuralist 'critique of historicism' and finds in it 'an antipathy to the notion that there is an overall pattern
in history'. The examples that Sarup provides of such anti-historicism are
Foucault, who 'writes about history without having the notion of progress', and
Derrida, who 'says there is no end point in history'. All the same, identifying
historicism with social evolutionism, that is, with the notion that some kind of
process is working itself out through the course of history, is a relatively recent
usage. It is attributable, it would seem, to Popper. An earlier usage takes
'historicism' to mean precisely the opposite. It represents a rejection of social
evolutionism with the consequent demand that every historical stage, situation
or phenomenon be judged on its own terms. An even earlier usage has the term
simply emphasising the radical importance of history for any understanding of
humans and their situation. Human beings are essentially historical beings and
no phenomenon can be adequately comprehended apart from its historical
context. In this last sense, historicism is synonymous with historicality, so that
'antihistoricist' (or 'non-historicist') is to be understood as 'ahistorical'. 'Historicist' can be applied to Dilthey in each of these last two senses.

13 The basic meaning of the Greek word λογos is 'word'. Heidegger is here referring
to the function of '-logy' in the word 'phenomenology'. As in similar constructions (theology as the knowledge or study of God, anthropology as the knowledge
or study of human beings), here too '-logy' denotes study or knowledge—in this
case, of phenomena. What Heidegger is stressing is that gaining knowledge in
phenomenology has an essentially hermeneutic character. It has, he says, 'the
character of a ἑρμηνευειν', which, as we have already noted, means 'to interpret'.

The word 'Dasein' is a common German term, almost a colloquialism, for
'existence'. It means literally 'being-there'. Heidegger uses it to denote 'human

being'—not as a human subject *per se*, but as the *locus* where Being manifests itself.

14 Jay paints a different picture. While admitting 'the magnitude of the Frankfurt School's challenge to the conventional wisdom of American social thought' (1973, p. 297), he lays the blame for the Institute's isolation in the USA rather squarely at the feet of the Institute itself, writing of its 'zealous preservation of its outsider status' (1973, p. 292).

15 In this attempt to do some 'sorting out', the particular debt I owe to Andrew Milner's *Contemporary Cultural Theory: An Introduction* (1991) will be obvious.

16 In describing structuralism, Milner uses the word 'anti-historicist'. In note 12 above we have taken account of three different senses of the word 'historicism'. In claiming that structuralisms are antihistoricist because they 'typically inhabit a never ending theoretical present', Milner would appear to be using the term in the third of these senses, that is, as underlining the essentially historical character of all things human. Hence the substitution of 'ahistorical' for Milner's 'anti-historicist'.

17 In Freudian theory, condensation and displacement are mechanisms whereby repressed desires can be formulated in ways acceptable to the psychic censor. In condensation, qualities pertaining to unacceptable elements merge with qualities relating to acceptable elements. For this to happen, there needs to be some kind of likeness between them. Metaphor too emphasises similarity, since it is a figure of speech that relates two unlikely items so as to suggest an identity between them (ship and camel in the metaphor 'ship of the desert'). In displacement, on the other hand, psychic energy shifts from an unacceptable element to an acceptable element. For this to happen, there needs to be some form of proximity between the elements. Now metonymy can be seen as emphasising contiguity of this kind. It is a figure of speech wherein a part or an attribute stands for the whole ('She has been on the stage for twenty years', with 'stage' representing the theatrical profession). In metonymy, the part or attribute needs to be observable side by side with the whole it will come to represent. Hence Lacan's linking of condensation to metaphor and displacement to metonymy.

BIBLIOGRAPHY

Adorno, T.W. 1973 *Negative Dialectics*, Routledge & Kegan Paul, London
——1974 *Minima Moralia: Reflections from Damaged Life*, NLB, London
——1977 'The actuality of philosophy' *Telos* vol. 31, Spring, pp. 120–33
——1981 *Prisms*, MIT Press, Cambridge
——1984 *Aesthetic Theory*, Routledge, Boston
Alcoff, L. & Potter, E. 1993 'Introduction: When feminisms intersect epistemology' *Feminist Epistemologies*, eds L. Alcoff & E. Potter, Routledge, New York, pp. 1–14
Alinsky, S. 1972 *Rules for Radicals: A Practical Primer for Realistic Radicals*, Vintage Books, New York
Althusser, L. 1977 *For Marx*, New Left Books, London
Apel, K. 1980 *Towards a Transformation of Philosophy*, Routledge & Kegan Paul, London
——1984 *Understanding and Explanation*, MIT Press, Cambridge
Armstrong, E.G. 1976 'On phenomenology and sociological theory' *British Journal of Sociology* vol. 27, no. 2, June, pp. 251–3
Aron, R. 1965 *Main Currents in Sociological Thought* vol. I, Penguin, Harmondsworth
Assiter, A. 1996 *Enlightened Women: Modernist Feminism in a Postmodern Age*, Routledge, London
Bannet, E.T. 1989 *Structuralism and the Logic of Dissent: Barthes, Derrida, Foucault, Lacan*, Macmillan, Basingstoke
Barthes, R. 1972 *Mythologies*, Jonathan Cape, London
——1975 *The Pleasure of the Text*, Hill & Wang, New York
——1976 *Sade/Fourier/Loyola*, Hill & Wang, New York
——1977 *Image—Music—Text*, Fontana/Collins, London
Becker, H. 1963 *Outsiders: Studies in the Sociology of Deviance*, Free Press, New York
Benjamin, W. 1969 *Illuminations*, Schocken, New York
Benner, P. 1985 'Quality of life: A phenomenological perspective on explanation, prediction, and understanding in nursing science' *Advances in Nursing Science* vol. 8, no. 1, pp. 1–14

Benston, M. 1969 'The political economy of women's liberation' *Monthly Review* vol. 21, no. 4, September, pp. 13–27

Berger, P.L. & Luckmann, T. 1967 *The Social Construction of Reality: A Treatise in the Sociology of Knowledge*, Anchor Books, Garden City

Blackburn, S. 1994 *The Oxford Dictionary of Philosophy*, Oxford University Press, Oxford

Blaikie, N. 1993 *Approaches to Social Enquiry*, Polity, Cambridge

Bloch, M. 1983 *Marxism and Anthropology*, Oxford University Press, Oxford

Blumer, H. 1969 *Symbolic Interactionism: Perspective and Method*, Prentice Hall, Englewood Cliffs

Bogdan, D. 1990 'In and out of love with literature' *Beyond Communication: Reading Comprehension and Criticism*, eds D. Bogdan & S.B. Straw, Boynton/Cook, Portsmouth, pp. 109–37

Bourne, R. 1977 *The Radical Will: Selected Writings 1911–1918*, ed. O. Hansen, Urizen Books, New York

Brenkman, J. 1987 *Culture and Domination*, Cornell University Press, Ithaca

Brentano, F. 1973 *Psychology from an Empirical Standpoint*, Routledge & Kegan Paul, London

Bruner, J. 1986 *Actual Minds, Possible Worlds*, Harvard University Press, Cambridge

Buck-Morss, S. 1977 *The Origin of Negative Dialectics*, Macmillan, New York

Caputo, J.D. 1982 *Heidegger and Aquinas: An Essay on Overcoming Metaphysics*, Fordham University Press, New York

Champagne, R. 1984 *Literary History in the Wake of Roland Barthes: Re-Defining the Myths of Reading*, Summa Publications, Birmingham

Chester, G. 1979 'I call myself a radical feminist' *Feminist Practice: Notes from the Tenth Year*, eds Organising Collective, Theory Press, London, pp. 12–15

Cioran, E.M. 1976 *The Temptation to Exist*, Quadrangle/The New York Times Book Co., New York

Cixous, H. 1981 'The laugh of the Medusa' *New French Feminisms*, eds E. Marks & I. de Courtivron, Schocken Books, New York, pp. 245–64

Cixous, H. & Clement, C. 1986 *The Newly Born Woman*, University of Minnesota Press, Minneapolis

Clough, P.T. 1994 *Feminist Thought: Desire, Power, and Academic Discourse*, Blackwell, Oxford

Connerton, P. 1980 *The Tragedy of Enlightenment: An Essay on the Frankfurt School*, Cambridge University Press, Cambridge

Coser, L.A. 1971 *Masters of Sociological Thought: Ideas in Historical and Social Context*, Harcourt Brace Jovanovich, New York

Craib, I. 1984 *Modern Social Theory: From Parsons to Habermas*, Wheatsheaf Books, Brighton

Crook, S. 1991 *Modernist Radicalism and Its Aftermath: Foundationalism and Anti-Foundationalism in Radical Social Theory*, Routledge, London

Crotty, M. 1995 'Phenomenology as radical criticism' *Proceedings, Asia-Pacific Human Science Research Conference*, eds F. Kretlow, D. Harvey, J. Grubb, J. Raybould, G. Sandhu & H. Dosser, Monash University, Churchill, pp. 87–97

——1996a *Phenomenology and Nursing Research*, Churchill Livingstone, Melbourne

——1996b 'Doing phenomenology' *Qualitative Research Practice in Adult Education*, eds P. Willis & B. Neville, David Lovell Publishing, Melbourne, pp. 272–82

——1997 'Tradition and culture in Heidegger's *Being and Time*' *Nursing Inquiry* vol. 4, no. 2, June, pp. 88–98

Dalla Costa, M. & James, S. 1972 *The Power of Women and the Subversion of the Community*, Falling Wall Press, Bristol

Dallmayr, F. 1997 'The politics of nonidentity: Adorno, postmodernism—and Edward Said' *Political Theory* vol. 25, no. 1, February, pp. 33–56

de Beauvoir, S. 1953 *The Second Sex*, Jonathan Cape, London

Denzin, N.K. 1978 'The methodological implications of symbolic interactionism for the study of deviance' *Contemporary Social Theories*, ed. A. Wells, Goodyear, Santa Monica, pp. 99–108

Denzin, N.K. & Lincoln, Y.S. (eds) 1994 *Handbook of Qualitative Research*, Sage, Thousand Oaks

Derrida, J. 1976 *Of Grammatology*, Johns Hopkins University Press, Baltimore

——1977 'Limited Inc abc' *Glyph 2*, Johns Hopkins University Press, Baltimore, pp. 162–254

——1981 *Positions*, Johns Hopkins University Press, Baltimore

de Saussure, F. 1974 *Course in General Linguistics*, Fontana, London

Dewey, J. 1929 *Experience and Nature*, Open Court, La Salle

Dews, P. 1987 *Logics of Disintegration: Post-Structuralist Thought and the Claims of Critical Theory*, Verso, London

Dickens, D.R. 1994 'North American theories of postmodern culture' *Postmodernism and Social Inquiry*, eds D.R. Dickens & A. Fontana, Guilford Press, New York, pp. 76–100

Dilthey, W. 1976a 'The rise of hermeneutics' *Critical Sociology: Selected Readings*, ed. P. Connerton, Penguin, Harmondsworth, pp. 104–16

——1976b *Selected Writings*, Cambridge University Press, Cambridge

Donoghue, D. 1994 *The Old Moderns*, Alfred A. Knopf, New York

Durkheim, É. 1964 *The Rules of Sociological Method*, Free Press, New York

——1976 *The Elementary Forms of the Religious Life*, George Allen & Unwin, London

Eco, U., with Rorty, R., Culler, J. & Brooke-Rose, C. 1992 *Interpretation and Overinterpretation*, ed. S. Collini, Cambridge University Press, Cambridge

Farber, M. 1991 'Phenomenology' *The Concise Encyclopedia of Western Philosophy and Philosophers* revised edn, eds J.O. Urmson & J. Rée, Routledge, London, pp. 233–5

Farganis, S. 1986 *Social Reconstruction of the Feminine Character*, Rowman & Littlefield, Totowa

Feyerabend, P. 1987 *Farewell to Reason*, Verso, London

——1991 *Three Dialogues on Knowledge*, Basil Blackwell, Cambridge

——1993 *Against Method* 3rd edn, Verso, London

——1996 *Killing Time*, University of Chicago Press, Chicago

Fink-Eitel, H. 1992 *Foucault: An Introduction*, Pennbridge Books, Philadelphia

Firestone, S. 1970 *The Dialectic of Sex*, Bantam Books, New York

Fischer, E. 1973 *Marx in His Own Words*, Penguin, Harmondsworth

Fish, S. 1990 'How to recognize a poem when you see one' *Ways of Reading: An Anthology for Writers* 2nd edn, eds D. Bartholomae & A. Petrosky, Bedford Books of St Martin's Press, Boston, pp. 178–91

Fonow, M.M. & Cook, J.A. 1991 'Back to the future: A look at the second wave of feminist epistemology and methodology' *Beyond Methodology: Feminist Scholarship as Lived Research*, eds M.M. Fonow & J.A. Cook, Indiana University Press, Bloomington, pp. 1–15

Foucault, M. 1967 *Madness and Civilization: A History of Insanity in the Age of Reason*, Tavistock, London

——1970 *The Order of Things: An Archaeology of the Human Sciences*, Tavistock, London

——1972 *The Archaeology of Knowledge*, Tavistock, London

——1973 *The Birth of the Clinic: An Archaeology of Medical Perception*, Tavistock, London

——1977 'Revolutionary action: Until now' *Language, Counter-Memory, Practice*, ed. D.F. Bouchard, Cornell University Press, New York, pp. 218–34

——1980 *Power/Knowledge: Selected Interviews and other Writings*, Harvester, Brighton

Freeman-Moir, J. 1992 'Reflections on the methods of marxism' *Educational Philosophy and Theory* vol. 24, no. 2, pp. 98–128

Freire, P. 1972a *Pedagogy of the Oppressed*, Penguin, Harmondsworth

——1972b *Cultural Action for Freedom*, Penguin, Harmondsworth

——1976 *Education: The Practice of Freedom*, Writers & Readers Publishing Cooperative, London

——1985 *The Politics of Education: Culture, Power and Liberation*, Macmillan, London

——1993 *Pedagogy of the City*, Continuum, New York

Friedan, B. 1974 *The Feminine Mystique*, Dell, New York

——1981 *The Second Stage*, Summit Books, New York

Gadamer, H-G. 1989 *Truth and Method* 2nd edn, Crossroad, New York

Geertz, C. 1973 *The Interpretation of Cultures*, Basic Books, New York

Gergen, K.J. 1985 'The social constructionist movement in modern psychology' *American Psychologist* vol. 40, pp. 266–75

Gergen, K.J. & Gergen, M.M. 1991 'Toward reflexive methodologies' *Research and Reflexivity*, ed. F. Steier, Sage, Newbury Park, pp. 76–95

Gerhart, M. & Russell, A. 1984 *Metaphoric Process: The Creation of Scientific and Religious Understanding*, Texas Christian University Press, Fort Worth

Giddens, A. 1976 *New Rules of Sociological Method: A Positive Critique of Interpretative Sociologies*, Hutchinson, London

——1979 *Studies in Social and Political Theory*, Hutchinson, London

——1991 *Modernity and Self-Identity: Self and Society in the Late Modern Age*, Stanford University Press, Stanford

Gilligan, C. 1982 *In a Different Voice: Psychological Theory and Women's Development*, Harvard University Press, Cambridge

Glaser, B.G. & Strauss, A.L. 1967 *The Discovery of Grounded Theory: Strategies for Qualitative Research*, Aldine, Chicago

Goffman, E. 1959 *The Presentation of Self in Everyday Life*, Doubleday, New York

Goodman, N. 1978 *Ways of Worldmaking*, Hackett, Indianapolis

——1984 *Of Mind and Other Matters*, Harvard University Press, Cambridge

Goodman, N. & Elgin, C. 1988 *Reconceptions in Philosophy and Other Arts and Sciences*, Hackett, Indianapolis

Greenwood, J. 1994 'Action research and action researchers: Some introductory considerations' *Contemporary Nurse* vol. 3, no. 2, pp. 84–92

Guba, E.G. & Lincoln, Y.S. 1989 *Fourth Generation Evaluation*, Sage, Newbury Park

——1994 'Competing paradigms in qualitative research' *Handbook of Qualitative Research*, eds N.K. Denzin & Y.S. Lincoln, Sage, Thousand Oaks, pp. 105–17

Guerin, W.L, Labor, E.G., Morgan, L. & Willingham, J.R. 1979 *A Handbook of Critical Approaches to Literature* 2nd edn, Harper, New York

Habermas, J. 1970a 'On systematically distorted communication' *Inquiry* vol. 13, no. 3, pp. 205–18

——1970b 'Toward a theory of communicative competence' *Inquiry* vol. 13, no. 4, pp. 360–76

——1972 *Knowledge and Human Interests*, Heinemann, London

——1973 'Wahreitstheorin' *Wirklichkeit und Reflexion*, ed. H. Fahrenbach, Neske, Pfullingen, pp. 211–66

——1979 *Communication and the Evolution of Society*, Beacon Press, Boston

——1984 *The Theory of Communicative Action* vol. 1 *Reason and the Rationalization of Society*, Beacon Press, Boston

——1987 *The Philosophical Discourse of Modernity*, MIT Press, Cambridge

——1988 *On the Logic of the Social Sciences*, MIT Press, Cambridge

Hamlyn, D.W. 1995 'Epistemology, history of' *The Oxford Companion to Philosophy*, ed. T. Honderich, Oxford University Press, Oxford, pp. 242–5

Hammersley, M. 1985 'Ethnography: What it is and what it offers' *Research and Evaluation Methods in Special Education*, eds S. Hegarty & P. Evans, Nefar-Nelson, Philadelphia, pp. 152–63

Hanson, N.R. 1972 *Patterns of Discovery*, Cambridge University Press, Cambridge

Harding, S. 1983 'Is gender a variable in conceptions of rationality?' *Beyond Domination: New Perspectives on Women and Philosophy*, ed. C.C. Gould, Rowman & Allanheld, Totowa, pp. 43–63

——1987 'Introduction: Is there a feminist methodology?' *Feminism and Methodology*, ed. S. Harding, Open University Press, Milton Keynes, pp. 1–14

Hardison Jr, O.B. 1989 *Disappearing through the Skylight: Culture and Technology in the Twentieth Century*, Penguin, New York

Harré, R. (ed.) 1986 *The Social Construction of Emotions*, Basil Blackwell, Oxford

Harrison, P.R. 1991 'Nietzsche' *Social Theory: A Guide to Central Thinkers*, ed. P. Beilharz, Allen & Unwin, Sydney, pp. 175–80

Hartmann, H. 1981 'The unhappy marriage of Marxism and feminism: Towards a more progressive union' *Women and Revolution: A Discussion of the Unhappy Marriage of Marxism and Feminism*, ed. L. Sargent, South End Press, Boston, pp. 1–41

Hawkes, T. 1977 *Structuralism and Semiotics*, Methuen, London

Heidegger, M. 1949 'Hölderlin and the essence of poetry' *Existence and Being*, ed. W. Brock, Regnery, Chicago, pp. 270–91

——1959 *An Introduction to Metaphysics*, Yale University Press, New Haven

——1962 *Being and Time*, Basil Blackwell, Oxford

——1971 *On the Way to Language*, Harper & Row, New York

——1975 *Poetry, Language, Thought*, Harper Colophon, New York

——1977 *Basic Writings*, ed. D.F. Krell, Harper & Row, New York

——1989 *Beiträge zur Philosophie* vol. 65 *Gesamtausgabe*, ed. F.-W. von Hermann, Klostermann, Frankfurt am Main

Heron, J. 1992 *Feeling and Personhood: Psychology in Another Key*, Sage, London

Hirsch, E.D. 1967 *Validity in Interpretation*, Yale University Press, New Haven

——1987 *Cultural Literacy: What Every American Needs to Know*, Houghton Mifflin, Boston

Horkheimer, M. 1973 'Foreword' *The Dialectical Imagination: A History of the Frankfurt School and the Institute of Social Research 1923–1950* by M. Jay, Heinemann, London

——1974 *Eclipse of Reason*, Seabury, New York

——1982 *Critical theory: Selected Essays*, Continuum, New York

Horkheimer, M. & Adorno, T.W. 1972 *Dialectic of Enlightenment*, Continuum, New York

Horowitz, I.L. 1966 'Introduction: The intellectual genesis of C. Wright Mills' *Sociology and Pragmatism: The Higher Learning in America* by C. Wright Mills, Oxford University Press, New York, pp. 11–31

Humphrey, N. 1993 *A History of the Mind*, Vintage, London

Husserl, E. 1931 *Ideas: General Introduction to Pure Phenomenology*, George Allen & Unwin, London

——1970a *Logical Investigations* vols I–II, Routledge & Kegan Paul, London

——1970b *The Crisis of European Sciences and Transcendental Phenomenology*, Northwestern University Press, Evanston

Huyssen, A. 1988 *After the Great Divide: Modernism, Mass Culture and Postmodernism*, Macmillan, London

Jaggar, A. 1989 'Love and knowledge: Emotion in feminist epistemology' *Women, Knowledge and Reality: Explorations in Feminist Philosophy*, eds A. Garry & M. Pearsall, Unwin Hyman, Boston, pp. 129–55

James, H. 1956 *Autobiography*, ed. F.W. Dupee, Criterion, New York

——1962 *The Art of the Novel*, ed. R.P. Blackmur, Scribner's, New York

——1969 *The American Scene*, Indiana University Press, Bloomington

James, W. 1950 'What pragmatism means' *Pragmatism and American Culture*, ed. G. Kennedy, Heath & Co., Lexington, pp. 1–23

Jay, M. 1973 *The Dialectical Imagination: A History of the Frankfurt School and the Institute of Social Research 1923–1950*, Heinemann, London

Johnson, P. 1984 *Marxist Aesthetics: The Foundations within Everyday Life for an Emancipated Consciousness*, Routledge & Kegan Paul, London

Kearney, R. 1991 'Ricoeur' *The Concise Encyclopedia of Western Philosophy and Philosophers* revised edn, eds J.O. Urmson & J. Rée, Routledge, London, pp. 277–8

Kincheloe, J.L. & McLaren, P.L. 1994 'Rethinking critical theory and qualitative research' *Handbook of Qualitative Research*, eds N.K. Denzin and Y.S. Lincoln, Sage, Thousand Oaks, pp. 138–57

Kipnis, L. 1989 'Feminism: The political conscience of postmodernism?' *Universal Abandon? The Politics of Postmodernism*, ed. A. Ross, Edinburgh University Press, Edinburgh, pp. 149–66

Knapp, S. & Michaels, W.B. 1985 'Pragmatism and literary theory III: A reply to Richard Rorty, What is pragmatism?' *Critical Inquiry* vol. 11, March, pp. 466–73

Kristeva, J. 1982 *Powers of Horror: An Essay on Abjection*, Columbia University Press, New York

——1984 *Revolution in Poetic Language*, Columbia University Press, New York

——1986 *The Kristeva Reader*, ed. T. Moi, Basil Blackwell, Oxford

Kuhn, T.S. 1970 *The Structure of Scientific Revolutions* revised edn, University of Chicago Press, Chicago

——1977 *The Essential Tension*, University of Chicago Press, Chicago

Larrabee, M.J. 1990 'The contexts of phenomenology as theory' *Human Studies* vol. 13, pp. 195–208

Lash, S. 1991 'Introduction' *Post-Structuralist and Postmodernist Sociology*, ed. S. Lash, Edward Elgar, Aldershot

Lather, P. 1991 *Getting Smart: Feminist Research and Pedagogy within the Postmodern*, Routledge, New York

Lechte, J. 1994 *Fifty Key Contemporary Thinkers: From Structuralism to Postmodernity*, Routledge, London

Lévi-Strauss, C. 1966 *The Savage Mind*, University of Chicago Press, Chicago

Lewis, J. 1975 *Max Weber and Value-Free Sociology: A Marxist Critique*, Lawrence & Wishart, London

Lichtheim, G. 1968 *The Origins of Socialism*, Weidenfeld & Nicolson, London

Lyotard, J-F. 1984 *The Postmodern Condition: A Report on Knowledge*, University of Minnesota Press, Minneapolis

——1991 *Phenomenology*, State University of New York Press, Albany

McCarthy, T. 1984 *The Critical Theory of Jürgen Habermas* 2nd edn, Polity, Cambridge

Macionis, J.J. 1991 *Sociology* 3rd edn, Prentice Hall, Englewood Cliffs

McLellan, D. 1995a 'Althusser, Louis' *The Oxford Companion to Philosophy*, ed. T. Honderich, Oxford University Press, Oxford, pp. 22–3

——1995b 'Marxist philosophy' *The Oxford Companion to Philosophy*, ed. T. Honderich, Oxford University Press, Oxford, pp. 526–8

MacLure, M. 1995 'Postmodernism: A postscript' *Educational Action Research* vol. 3, no. 1, pp. 105–6

Macquarrie, J. 1973 *Existentialism*, Penguin, Harmondsworth

MacRae, D.G. 1974 *Weber*, Fontana/Collins, London

Mannheim, K. 1936 *Ideology and Utopia: An Introduction to the Sociology of Knowledge*, Harcourt, Brace & World, New York

Marcel, G. 1952 *Metaphysical Journal*, Rockliff, London

——1963 *The Existential Background of Human Dignity*, Harvard University Press, Cambridge

——1964 *Creative Fidelity*, Farrar, Straus & Giroux, New York

——1965 *The Philosophy of Existentialism* 5th edn, Citadel, New York

Marcus, G.E. 1994 'What comes (just) after "post"? The case of ethnography' *Handbook of Qualitative Research*, eds N.K. Denzin & Y.S. Lincoln, Sage, Thousand Oaks, pp. 563–74

Marcuse, H. 1968 *Negations: Essays in Critical Theory*, Allen Lane/Penguin, London

Marías, J. 1967 *History of Philosophy*, Dover, New York

Marshall, G. (ed.) 1994 *The Concise Oxford Dictionary of Sociology*, Oxford University Press, Oxford

Marton, F. 1986 'Phenomenography: A research approach to investigating different understandings of reality' *Journal of Thought* vol. 21, no. 3, Fall, pp. 28–49

Marx, K. 1961 *Selected Writings in Sociology and Social Philosophy* 2nd edn, eds T.B. Bottomore & M. Rubel, Penguin, Harmondsworth

——1963 *The Poverty of Philosophy*, International Publishers, New York

——1964 *Economic and Philosophic Manuscripts of 1844*, International Publishers, New York

Marx, K. & Engels, F. 1937 *The Communist Manifesto*, Lawrence & Wishart, London

——1969 *Selected Works* vol. I, Progress Publishers, Moscow

Maynard, M. 1994 'Methods, practice and epistemology: The debate about feminism and research' *Researching Women's Lives from a Feminist Perspective*, eds M. Maynard and J. Purvis, Taylor & Francis, London, pp. 10–26

Mead, G.H. 1934 *Mind, Self and Society*, University of Chicago Press, Chicago

——1964 *Selected Writings*, ed. A.J. Reck, Bobbs-Merrill, New York

Merleau-Ponty, M. 1962 *Phenomenology of Perception*, Routledge & Kegan Paul, London

——1964 *Signs*, Northwestern University Press, Evanston

Merquior, J.G. 1986 *From Prague to Paris: A Critique of Structuralist and Post-Structuralist Thought*, Verso, London

Mészáros, I. 1989 *The Power of Ideology*, New York University Press, New York

Mies, M. 1991 'Women's research or feminist research? The debate surrounding feminist science and methodology' *Beyond Methodology: Feminist Scholarship as Lived Research*, eds M.M. Fonow & J.A. Cook, Indiana University Press, Bloomington, pp. 60–84

Millett, K. 1970 *Sexual Politics*, Doubleday, New York

Milner, A. 1991 *Contemporary Cultural Theory: An Introduction*, Allen & Unwin, Sydney

Mitchell, J.C. 1977 'The logic and methods of sociological inquiry' *Introducing Sociology* 2nd edn, ed. P. Worsley, Penguin, Harmondsworth, pp. 73–121

Mumford, L. 1950 'The pragmatic acquiescence' *Pragmatism and American Culture*, ed. G. Kennedy, D.C. Heath & Co., Lexington, pp. 36–49

Natanson, M.A. 1973 *Edmund Husserl: Philosopher of Infinite Tasks*, Northwestern University Press, Evanston

Nelson, C., Treichler, P.A. & Grossberg, L. 1992 'Cultural studies' *Cultural Studies*, eds L. Grossberg, C. Nelson and P.A. Treichler, Routledge, New York, pp. 1–16

Oakley, A. 1974 *The Sociology of Housework*, Martin Robertson, London

O'Connor, R. 1979 'Ortega's reformulation of Husserlian phenomenology' *Philosophy and Phenomenological Research* vol. 40, no. 1, September, pp. 53–63

Okrent, M. 1988 *Heidegger's Pragmatism: Understanding, Being, and the Critique of Metaphysics*, Cornell University Press, Ithaca

Ortega y Gasset, J. 1958 *Man and Crisis*, Norton, New York

——1963 *Concord and Liberty*, Norton, New York

——1964 *Obras Completas* vol. 6, 6th edn, Revista de Occidente, Madrid

Outhwaite, W. 1994 *Habermas: A Critical Introduction*, Polity, Cambridge

Palmer, R. 1969 *Hermeneutics: Interpretation Theory in Schleiermacher, Dilthey, Heidegger, and Gadamer*, Northwestern University Press, Evanston

Peirce, C.S. 1931–58 *The Collected Papers of Charles Sanders Peirce* vols 1–6 eds C. Hartshorne & P. Weiss, vols 7–8, ed. A. Burks, Harvard University Press, Cambridge

Popper, K.R. 1957 *The Open Society and Its Enemies*, Routledge & Kegan Paul, London

——1959 *The Logic of Scientific Discovery*, Basic Books, New York

——1963 *Conjectures and Refutations: The Growth of Scientific Knowledge*, Routledge & Kegan Paul, London

——1972 *Objective Knowledge: An Evolutionary Approach*, Clarendon Press, Oxford

Popper, K.R. & Eccles, J.C. 1977 *The Self and Its Brain*, Springer International, New York

Posnock, R. 1991 *The Trial of Curiosity: Henry James, William James, and the Challenge of Modernity*, Oxford University Press, New York

Psathas, G. 1973 'Introduction' *Phenomenological Sociology: Issues and Applications*, ed. G. Psathas, Wiley, New York, pp. 1–21

Rasmussen, D.M. 1990 *Reading Habermas*, Basil Blackwell, Cambridge

Rée, J. 1991 'Post-modernism' *The Concise Encyclopedia of Western Philosophy and Philosophers* revised edn, eds J.O. Urmson & J. Rée, Routledge, London, p. 256

Rescher, N. 1995 'Pragmatism' *The Oxford Companion to Philosophy*, ed. T. Honderich, Oxford University Press, Oxford, pp. 710–13

Rich, A. 1990 'When we dead awaken: Writing as re-vision' *Ways of Reading: An Anthology for Writers* 2nd edn, eds D. Bartholomae & A. Petrosky, Bedford Books of St Martin's Press, Boston, pp. 482–96

Richards, J.R. 1982 *The Sceptical Feminist: A Philosophical Enquiry*, Penguin, Harmondsworth

Richardson, W. 1963 *Heidegger: Through Phenomenology to Thought*, Martinus Nijhoff, The Hague

Ricoeur, P. 1974 *The Conflict of Interpretations: Essays in Hermeneutics*, Northwestern University Press, Evanston

——1976 *Interpretation Theory, Discourse and the Surplus of Meaning*, Texas Christian University Press, Fort Worth

——1981 *Hermeneutics and the Human Sciences*, Cambridge University Press, Cambridge

Rochberg-Halton, E. 1986 *Meaning and Modernity: Social Theory in the Pragmatic Attitude*, University of Chicago Press, Chicago

Roderick, R. 1986 *Habermas and the Foundations of Critical Theory*, Macmillan, Basingstoke

Rogers, M.F. 1981 'Taken-for-grantedness' *Current Perspectives in Social Theory* vol. 2, pp. 133–51

Rorty, R. 1983 'Review: A Stroll with William James by Jacques Barzun' *The New Republic* vol. 9, May, pp. 31–3

Rue, L. 1994 *By the Grace of Guile: The Role of Deception in Natural History and Human Affairs*, Oxford University Press, New York

Rundell, J. 1991 'Jürgen Habermas' *Social Theory: A Guide to Central Thinkers*, ed. P. Beilharz, Allen & Unwin, St Leonards, pp. 133–40

——1995 'Gadamer and the circles of interpretation' *Reconstructing Theory: Gadamer, Habermas, Luhmann*, ed. D. Roberts, Melbourne University Press, Melbourne

Sadler Jr, W.A. 1969 *Existence and Love: A New Approach in Existential Phenomenology*, Charles Scribner's Sons, New York

Sartre, J-P. 1956 *Being and Nothingness: An Essay on Phenomenological Ontology*, Philosophical Library, New York

Sarup, M. 1993 *An Introductory Guide to Post-Structuralism and Postmodernism* 2nd edn, University of Georgia Press, Athens

Saul, J.R. 1992 *Voltaire's Bastards: The Dictatorship of Reason in the West*, Free Press, New York

Sawicki, J. 1991 *Disciplining Foucault: Feminism, Power, and the Body*, Routledge, New York

Schutz, A. 1967 *The Phenomenology of the Social World*, Northwestern University Press, Evanston

——1973 *Collected Papers 1 The Problem of Social Reality* 4th edn, Martinus Nijhoff, The Hague

Schwandt, T.A. 1994 'Constructivist, interpretivist approaches to human inquiry' *Handbook of Qualitative Research*, eds N.K. Denzin & Y.S. Lincoln, Sage, Thousand Oaks, pp. 118–37

Seigfried, C.H. 1991 'Where are all the pragmatist feminists?' *Hypatia* vol. 6, no. 2, Summer, pp. 1–20

Silverman, E.K. 1990 'Clifford Geertz: Towards a more "thick" understanding' *Reading Material Culture: Structuralism, Hermeneutics and Post-Structuralism*, ed. C. Tilley, Basil Blackwell, Oxford

Simpson, G. 1982 'Auguste Comte 1798–1857' *Origins and Growth of Sociological Theory*, eds A.O. Donini & J.A. Novack, Nelson-Hall, Chicago, pp. 60–81

Spiegelberg, H. 1981 *The Context of the Phenomenological Movement*, Martinus Nijhoff, The Hague

——1982 *The Phenomenological Movement: A Historical Introduction* 3rd edn, Martinus Nijhoff, Boston

Stanley, L. & Wise, S. 1983 *Breaking out: Feminist Consciousness and Feminist Research*, Routledge & Kegan Paul, London

——1990 'Method, methodology and epistemology in feminist research processes' *Feminist Praxis: Research, Theory and Epistemology in Feminist Sociology*, ed. L. Stanley, Routledge, London, pp. 20–60

Straw, S.B. 1990a 'Conceptualizations of communication in the history of literary theory: Readers apprehending texts and authors' *Beyond Communication: Reading Comprehension and Criticism*, eds D. Bogdan and S.B. Straw, Boynton/Cook, Portsmouth, pp. 49–66

——1990b 'Challenging communication: Reader's reading for actualization' *Beyond Communication: Reading Comprehension and Criticism*, eds D. Bogdan and S.B. Straw, Boynton/Cook, Portsmouth, pp. 67–89

Straw, S.B. & Sadowy, P. 1990 'Dynamics of communication: Transmission, translation and interaction in reading comprehension' *Beyond Communication: Reading Comprehension and Criticism*, eds D. Bogdan and S.B. Straw, Boynton/Cook, Portsmouth, pp. 21–47

Sturrock, J. 1993 *Structuralism*, Fontana, London

Tar, Z. 1977 *The Frankfurt School: The Critical Theories of Max Horkheimer and Theodor W. Adorno*, John Wiley & Sons, New York

Tertulian, N. 1985 'Lukács, Adorno and classical German philosophy' *Telos* vol. 63, Spring, pp. 79–96

Thayer, H.S. 1968 *Meaning and Action: A Critical History of Pragmatism*, Bobbs-Merrill, Indianapolis

Tong, R. 1995 *Feminist Thought: A Comprehensive Introduction*, Routledge, London

Walzer, M. 1989 *The Company of Critics*, Peter Halban, London

Waters, M. 1989 *Sociology One: Principles of Sociological Analysis for Australians*, Longman Cheshire, Melbourne

Waugh, P. 1992 'Modernism, postmodernism, feminism: Gender and autonomy theory' *Postmodernism: A Reader*, ed. P. Waugh, Edward Arnold, London, pp. 189–204

Weber, M. 1949 *The Methodology of the Social Sciences*, Free Press, Glencoe

——1962 *Basic Concepts in Sociology*, Peter Owen, London

——1968 *On Charisma and Institution Building: Selected Papers*, ed. S.N. Eisenstadt, University of Chicago Press, Chicago

——1970 *From Max Weber: Essays in Sociology*, eds H.H. Gerth & C.W. Mills, Oxford University Press, New York

Weiss, J. 1986 *Weber and the Marxist World*, Routledge & Kegan Paul, London

Wiggershaus, R. 1994 *The Frankfurt School: Its History, Theories, and Political Significance*, MIT Press, Cambridge

Wild, J. 1955 *The Challenge of Existentialism*, Indiana University Press, Bloomington

Wittgenstein, L. 1968 *Philosophical Investigations* 3rd edn, Macmillan, New York

Wolff, K.H. 1984 'Surrender-and-catch and phenomenology' *Human Studies* vol. 7, no. 2, pp. 191–210

——1989 'From nothing to sociology' *Philosophy of the Social Sciences*, vol. 19, pp. 321–39

Wolin, R. 1992 *The Terms of Cultural Criticism: The Frankfurt School, Existentialism, Poststructuralism*, Columbia University Press, New York

Yates, T. 1990 'Jacques Derrida: "There is nothing outside of the text"' *Reading Material Culture: Structuralism, Hermeneutics and Post-Structuralism*, ed. C. Tilley, Basil Blackwell, Oxford, pp. 206–80

Zaner, R.M. 1970 *The Way of Phenomenology: Criticism as a Philosophical Discipline*, Pegasus, New York

INDEX